T4-AJW-111

WALT DISNEY WORLD®

with Kids

2001

KIM WRIGHT WILEY

Prima Publishing
3000 Lava Ridge Court • Roseville, California 95661
(800) 632-8676 • www.primalifestyles.com

To my children,
Leigh and Jordan,
the best ride-testers in the business.

© 2000 by Kim Wright Wiley

All rights reserved. No part of this book may be reproduced or transmitted in any form or by any means, electronic or mechanical, including photocopying, recording, or by any information storage or retrieval system, without written permission from Prima Publishing, except for the inclusion of quotations in a review.

PRIMA PUBLISHING and colophon are registered trademarks of Prima Communications, Inc.

All products mentioned in this book are trademarks of their respective companies.

Every effort has been made to make this book complete and accurate as of the date of publication. In a time of rapid change, however, it is difficult to ensure that all information is entirely up-to-date. Although the publisher and author cannot be liable for any inaccuracies or omissions in this book, they are always grateful for corrections and suggestions for improvement.

Interior and maps designed by designLab-Seattle

Editorial Assistant: Felicia B. Howie

ISBN: 0-7615-2418-5

ISSN: 1083-2424

01 02 03 HH 10 9 8 7 6 5 4 3 2

Printed in the United States of America

How to Order

Single copies may be ordered from Prima Publishing, 3000 Lava Ridge Court, Roseville, CA 95661; telephone (800) 632-8676, ext. 4444. Quantity discounts are also available. On your letterhead, include information concerning the intended use of the books and the number of books you wish to purchase.

Visit us online at www.primalifestyles.com

Contents

Chapter 1   Before You Leave Home   1

Chapter 5 The Magic Kingdom — 139

Chapter 6 Epcot Center — 179

Chapter 7   Disney-MGM Studios Theme Park   215

Chapter 8   The Animal Kingdom   241

Chapter 9 The Disney World Water Parks 261

Chapter 10 The Rest of the World 281

Chapter 15 Islands of Adventure 409

Chapter 16 Life Beyond Disney World:
Sea World and Other Orlando Attractions 431

HELPFUL PHONE NUMBERS

All Orlando numbers have a 407 area code. Be sure to make all resort reservations through the W-DISNEY number and use the resort's direct line only to call Guest Services, to call the child-care centers, or to reach a registered guest.

General Disney World Information	824-4321
Florida Relay Service	TDD/TDY 800-955-8771
Voice	800-955-8770
General Accommodation Information	W-DISNEY (934-7639)
Priority Seating	WDW-DINE (939-3463)
ABC Mothers	857-7447
Alamo Car Rental	877-252-6600
All-Star Movies Resort	939-7000
All-Star Music Resort	939-6000
All-Star Sports Resort	939-5000
American Airlines	800-321-2121
Avis Car Rental	800-331-1212
Beach Club Resort	934-8000
BoardWalk Resort	939-5100
Camp Sea World	800-406-2244/363-2380
Caribbean Beach Resort	934-3400
Contemporary Resort	824-1000
Coronado Springs Resort	939-1000
Delta Airlines	800-872-7786
Delta Orlando Resort	800-776-3358/351-3340
Disney Cruise Line	800-511-1333/566-7000
Disney Institute Villas	827-1100
Disney Institute Programs	800-746-5858
Disney Travel Company	800-828-0228
Dixie Landings	934-6000
Dolphin Resort	934-4000
Downtown Disney	828-3058
Embassy Suites	800-EMBASSY/239-1144
Fort Wilderness Campground	824-2900
Gatorland	800-393-JAWS/855-5496

Golf Information	WDW-GOLF (939-4653)
Grand Floridian Resort	824-3000
Hertz Car Rental	800-654-3131
Hilton Disney Village	800-782-4414/827-4000
Holiday Inn Sunspree	800-HOLIDAY/239-4500
Hyatt Grand Cypress	800-233-1234/239-1234
Islands of Adventure	363-8000
Kennedy Space Center	452-2121
KinderCare	827-5444
Magic Kingdom Club Reservations	824-2600
Main Street Physicians	396-1195
Mears Shuttle Service	423-5566
National Car Rental	800-227-7368
Old Key West Resort	827-7700
Orlando Science Center	896-7151
Orlando Visitor's Bureau	800-255-5786
Pleasure Island	934-7781
Polynesian Resort	824-2000
Port Orleans Resort	934-5000
River Country	824-2760
Sea World Information	351-3600
Sports Information	824-2621
Super Sitters	382-2558
Swan Resort	934-3000
Tennis Information	824-3578
TicketMaster	839-3900
Tour Information	939-TOUR (939-8687)
Typhoon Lagoon	560-4141
Universal Studios	888-U ESCAPE (837-2273)
USAir	800-455-0123
Wet 'n Wild	800-992-WILD/351-9453
Wide World of Sports	363-6600
Wilderness Lodge	824-3200
Yacht Club	934-7000

LIST OF MAPS

LIST OF QUICK GUIDE REFERENCE TABLES

ABBREVIATIONS, TERMS, AND ICONS

Abbreviations and Terms

WDW	Walt Disney World
The major parks	The Magic Kingdom, Epcot Center, Disney-MGM Studios, and Animal Kingdom
The minor parks	Typhoon Lagoon, River Country, Pleasure Island, and Blizzard Beach
MK	Magic Kingdom
AK	Animal Kingdom
MGM	The Disney-MGM Studios Theme Park
Downtown Disney	A shopping, dining, and entertainment complex composed of Pleasure Island, the Marketplace, and the West Side
TTC	Ticket and Transportation Center: The monorail version of a train station, where riders can transfer to monorails bound for Epcot, the Magic Kingdom, or monorail-line hotels. You can also catch buses at the TTC bound for the parks, the on-site hotels, and Downtown Disney.

Icons

 Helpful Hint   Insider's Secret

 Money-Saving Tip   Scare Factor

 Time-Saving Tip

Preface

How Has Walt Disney World Changed?

The simple answer is, it's gotten bigger. And they're still building.

In the 10 years since I began researching the first version of this guide, Disney has added one major park, three minor ones, five hotels, a cruise line, and more attractions and eateries than I can count. It was once possible for a fleet-footed and well-prepared family to see most of Walt Disney World in a four- or five-day stay. But this is no longer true. As the Disney complex expands, it is more vital than ever that you target in advance what you most want to see, work these priorities into your schedule, and then relax. Anything beyond that is pure gravy.

Many tourists treat Orlando as if it were a kiddie version of Vegas; that is, you go there to play the numbers, and a family that hits 24 attractions a day must, by definition, be having four times as much fun as a family that sees six things a day. Not so. You'll find a lot of crying kids and exasperated parents by midafternoon, largely because everyone is frantic with the idea that because this trip is so expensive you'd darn well better squeeze the most out of every minute.

With this in mind, I've dropped my touring plans from this version of the book and replaced them with advice on how you can customize a general touring plan for your own family. I've made these changes because, while it's nice to be able to shave 22 seconds off your morning dash to Splash Mountain by ducking through the restroom tunnel in Adventureland, the most successful plan seems to boil down to a few simple guidelines.

You'll have twice as much fun with half as much stress if you follow these five tips:

1. Plan your trip for times of the year when the parks are less crowded. When people write to me about having bad experiences at Walt Disney World, it seems that about 90 percent of the disasters occur in July.
2. Order maps and tickets and arrange all reservations or priority seating well in advance. Every phone call you make from home is a line you won't have to stand in later.
3. Read up on attractions and let each family member choose the two or three things per park that are absolute must-sees. An amazing number of parents plan this trip for the kids, neglecting to ask them what they want to do.
4. Accept your differences and be willing to split up occasionally. Forcing a 14-year-old on It's a Small World or strapping a 6-year-old into Alien Encounter in the interest of family togetherness will guarantee at least one tantrum per hour.
5. Arrive at the parks very early, go back to your hotel for a nap or swim in the afternoon, and return to the parks at night. Walt Disney World can be exhausting, and regular rest stops are key.

What hasn't changed in 10 years is my belief that Walt Disney World is the best family travel destination on the planet. There is truly something for everyone within these gates, and the spectacular, awe-inspiring rides are counterbalanced with sweet, small moments of joy that often linger in the mind for years. When you check into your hotel the first night and find you can see the IllumiNations fireworks from your balcony . . . when Merlin picks your 5-year-old to pull the sword from the stone and be declared ruler of all England . . . when they release the doves at the end of the Beauty and the Beast show . . . or when your 13-year-old actually smiles—then, trust me, you'll remember why you came to Disney.

CHAPTER

1

Before You Leave Home

1. Coronado Springs Resort
2. Wide World of Sports
3. Swan Resort
4. Dolphin Resort
5. Yacht & Beach Club Resorts
6. Disney's BoardWalk, BoardWalk Inn & Villas
7. Magic Kingdom Main Entrance
8. Car Care Center
9. Transportation & Ticket Center Parking
10. Transportation & Ticket Center
11. Polynesian Resort
12. The Grand Floridian
13. Contemporary Resort
14. Wilderness Lodge
15. Fort Wilderness Campground
16. Dixie Landings Resort
17. Port Orleans Resort
18. Old Key West Resort
19. Lake Buena Vista Golf Course
20. Disney Institute
21. Disney Institute Villas
22. Disney's West Side
23. Pleasure Island
24. Caribbean Beach Resort

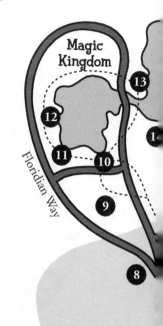

Magic Kingdom

Floridian Way

← To U.S. 27 (192)

25. Animal Kingdom Lodge
26. Disney Village Hotels
27. All-Star Resorts

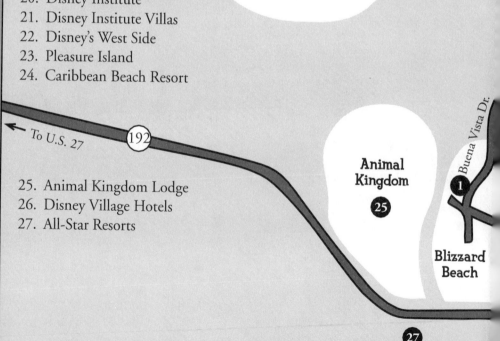

Animal Kingdom

Buena Vista Dr.

Blizzard Beach

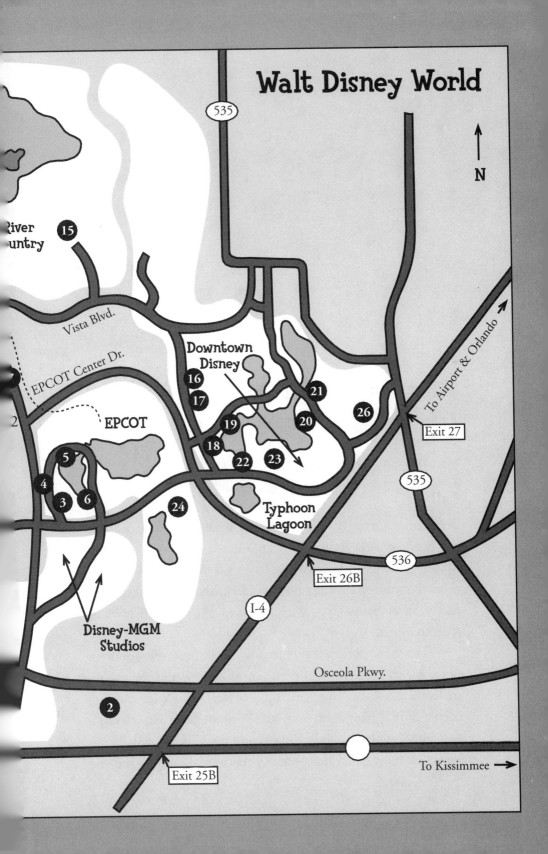

Walt Disney World

535

↑
N

River
ountry
15

Vista Blvd.

Downtown Disney

EPCOT Center Dr.

16

17

21

EPCOT

26

19

20

Exit 27

To Airport & Orlando

18

5

22 **23**

535

4

3 **6**

24

Typhoon Lagoon

536

Exit 26B

I-4

Disney-MGM Studios

Osceola Pkwy.

2

To Kissimmee →

Exit 25B

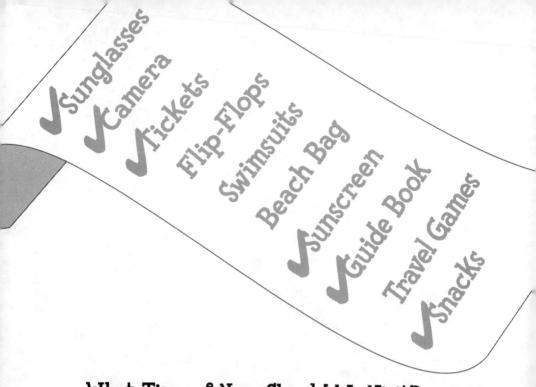

Sunglasses ✓
Camera ✓
Tickets ✓
Flip-Flops
Swimsuits
Beach Bag
Sunscreen ✓
Guide Book ✓
Travel Games
Snacks ✓

What Time of Year Should We Visit?

Crowd levels at Walt Disney World vary seasonally, so one of the most important decisions you will make while planning your trip is deciding when to go.

Fall

September through mid-December is the best time of year for families with young children. Crowds are light—around 30,000 visitors a day, compared to 60,000 in the summer months—and many area hotels offer discounted rates. Even the weather cooperates, with highs in the 80s and lows in the 60s.

There are disadvantages to a fall visit, however. You may not want to take your children out of school, and the theme parks do close earlier at this time of year. The Magic Kingdom, Animal Kingdom, and MGM often close as early as 6 P.M., although Epcot generally remains open until 9 P.M. These earlier closings mean that some of the special evening presentations, such as the evening parade in the Magic Kingdom, are suspended during the off-season.

Fall is also hurricane season in Florida, so there is some risk you'll schedule your trip for the exact week that Hurricane Laluna pounds the coast. But Orlando is an hour inland, which means that even the worst coastal storms usually yield only rain at Disney World. Furthermore, there are more rainy days in the summer months than there are in the fall, so in general the advantages of autumn touring far outweigh the disadvantages.

Spring

If a fall visit isn't possible, spring is nearly as nice. With the exceptions of the holiday weeks around Presidents' Day, spring break, and Easter, springtime crowds average around 40,000—not as small as in fall but still far better than in summer. And the weather is sublime, with highs in the 70s, lows in the 60s, and less rainfall than in any other season.

Disney maintains longer park hours in spring than in fall, but schedules vary widely in the weeks between January and May. To check projected hours of operation, call 407-824-4321 before you leave home.

Summer

The good news about summer is that everything is open and operational, and the parks run very long hours. The bad news is that it is hot and crowded, so crowded that the wait for many rides can be as long as 90 minutes.

If your children's school schedule dictates that you must visit in summer, the

Helpful Hint

If your children are preschoolers or younger, avoid summers like the plague.

first two weeks of June and the last two weeks of August are your best bet. Check out "Special Tips for Extra-Crowded Times" in Chapter 3.

Winter

Winter is a mixed bag. The absolute worst times are holidays. Christmas and New Year's can pull in 80,000 visitors per day, and even extended hours can't compensate for crowds of this size. Although special parades and shows are always planned, you're better off at home watching them on TV.

But if you avoid the holiday weeks, winter can be an ideal time for touring. January and February are pleasantly cool; and Disney World is relatively uncrowded, although the water parks are sometimes closed during this period, and the parks run the same shortened schedule as in fall.

Helpful Hint
Special holiday packages, which include price breaks on lodging, a party with the characters, and access to the Christmas parades and shows, run from the end of November to mid-December.

The first two weeks of December are another good option. Disney World is fetchingly decorated at Christmas, and the decorations go up just after Thanksgiving. So if you make an early December visit, you'll have all the trees and wreaths and carolers you could wish for—as well as a nearly deserted theme park.

How Long Should We Stay?

It will take at least five days for a family with young kids to tour the Magic Kingdom, Epcot, the Animal Kingdom, and

MGM. Park Hopper Plus passes—which admit holders to Pleasure Island, Typhoon Lagoon, Blizzard Beach, and River Country, as well as the major theme parks—are the best buy.

If you plan to spend a lot of time at the minor theme parks, especially the water parks, schedule six days. Six days are also necessary for families who enjoy boating, tennis, swimming, or golf—or those who would like to tour at a more leisurely pace.

If you wish to visit other area attractions such as Sea World or Universal Orlando, allow no less than a week.

Should We Take the Kids Out of School?

Even if you're sold on the advantages of fall and spring touring, you may be reluctant to take your children out of school for a week. There are ways to highlight the educational aspects of a trip to Disney World; let's look at few.

Work together with the teacher to create a plan so that your child can avoid falling behind. Ideally, half of the makeup work should be done before you leave—the post-trip blues are bad enough without facing three hours of homework each night of the first week you're back.

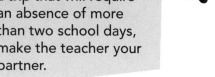

Insider's Secret

If you're considering a trip that will require an absence of more than two school days, make the teacher your partner.

Also, timing is everything. Don't plan your trip for the week the school is administering exams or standardized testing. Check with the teacher to see if there are better times for your child to be absent.

To make up for being absent on school days, have your child do a project related to the trip. Here are some suggestions:

Epcot Projects

The greenhouse tour in the Land pavilion is full of information on space-age farming.

Marine biology is the theme of the Living Seas pavilion.

Missing health class? The Wonders of Life pavilion is devoted to that greatest of all machines, the human body.

Interested in geography? Some students have done reports on the cultures of countries represented in the World Showcase.

Innoventions, although often described as the world's hippest arcade, is also a preview of future technology.

Animal Kingdom Projects

Cretaceous Trail—a path filled with plants and animals that have survived from the Cretaceous period—is an excellent intro to botanical evolution.

Conservation Station is the park's research and education hub, where kids can tour veterinary labs, use the Eco-web to find the conservation organization closest to their home, and watch interactive videos about endangered animals.

Younger kids might like to simply do a report on one of the animals they see on Kilimanjaro Safaris.

Along with reports on the subjects listed, your child might also want to make a scrapbook or collection display.

The mother of one preschooler helped him create an "ABC" book before he left home, and he then spent his week at Disney World collecting souvenirs for each page—Goofy's autograph on the "G" page, a postcard of a Japanese pagoda on the "P" page, and so on. An older child might gather fallen leaves from the various trees and bushes imported from the countries represented in the World Showcase. Or a young photographer could demonstrate his proficiency with various lighting techniques by photographing the Cinderella Castle in early morning, at noon, at sunset, and after dark. You can even work on math if you give your kids a set amount of mythical money to spend (such as $1,000). Then let them keep track of expenses, deducting them from their starting total and making decisions about what they can and cannot afford on their budget.

If your kids are old enough to benefit from a more formal program, consider a day at Camp Disney. You can use the brochure to help explain to the child's teacher exactly what will be covered in the course and give you both ideas on what sort of project would be best. My 12-year-old daughter took so many pictures during her Disney Made Wild experience that she was able to put together a whole book, which she presented to her biology class upon her return.

Camp Disney at the Disney Institute

Disney's half- and full-day seminars for kids are now collectively grouped under the label "Camp Disney" and are run from the Disney Institute. This is dynamite stuff—giving young students the chance to go backstage before a live show or into the animation studios and costuming tunnels. It's what the tourists never see!

Insider's Secret

In addition to being inspirational and educational, Camp Disney programs effectively break up the week. Just when you're all on each other's nerves from an overdose of togetherness, you can farm the kids out for a great day at the Institute and take a couple of adult-oriented classes yourself.

Not every program is offered every day, and offerings are constantly being updated and changed. Call the Disney Institute (800-746-5858) to order an information packet; call 407-WDW-TOUR (939-8687) or visit the Web site at www.disneyinstitute.com for more detailed information. The reservations staff will be able to fully describe the programs and help you pick the one that is best suited for your children.

A full-day class or two half-day classes are $99, half-days are $69, and lunch is included in the longer programs.

Classes change constantly, so call the Institute before you make any promises. Here are the current offerings:

Programs for Kids 7 to 10

Classes last 3.5 hours.

Broadway Bound

Kids dance, sing, act, and even learn how to audition in this lively class, which takes them behind the scenes at both the Magic Kingdom and MGM.

Face Magic

Learn how artists create illusions and special effects through the use of makeup and lighting. At MGM, students get a

chance to apply what they've learned by painting their own faces. You'll drop off David and pick up Dracula.

ArtSurround

Epcot is the backdrop for this seminar on how art is inspired by nature, emotions, and music. After seeing how the pros do it, kids get a chance to create art using bubbles, paint, and some rather unusual supplies.

Programs for Kids 11 to 15

Classes last 3.5 hours.

Animation

Kids learn the tricks of the trade that Disney artists use in order to create the magic in the films and theme parks. They go backstage at the animation studio, paint a cel, and learn tips on how to draw the characters.

The Magic Behind the Show

Students go behind the scenes at the Magic Kingdom to see how a live show is prepared and rehearsed, as well as look at the technical side of production. Kids go into the infamous Magic Kingdom "tunnel" to see the world's largest costume department and meet cast members who talk about the roles they play in the world of show business, Disney style.

Disney Made Wild

For those who prefer the earthy to the artsy, discover how nature inspires the magic of Disney. Visit a natural Florida environment, learn how nature can stimulate the imagination, and unearth the adventurer within.

Other Orlando Educational Programs

Disney World isn't the only place in Orlando that can be educational. Consider one of the following:

Sea World

Sea World offers daily tours and classes, as well as weeklong and overnight programs during summer and holidays. You'll find details in Chapter 16. Call 407-351-3600 for a brochure.

Orlando Science Center

This impressive facility has oodles of hands-on exhibits, one-day programs for kids of all ages, and evening planetarium shows. If you request the brochure, you'll find that something is happening all the time and that the prices are reasonable. All programs must be booked in advance.

Admission to the center is $12.50 for adults, $11.50 for seniors, and $9.25 for kids 3 to 11. Classes are individually priced. Call 407-896-7151.

Kennedy Space Center

Orlando is only about an hour from Kennedy Space Center, so it's an easy day trip. Kids will enjoy the Rocket Garden, which holds eight rockets from the Mercury through Gemini programs, and the new Apollo/Saturn V Center, where you can see Saturn V, the most powerful rocket ever built. The films, projected on the five-story-high screen in the IMAX theater, are also a highlight. Call the Center before you leave home and see if a launch is scheduled while you'll be in Florida. If so, plan your trip for that day. The crowds will be heavier, but your kids will experience a rare thrill.

Crew passes, which include a shuttle tour of the Space Center as well as the IMAX film, are $19 for adults and $15 for kids 3 to 11. One word of warning: The Space Center is not a theme park and therefore is not as user-friendly as Disney World. "The most inefficient line and ticketing system I've ever seen," wrote one father. Call 407-452-2121.

Should We Buy a Package?

This is a toughie. There are advantages to package trips, most notably that it is possible to save a good deal of money. It's also helpful to know up front what your vacation will cost. Often packages require hefty prepayments, which are painful at the time—but at least you don't return home with your credit card utterly maxed out.

Package trips can have drawbacks, however. Like buying a fully loaded car off a dealer's lot, you may find yourself paying for options you don't want and don't need. Packages are often padded with perks such as reduced golf greens fees, which are of interest to only a few families, or rental cars, which you may not need if you're staying on-site. At the other end of the spectrum are deeply discounted packages that place you in rundown or out-of-the-way hotels.

> **Money-Saving Tip**
> Be doubly wary of the very cheap packages offered in Sunday papers. If a deal sounds too good to be true, it probably is.

Disney's Resort Package Vacations

Several families responding to our survey were sold on Disney's own packages, such as the Grand Plan, which houses guests in the swank Grand Floridian or the almost-as-swank Yacht and Beach Clubs and includes all food, all tickets, and unlimited golf, boating, and other sporting facilities, in addition to such extras as babysitting, stroller rental, a personalized itinerary, tuition in one of the Disney Institute programs—and a Fantasia alarm clock. As a reservation agent laughingly told me, "This one even includes the kitchen sink." Such luxury, needless to say, doesn't come cheap. A family of four staying five days at the Grand Floridian on the Grand Plan can expect to pay $4,400.

If all this sounds a bit much, Disney also offers a variety of less expensive packages that lodge families at one of the on-site mid-priced hotels, such as Dixie Landings, Port Orleans, or the Caribbean Beach Resort. You can opt for meals or not; five days for a family of four without food would be about $1,900. Call 407-W-DISNEY to request a brochure and videotape outlining all the options or 800-828-0228 to book directly with the Walt Disney Travel Company.

Magic Kingdom Club Packages

Those who hold a Magic Kingdom Club Gold Card have packages developed solely for them, ranging once again from the all-inclusive to the more affordably priced. The difference is that the Magic Kingdom Club packages are 10 to 20 percent cheaper than comparable Disney packages, so if you're seriously considering booking a package, get thee posthaste to a telephone and dial 800-56-DISNEY. Once you purchase your Gold Card, you're in the Magic Kingdom Club automatically; Disney uses the terms "cardholder" and "club member" interchangeably, which can be a bit confusing. See "Magic Kingdom Club Gold Cards" later in this chapter.

Money-Saving Tip
Paying the $50 for the two-year club membership would be smart, especially if you're traveling during the off-season, when the deepest discounts are in effect.

Airline Packages

If you're flying, check out the airline's own packages, which include airfare, theme park tickets for Disney and other Orlando attractions, car rental, and lodging at either on-site or off-site hotels. Again, there's a huge range of amenities— you can have valet parking and use of a camcorder if you're willing to pay for them. And again, the packages can be fine-tuned to meet your needs. If you'll be flying Delta, call 800-872-7786 for a brochure; the number for USAir is 800-455-0123; American Airlines is 800-321-2121.

> **Insider's Secret**
> The airlines control a limited number of on-site hotel rooms, so call at least six months in advance if you have your heart set on a Disney resort.

Cruise Packages

The Walt Disney Company's cruise ships, Disney Magic and Disney Wonder, offer families the chance to combine a Bahamas cruise with a Disney World vacation.

Families may opt to spend either three or four nights at sea, and the remainder of the week is spent in Orlando. Park admissions are included in the packages, as is airfare, a rental car, and your meals while on board ship. During the cruise segment of the week, you'll find a staggeringly full program for children, including dawn-to-dusk kids' clubs, special menus, parties and mixers geared toward teens and preteens, and the Disney characters. Youth counselors squire the kids around, giving worn-out parents the chance to collapse on deck chairs.

You can book the cruises through your travel agent or by calling 800-511-1333. See Chapter 12 for more information.

Travel Agents

If you'd like to stay on-site but you're not accustomed to using a travel agent, don't worry. Any discounts an agent would be able to get on a Disney resort would be minimal, so you'll come out about as well handling the reservations yourself. Simply call 407-W-DISNEY, and the representative will explain your options.

Money-Saving Tip

Travel agents are most helpful to families staying off-site. Agents are often aware of Orlando hotels that offer packages, and they are a good source of comparative rate shopping. Large travel agencies sometimes put together their own packages, which include airfare, lodging at an off-site hotel, and a rental car. If you need all three of these components, you'll probably come out cheaper buying a package through your local agent than trying to book all three separately.

Cheapie Deals

These are frequently seen in the travel sections of major newspapers and offer extremely low rates. But proceed with caution. The hotels are sometimes as far as 50 miles away from the Disney gates. (With a rental car and an alarm clock, even this obstacle can be overcome—but you should know what you're up against.) Other pitfalls include tickets that can be used only at certain times of the year or extremely inflexible touring arrangements that require you to ride from attraction to attraction in slow-moving, overloaded buses.

Another drawback is that the hotels featured may not be in a very desirable area of town. Orlando has not suffered the degree of tourist-targeted crime that we've read about in other Florida cities, but unless either you or your travel agent is familiar with the area where the hotel is located, be wary. A family interested in saving money would be far better off driving and camping at Fort Wilderness or trying the All-Star Resorts than signing up for one of these packages.

Magic Kingdom Club Gold Cards

If your family is really dizzy for Disney, it makes economic sense to purchase a Magic Kingdom Club Gold Card. You can receive a brochure outlining packages and other benefits or order a Magic Kingdom Club Gold Card by calling 800-56-DISNEY. The cost of a two-year membership is $50, $45 thereafter.

The biggest perk is the discounts on rooms at on-site hotels. The 20 percent discounts coincide with the least-crowded times of the year, namely fall and winter, with 10 percent discounts at other times of the year. (The budget All-Star Resorts offer a flat 10 percent discount.) You can also expect 10 percent discounts at some theme park restaurants and dinner shows and merchandise bought through the Disney catalog and at Disney stores nationwide (except those in

Helpful Hint
Like the Fairy Godmother told Cinderella, there's one catch: If you are planning to visit either Disney World or Disneyland next year, you should order your Magic Kingdom Club Gold Card as soon as possible because you must have it in hand when you make your hotel reservation.

Orlando or Anaheim) and about a 5 percent price break on theme park tickets. Given the high price of Disney World lodging and dining, it's easy to see how club membership could pay for itself very quickly.

Only a certain block of rooms is set aside in each hotel for cardholders; call at least six months in advance if you want the best choice of dates and resorts.

Cardholders have their own travel agency that offers special package deals. Club members make their hotel reservations and get information on special packages by calling 407-824-2600. You'll get a brochure outlining all the perks and packages when you order your card.

Money-Saving Tip

If you're really lucky, you can receive the goodies listed previously without having to pay for the card. Many corporations hold Magic Kingdom Club Gold Cards, which qualify their employees for the discounts. State and federal employees are also covered. Check with your human resources or employee benefits department to see if your company is a member.

What Kind of Ticket Do We Need?

This decision, believe it or not, needs to be made long before you get to the theme park gates. First of all, prepare yourself for the news that, at least in the eyes of the Disney accountants, your 10-year-old is an adult. Then consider how many days you'll need the tickets, whether you'd like to visit the minor parks, and if you plan to visit more than one park in a

single day. (Most of the tips and touring plans in this book assume that you will.)

As we go to press, the following ticket options are available, and the prices quoted are before tax. Disney "adjusts"—that is, raises—prices on a regular basis, so you should always confirm prices and ticket options by calling 407-824-4321.

Seven-Day Park Hopper Plus

This pass admits holders to the four major parks, plus four visits to the minor ones. Children under 3 are admitted free.

- Adult: $296.00
- Child (3 to 9): $242.00

Six-Day Park Hopper Plus

Admits holders to the four major parks, plus three visits to the minor ones. Children under 3 are admitted free.

- Adult: $266.00
- Child (3 to 9): $217.00

Five-Day Park Hopper Plus

Admits holders to the four major parks, plus two visits to the minor ones. Children under 3 are admitted free.

- Adult: $236.00
- Child (3 to 9): $192.00

Five-Day Park Hopper Pass

Admits holder to the four major parks. Children under 3 are admitted free.

- Adult: $206.00
- Child (3 to 9): $167.00

Four-Day Park Hopper Pass

Admits holder to the four major parks. Children under 3 are admitted free.

- Adult: $176.00

- Child (3 to 9): $142.00

One-Day Ticket

Admits holder to one park only. Children under 3 are admitted free.

- Adult: $46.00

- Child (3 to 9): $37.00

It's also worth noting that the Park Hopper passes do not have to be used on consecutive days and, in fact, never expire. Assuming that your kids don't move from the child to the adult category in the meantime, you can return in five years and the unused days will still be valid. Even though Disney no longer issues the Four-Day Value Pass, they still honor it along with any other multiday passes they have discontinued issuing.

Money-Saving Tip

Guests at the on-site hotels should consider the Length-of-Stay Pass, which is good for a stay of any length from 4 to 10 days. The pass offers unlimited access to both the major and minor parks during the time you're staying at a Disney hotel, and, although the price is obviously tied to how long you stay, the cost is slightly cheaper than buying tickets at the gate.

Disney tickets are never discounted, so if you're offered cut-rate tickets, you should immediately smell a rat. Sometimes companies offer free or discounted tickets in order to lure you into time-sharing or other vacation club promotions. You'll waste a whole day trying to save 20 bucks.

Helpful Hint

One word of caution about buying tickets: The Guest Services desk at off-site hotels may not be run by your hotel at all but by a separate company that exists solely to sell tickets and bus fares to tourists. These companies offer their own version of the multiday passes, which they hawk aggressively, usually by telling you that it is much cheaper than the Disney ticket. It isn't. If you are offered a four-day ticket with access to River Country and Pleasure Island, this is a good buy ONLY if you're sure you'll never use that extra day provided on the five-day pass and you don't plan to visit Typhoon Lagoon or Blizzard Beach.

Time-Saving Tip

In the off-season, when the Magic Kingdom closes early, Disney sometimes offers a special "E ticket" to on-site guests. To be used in conjunction with a park hopper pass, the E ticket allows you into the Magic Kingdom on a night when it is closed to the general public. About 10 attractions are open, and only 5,000 E tickets are generally sold, meaning very short lines. The open rides include Space Mountain, Splash Mountain, and other big-name attractions, so the E ticket is most appealing to families with older kids. Few Fantasyland attractions are open.

Money-Saving Tip

Another rip-off to look out for: overpriced shuttle tickets at off-site hotels. The agents hawking these tickets may tell you that you'll save the "horrendous" cost of Disney parking by taking their shuttle, but the truth is that it costs $6 to park no matter how many people are in the car, and the bus tickets cost $3 to $7 per person. For a family of four, that adds up fast. Also, the shuttles offered by these independent services generally stop at several hotels, making your commute time much longer than if you stayed at a hotel offering a direct shuttle or drove your own car. Don't pay for this abuse.

Helpful Hint

Be careful when buying bus rides into the parks. For starters, many hotels offer free shuttle service, so if you've chosen your hotel carefully, there's no reason you should have to pay for transportation. But even if you need transportation, these independent shuttles may not be your best bet.

Advance Reservations and Ticket Purchases

Get maps of the theme parks and general touring information by calling 407-W-DISNEY. If you're traveling with someone who is elderly or in a wheelchair, request the "Guidebook for Disabled Visitors."

Tickets to the theme parks can be purchased by calling 407-W-DISNEY. MasterCard, Visa, and American Express are all accepted, and the tickets will be mailed to you. If you'd prefer to pay by check, call first to confirm prices, then mail your payment to

Money-Saving Tip
Theme park ticket prices change about every six months. Always call to confirm prices. Once you purchase tickets, however, the price is fixed, so buy in advance when you can.

WDW Tickets
P.O. Box 10030
Lake Buena Vista, FL 32830-0030

Helpful Hint
Booking mistakes are rare, but it never hurts to call and confirm room reservations before you leave home.

Many area hotels, including all Disney hotels, allow guests to purchase theme park tickets at check-in. Inquire when you make reservations. If you live near a Disney store, you can buy theme park tickets there.

Room reservations for on-site hotels should be made at least six months in advance, especially if you're staying at one of the budget hotels or traveling during a busy season. Dial 407-W-DISNEY for information on all Disney-owned hotels.

Room reservations for off-site hotels can usually be made later, perhaps a month before you plan to arrive in the off-season or three to four months in advance in the on-season.

> **Insider's Secret**
>
> Priority seating is a must for character breakfasts or if you're traveling in the on-season and would specifically like to try some of Disney World's more popular restaurants.

Only the wildly optimistic should arrive in Orlando with no reservations at all.

Disney dinner show reservations should also be made from home, and reservations are accepted up to two years in advance.

Disney restaurants no longer accept reservations, but you can arrange for priority seating 60 days in advance. Priority seating means that if you show up at the specified time, you'll be given the next available table; it's not as good as a reservation but does guarantee you'll be seated before the walk-ins. Wait times average 10 to 30 minutes under this system.

To arrange priority seating from home, call 407-WDW-DINE. Disney changes dining policy frequently, but the representative on the line will be able to explain your options.

If you would like to wait until you've checked in to your on-site hotel so you can see which restaurant looks the coolest, arrange priority seating through Guest Services or call direct from your hotel room.

You can also arrange priority seating in person on the day you plan to visit—by dropping by the actual restaurant in the Magic Kingdom, at the reservations booth at MGM, or at the WorldKey Information System beside Spaceship Earth at Epcot. By waiting until the last minute, you'll likely be closed out of the most popular eateries at peak dining times. But if you're traveling off-season or don't have a strong preference about when or where you eat, waiting until the last minute is okay.

Money-Saving Tip

Another great way to get discounts is to call the Orlando Visitor's Bureau at 800-255-5786 and request its Vacation Planner and Magicard. It takes three to four weeks to get the package, but the card qualifies you for discounts on hotels, off-site dinner shows, and non-Disney-area attractions.

Members of the Entertainment Club may be surprised to learn that some spiffy off-site hotels offer 50 percent discounts to cardholders, making an upscale resort as inexpensive as an interstate cheapie. But because only a certain number of rooms are set aside for club members, reservations must be made well in advance to get the discounts. (Becoming a member of the Entertainment Club is as simple as buying one of the discount coupon books in your hometown. The books generally cost between $35 and $50 and are best known for their restaurant coupons. Few people seem to realize that a nationwide directory of hotels offering 50 percent discounts can be found in the back.)

Decide in advance if you need a rental car. If you're staying off-site or if you plan to visit non-Disney attractions, the answer may be yes. Some rental car companies—Avis, Dollar, and National—have desks at the Orlando airport, with the cars in an adjacent lot. Others, such as Hertz or the huge and popular Alamo, are located away from the airport and require a separate shuttle ride. Waiting for the shuttle adds 20 minutes to your commute, both coming and going from the airport, but Alamo offers slightly lower rental fees to compensate. To reserve a car, call:

Alamo	877-252-6600
Avis	800-331-1212
Dollar	800-800-4000
Hertz	800-654-3131
National	800-227-7368

An average weekly rental fee for a compact is around $300. Don't be fooled by the quoted rate of $30 a day; by the time you add taxes and insurance, it's closer to $50. Quite a few families have reported they used their rental car less than they anticipated—"We paid $320 for the privilege of driving from the airport to our hotel and back," wrote one father—so rent a car only if you're staying off-site or visiting several non-Disney attractions. Cars can also be helpful if you plan to eat at or visit a variety of on-site hotels. Don't worry if you've never driven in Orlando; the town is built for tourists, and things are quite well marked. Route 417 South takes you directly to Disney from the airport, and the roads on Disney property are often circular; if you miss an exit, keep driving, and you'll soon get another chance.

More than three people in your party? You'll come out as well taking a taxi. They're always available outside the airport; the fare to a hotel near WDW should be about $30 to $40.

Helpful Hint

If you're staying on-site and visiting only Disney World, you may not need a rental car. Call Guest Services at the hotel where you'll be staying and ask the best way to get from the airport to the hotel. Some hotels run their own shuttles, and others use independent services such as Mears (407-423-5566). Shuttle cost is around $14 a person, $25 round trip.

Taxis can also transport you to off-site attractions such as Universal Studios or Sea World. Again, if there are more than three of you, a cab is generally as cheap as a shuttle—and a whole lot faster as well.

Helpful Hint
For the most up-to-date information of all, check Disney's Web site at www.disney.com.

It's always a good idea to read up on Disney as much as possible before you go. The company's own material is helpful, but there's an everything-is-wonderful tone, which is not much help to a family with limited vacation time who must make some hard choices about what to see and do. Your advance reading should include some "unofficial" sources, like this book.

Things to Discuss with Your Kids Before You Leave Home

It's important to include the kids when planning the vacation. Discuss the following topics before you leave home:

The Trip Itself

There are two schools of thought on just how far in advance of the trip you should let the kids in on the plan. Because many families make reservations six months in advance or more, it's easy to fall into a "waiting for Christmas" syndrome, with the kids nearly in a lather of anticipation weeks before you leave. In order to avoid the agony of a long countdown, one couple packed in secret and then woke the children up at 5 A.M. one morning and announced, "Get in the car, we're going to Disney World." The best method is probably somewhere in between the two extremes. Tell the kids at the time you make your reservations, but don't begin poring over the brochures in earnest until about two weeks before the trip.

The Layout of the Parks

Among the more than 300 families surveyed or interviewed for this book, there was a direct correlation between the amount of advance research they had done and how much they enjoyed the trip. Visitors who show up at Disney World without any preparation can still have fun, but their comment sheets were sprinkled with "Next time I'll know . . ." and "If only we had. . . ."

Kids 7 or older should have some idea of the layout of the parks. If you're letting preteens and teens roam about on their own, you should definitely brief them on the location of major attractions and where and when to meet up with the family again.

The pleasures of being prepared extend to preschoolers. If you purchase a few Disney World coloring books to enjoy on the trip down to Orlando or watch one of the Disney Channel specials featuring the parks, even the youngest child will arrive able to identify the Swiss Family Robinson Treehouse and Living Seas pavilion. A little knowledge before entering the gates helps you decide how to best spend your time and eliminates those "Whadda we do now?" debates.

The Classic Stories of Disney

If your children are under 7, another good pretrip purchase is a set of Disney paperbacks with audiotapes. Even though parental eyes may glaze over when Dumbo rewinds for its thirty-fourth straight hearing, these tapes and books help to pass the trip and familiarize kids with the characters and rides they'll be seeing once they arrive. (If you find kiddie tapes too annoying, you can always bring along headphones for the children to use.)

Some families rent Disney movies just before the trip as well. The videotape Disneyland Fun is especially good for getting the whole family revved up and in the mood. The featured park is Disneyland in California and not the Magic Kingdom in Florida, but the attractions are similar enough to make the tape an exciting preview. Renting *Honey, I Shrunk the Kids* before you leave will vastly improve your children's appreciation of Epcot's *Honey, I Shrunk the Audience* as well as the Honey, I Shrunk the Kids Adventure Zone at MGM.

Special Academic Projects

See "Should We Take the Kids Out of School?" earlier in this chapter for ideas on special projects and seminars.

Souvenirs and Money

Will you save all souvenir purchases for the last day? Buy one small souvenir every day? Are the children expected to spend their own money, or will Mom and Dad spring for the T-shirts? Whatever you decide will depend on your pocketbooks and your particular interpretation of fiscal responsibility, but do set your rules before you're in the park. Otherwise the selection of goodies will lure you into spending far more than you anticipated.

One excellent technique for limiting impulse buys is to request Disney Dollars at the time you order your theme park tickets. Disney Dollars come in denominations of $1 (Mickey), $5 (Goofy), and $10 (Minnie or Simba) and are accepted throughout the theme parks, shops, restaurants, and resorts of Disney World. Some wily parents have managed to convince their tots that these bills are the only currency the parks accept and have given them a certain number of Disney Dollars before leaving home, explaining that this money and this money alone is for souvenirs. You can purchase Disney Dollars at all Disney stores or by writing to

Walt Disney World Ticket Mail Order
P.O. Box 10030
Lake Buena Vista, FL 32830-0030

The Scare Factor

Finally, give some thought to the scare factor.

How frightening a ride is can be tough to gauge because Disney World scariness comes in two forms. First there are atmospheric rides, ranging from the shadows and cardboard witch of Snow White's Scary Adventures to the full-throttle scream-o-rama known as Alien Encounter. The other kind of fear is motion related: Space Mountain and the other coasters are obviously risky, but don't overlook the fact that some people lose their lunch on sweet little charmers like the Mad Tea Party. For some people, the motion simulation rides are more disturbing than the coasters. Body Wars in Epcot, for example, scarcely moves, but the visual effects leave some people wrecked for the day.

The Scare Factor
While a mediocre meal or boring show can be a disappointment, misjudging the intensity of a ride can leave you with a terrified or nauseated child—thus ruining the whole day.

Age is often not the determining factor, since some 6-year-olds are fearless and some 11-year-olds are easily unnerved. Disney's only guidance comes in the form of height requirements (listed below), but

saying that a 41-inch-tall 5-year-old *can* ride Big Thunder Mountain is no indication that he *should* ride Big Thunder Mountain. Read the ride descriptions to find out what kind of scary you're dealing with; children who are terrified of a creepy ride like the Alien Encounter may adore the high-speed Test Track, and some kids who love the Haunted Mansion panic when Dumbo lifts off. I include scare-factor ratings after each ride description, based primarily on feedback I've received from the families I've surveyed.

Height Requirements

In the Magic Kingdom:
Alien Encounter	44 inches (and child must be 7 years old)
Big Thunder Mountain	40 inches
Space Mountain	44 inches
Splash Mountain	40 inches

At Epcot
Test Track	40 inches

At MGM:
Star Tours	40 inches
Tower of Terror	40 inches
Rock 'n' Roller Coaster	48 inches

At Animal Kingdom:
Countdown to Extinction	46 inches (and child must be 7 years old)

If you're still unsure, employ these strategies:

ℯ The baby swap
   No, this does not mean that you can trade your shrieking 1-year-old for that angelically napping infant behind you!

If you have doubts whether a ride is appropriate for your child, inform the attendant that you may need to do a baby swap. As you approach the attraction, one parent rides and returns with the verdict. If the first parent thinks the child will do okay, the second parent immediately boards and rides with the child.

Insider's Secret

You can also use the "baby swap" method if you're traveling with a child who is definitely too young to ride major attractions. One parent rides, and then the other hands the baby through and immediately boards the ride.

If the first parent thinks the ride is too wild, the second parent passes the child through to the first and then rides himself. Granted, it's not as much fun as riding together, but it beats starting the day with a terrified child.

❧ Build up ride intensity throughout the day

Not sure if your 7-year-old is up to a roller coaster? Start her off with something relatively mild like Goofy's Barnstormer or Pirates of the Caribbean. If she handles these okay, proceed on to Splash Mountain or Big Thunder Mountain Railroad. Who knows, you may close out the day on Space Mountain.

This advice runs counter to the touring tips you'll find later in the book that recommend that you ride the big-deal attractions first thing in the morning. But it's better to ease a nervous kid in slowly, even if you risk long lines at the end of the day. You can reduce the wait somewhat if you ride major attractions during the evening parade, which draws most of the crowd back to Main Street.

☙ Avoid motion sickness

Obviously, avoid riding a bumpy attraction just after eating. If you begin to feel sick on a ride like Body Wars, where the visual effects are so convincing that many people become queasy, stare at something inside the cabin instead of the screen. If you focus on the back of the seat in front of you, your nausea will likely subside.

Some families routinely take motion sickness pills in the morning before heading to the parks.

Don't Leave Home Without . . .

✔ Comfortable shoes. This is no time to be breaking in new Nikes.

✔ Minimal clothing. Many hotels have laundry facilities, and you can always wash out underwear in the sink. Most families make the mistake of overpacking, not figuring in all the souvenirs they'll be bringing back. (Guest Services reports that many families buy so much stuff they end up shipping their dirty clothes home via UPS.) Disney T-shirts are not only great for touring but can serve as swimsuit cover-ups and pajamas as well. And unless you're planning a special evening out at Victoria and Albert's, casual clothing is acceptable everywhere.

Helpful Hint
Juiceboxes. Not only are they handy in the car for the trip down, but you might also want to keep a couple in your bag while touring, because bottled water is $2.50 a drink and kids can become dehydrated rapidly.

✔ Lightweight jackets. It rains in Orlando off and on year-round, so jackets should be water-resistant too.

✔ Basic necessities. These include disposable diapers, baby formula, film, and blank camcorder tapes. All these are available within Disney World, but at premium prices.

✔ Sunscreen. Keep a tube with you and reapply it often. Sunburn is the number-one complaint at the first-aid clinic in the Magic Kingdom. You need sunburn protection all through the year in Orlando, not just during the summer.

✔ A waist pouch or fanny pack. This is a good alternative to dragging along a purse while touring, and it frees up your hands for boarding rides, pushing strollers, and holding on to your kids.

✔ Sunglasses. The Florida sun is so blindingly bright that more than once I've reached into my purse for my sunglasses only to realize I already had them on. Kids too young for sunglasses need wide-billed caps to cut down on the glare.

✔ Strollers. If you're staying at one of the more sprawling resorts—such as the Caribbean Beach, All-Star, Dixie Landings, or Coronado Springs resorts, or the Fort Wilderness Campground—you'll need your own stroller just to get around your hotel.

But if your children are preschoolers and will need a stroller only one or two days of the trip (most likely at Epcot), rental is not a bad option.

How to Get Up-to-Date Information Before You Leave

If you need information before you leave home, write to

> Walt Disney World Guest Information
> P.O. Box 10040
> Lake Buena Vista, FL 32830-0040

or subscribe to *Disney Magazine.* To order, write to

> Disney Magazine
> P.O. Box 37263
> Boone, IA 50037-2263

If you want to get information online, the Disney World home page is at www.disney.com/disneyworld/index2.html. Disney's Web site at www.disney.com has links to all the Disney Web sites worldwide.

At the Hotel

If you need information once you check in to your hotel, both on-site and off-site hotels provide material upon check-in. Study the maps and brochures on your first evening. Guest Services in both on-site and off-site hotels are equipped to answer most questions. The on-site hotels offer nonstop Disney

Helpful Hint
On-site hotels also provide continuous information about park operating hours, special events, and touring tips on your room TV, including an especially helpful program about dinner theaters and special shows, called "Disney Nights."

programming about the parks—including laughably obvious "tips" like "You'll need a ticket to enter the theme parks."

Some of the large off-site hotels have their own entertainment information channels, which keep you up-to-date on not only Disney but also all other Orlando-area attractions.

Magic Kingdom radio is 1030 AM. Epcot is 810 AM. Tune in as you drive into the parks.

If you still have questions, call 407-824-4321. You'll go through minutes of button-pushing torment, but eventually a real live person will come on the line to tell you what time Epcot closes on May 7, the price of the Polynesian Revue for a 10-year-old, and how tall you have to be to ride Splash Mountain.

In the Parks

If you need information once you're in the parks, check with Guest Services, which is located near the main gate of all four major theme parks.

At Epcot, there are WorldKey Information Terminals (which operate like those located beside Spaceship Earth) on the bridges that connect Future World to the World Showcase and in the Germany pavilion. You'll have access to a Disney employee within seconds.

Or flag down the nearest person wearing a Disney name tag. The "cast members" at the theme parks are remarkably helpful and well informed.

The Frantic Factor

Although I'll rate rides throughout this book according to their "scare factor," I've often thought that I should include ratings on the "frantic factor" as well, measuring how hysterical the average parent is apt to become in any given situation.

I'm often asked to speak to parents' groups on the topic of family travel. Almost inevitably, someone asks me how to make a Disney vacation relaxing. These people are very earnest, but they may as well be asking me to recommend a nice ski lodge for their upcoming trip to Hawaii. The only honest response is, "If you want to relax, you're going to the wrong place." Disney World is a high-stimulation environment, a total assault on all five senses mixed in with a constant and mind-boggling array of choices. This is not the week to take your kids off Ritalin. This is not the week to try to come off cigarettes or discuss marital issues with your spouse. This is not the week to relax.

Actually, high stimulation and a lively pace can be fun and may even be the reason most people come to Disney World in the first place. Families who slip over the line from stimulated to frantic often do so because (1) they forget to build in adequate rest breaks, (2) they've planned their trip for the busiest times, (3) they're confused about the logistics of touring, or (4) they are hell-bent on taking it all in because "We're paying through the nose for this" and "Who knows when we'll get back?" This book is full of tips to help you avoid the first three mistakes, but your attitude is pretty much up to you. Just remember that doing it all is not synonymous with having the most fun, and if time is tight, limit your touring to those attractions that have the most appeal to your particular group. As for when you'll get back, who knows? But using this as a rationale for pushing anyone in the family past their personal exhaustion limit only guarantees that you'll never want to come back.

And if you're still fried at the end of the day, don't fret. Nearly every hotel in the Orlando area has a hot tub, and impromptu emotional support groups for parents tend to gather from 5 to 7 P.M. every day.

CHAPTER

2

Choosing
a Hotel

1. Coronado Springs Resort
2. Wide World of Sports
3. Swan Resort
4. Dolphin Resort
5. Yacht & Beach Club Resorts
6. Disney's BoardWalk, BoardWalk Inn & Villas
7. Main Entrance
8. Car Care Center
9. Transportation & Ticket Center Parking
10. Transportation & Ticket Center
11. Polynesian Resort
12. The Grand Floridian
13. Contemporary Resort
14. Wilderness Lodge
15. Fort Wilderness Campground
16. Dixie Landings Resort
17. Port Orleans Resort
18. Old Key West Resort
19. Lake Buena Vista Golf Course
20. Disney Institute
21. Disney Institute Villas
22. Disney's West Side
23. Pleasure Island
24. Caribbean Beach Resort

25. Animal Kingdom Lodge
26. Disney Village Hotels
27. All-Star Resorts

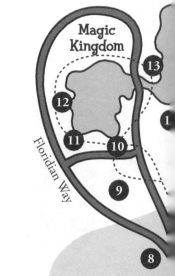

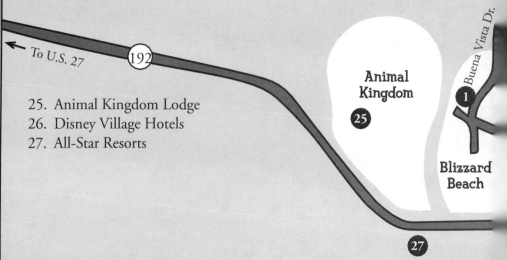

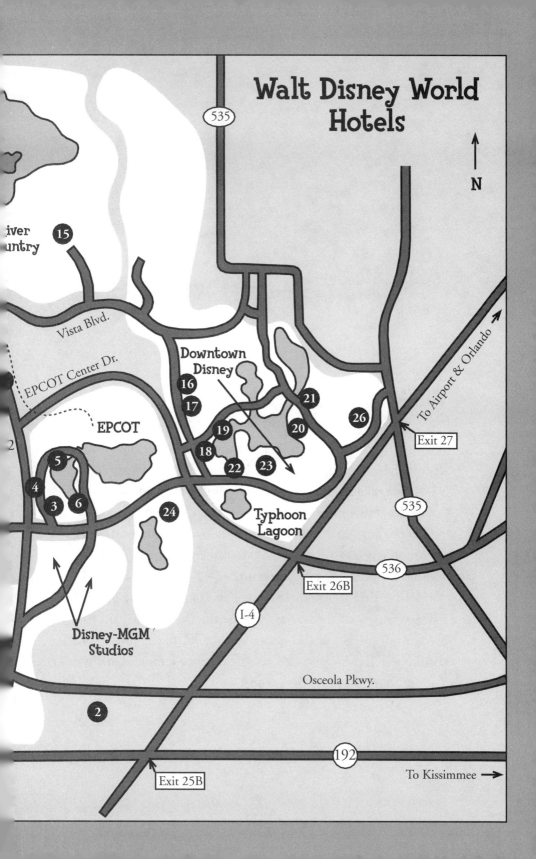

Guide to On-Site Hotels

The ratings for the hotels discussed in this chapter are based on three factors: the response of families I've personally surveyed; the percentage of repeat business a resort experiences, which is a reliable indicator of guest satisfaction; and the quality of the resort in relation to the price. Obviously, you'd expect more amenities and a higher employee-to-guest ratio at a $250-a-night resort than at a $100-a-night resort, so it's unfair to hold them to the same standard.

    With that in mind, I've rated the hotels on the basis of value versus cost; that is, are you getting what you paid for? Do the advantages of this resort make it worth the price? And would you recommend this resort to other families with the same amount of money to spend?

General Information About the On-Site Disney Hotels

@ A deposit equal to the price of one night's lodging is required within 14 days after making your reservation. You may pay by check or credit card. If you cancel at least 5 days in advance, your deposit will be fully refunded.

@ All Disney hotels operate under the family plan, meaning that kids 18 and under stay free with parents. The rooms at the budget and midpriced hotels, as well as the Swan, Dolphin, and Wilderness Lodge, are designed for four people; the other on-site hotels can easily fit five in a room. If your family is larger, consider either a villa or a trailer home.

@ Check-in time is 3 P.M. at most Disney resorts but 4 P.M. at the villas. You can drop off your bags and pick up your tickets and resort IDs in the morning, tour until midafternoon, and then return to your hotel to check in.

@ When you check in, you'll be issued a resort ID that allows you to charge meals, drinks, tickets, and souvenirs to your room and also gives you access to all Disney World transportation.

Time-Saving Tip
Checkout time is 11 A.M., but once again you needn't let this interfere with your touring. Check out early in the morning and store your bags with the concierge or valet parking. Then enjoy your last day in the parks. If you pay with a credit card, you can arrange for automatic checkout; an itemized charge statement is slipped under your door early on the morning you'll be leaving—a definite timesaver.

Quick Guide to

Hotel	Description
All-Star Resorts	Very popular, great price
Beach Club Resort	Homey, lovely, and not one bit fancy
BoardWalk Inn	Rooms are spacious, modern, and attractive
BoardWalk Villas	Great location, close to both Epcot and MGM
Caribbean Beach Resort	Solid value for the money
The Contemporary	Convenient and lively
Coronado Springs Resort	The price is right
Disney Institute Villas	Great for families
Dixie Landings Resort	Unbeatable ambience and amenities
Dolphin Resort	Beautiful resort, but expensive
Fort Wilderness Campground	Great for families who like to camp
The Grand Floridian	Expensive, but luxurious
Old Key West Resort	Lots of room, quiet
The Polynesian Resort	Relaxed and casual with a loyal, repeat clientele
Port Orleans Resort	Transports guests to the heart of the French Quarter
Swan Resort	Adult-oriented and expensive
Wilderness Lodge	Rustic looking, with an intimate feel
Yacht Club Resort	On the door of the Epcot World Showcase

NOTE: *The central reservations number for on-site hotels is 407-W-DISNEY.*

On-Site Hotels

Location	Rating	Price Range	Details on
Animal Kingdom	★★	$74 and up	Page 74
Epcot	★★★	$269–$430	Page 62
Epcot	★★★	$269–$360	Page 64
Epcot	★★	$269–$579	Page 66
Epcot	★★	$124–$169	Page 67
Magic Kingdom	★★	$219–$295	Page 61
Animal Kingdom	★★	$144–$189	Page 76
Downtown Disney	★	$204–$1,300	Page 72
Downtown Disney	★★★	$124–$169	Page 69
Epcot	★	$265–$410	Page 68
Magic Kingdom	★★	$36–$229	Page 59
Magic Kingdom	★★	$304–$515	Page 60
Downtown Disney	★★	$234–$1,155	Page 71
Magic Kingdom	★★★	$279–$425	Page 56
Downtown Disney	★★★	$124–$169	Page 69
Epcot	★	$265–$410	Page 68
Magic Kingdom	★★★	$185–$250	Page 57
Epcot	★★★	$269–$430	Page 62

Is It Worth the Expense to Stay On-Site?

Staying at one of the Disney-owned hotels is very convenient—and with rates as low as $74 a night at the All-Star Resorts, it's becoming more affordable each year.

Off-site hotels are fighting back with special price promotions and perks of their own, arguing that the Disney hotels still cost more and bring you only slightly closer to the action. On-site or off-site? Ask yourself the following questions; your answers will help you decide.

@ What time of year are you going, and how long are you staying?

If you're going in summer or during a major holiday, you'll need every extra minute, so it's worth the cost to stay on-site. (Another reason to book on-site in summer: In the Florida heat, it's nearly a medical necessity to keep young kids out of the sun in midafternoon, and a nearby hotel room makes that easier.) Likewise, if your visit will be for fewer than four days, you can't afford to waste time commuting, so staying on-site is worth considering.

@ Are you flying or driving?

If you're flying and doing only Disney World, it may make more economic sense to stay on-site and use Dis-

Insider's Secret

If your kids are still young enough to take naps, staying on-site makes it much easier to return to your room after lunch for a snooze. If they're preteens who are up to a full day in the parks, commute time is less of a factor.

ney World's transportation system in lieu of a rental car. But if you're driving to Orlando, consider an off-site location. You'll be able to drive into the parks at the hours that suit you without being dependent on those sometimes less-than-prompt off-site buses.

@ How strapped are you for cash?

If money isn't a major issue, stay on-site. If money is a primary consideration, you'll find your best deals at the budget hotels along Interstate 4. Exits 25 and 27, which flank the Disney exit, are chock-full of chain hotels and restaurants. Exit 27 alone has three Days Inns within two blocks of one another.

@ How much do your kids eat?

Food is expensive at Disney World, both in the parks and at the on-site hotels. If you're staying off-site, you can always eat at the numerous fast-food and family-style restaurants along I-4, Route 192, and International Drive. If you book a suite, fixing simple meals in your room is even cheaper, and kids can really load up at those complimentary buffet breakfasts so frequently offered at the off-site hotels.

@ Do you plan to visit other attractions?

If you'll be spending half your time at Sea World, Universal Orlando, or the other non–Disney World attractions, stay off-site, at least during those days. There's no need to pay top dollar for proximity to Disney if you're headed for Islands of Adventure.

@ Will your party be splitting up at times?

Does Dad want to play golf in the afternoon? Do you have teenagers who can spend a day at Blizzard Beach on their own? Will there be times when it would make sense for Dad to take the younger kids back to the hotel while Mom stays in the park with the older ones? Is your 5-year-old raring to go at dawn while your 15-year-old sleeps until noon? If so, stay on-site, where the use of the Disney World transportation system makes it easy for all of you to go your own way.

@ What's your tolerance level for hassles?

If you simply don't want to be bothered with interstate commutes, parking lots, carrying cash, and maps, stay on-site.

The Advantages of Staying On-Site

Disney World offers plenty of perks to lure visitors to their on-site hotels—and to make sure they keep coming back.

Early Entry Mornings

Under the Early Entry program, Disney allows on-site guests into one designated theme park a day an hour earlier than off-site guests. When you check in, you're given a brochure that tells you which park is open early on which day. Because visitors are almost always admitted to the theme parks 30 minutes before the stated opening time, this program means that on-site guests may find themselves inside the Magic Kingdom as early as 7:30 on mornings when the official opening time is 9 A.M.

At present the Magic Kingdom opens up early on Monday, Thursday, and Saturday. Epcot opens early on Tuesday and Friday, MGM on Wednesday and Sunday. The Animal Kingdom, which opens earlier than the other parks on all days of the week, is not included in the Early Entry Cycle. Confirm these days with the information you are given at check-in; like every thing else at WDW, they're subject to change.

Generally only one part of the park is open during the first hour. For example, in the Magic Kingdom it's presently Fantasyland and Tomorrowland, which means that you can ride Space Mountain, Dumbo, and the other attractions within these sections with minimal waits. Then when the ropes drop at the official opening time, allowing you into the other sections, you're already deep within the park. You can head straight for Splash Mountain or any other attraction that will be crowded later in the day.

Insider's Secret

Some families told us that because Disney has so many hotels, and thus so many on-site guests, they use reverse psychology and visit one of the parks not featured as that day's Early Entry park. "If the sheet says Epcot, everyone runs to Epcot like lemmings," writes one father.

There's little doubt that the park featured each day draws more people than it ordinarily would—and remains more crowded all day. The answer may be to visit the featured Early Entry park when it opens and stay until midmorning, during which time you visit the biggie attractions that are opened early. Then go to one of the other parks in the afternoon.

Priority Seating

On-site guests can arrange for priority restaurant seating both within the theme parks and at on-site hotels up to 60 days in advance. Some restaurants allow for 120 days in advance, so ask when making arrangements. Because there are so many on-site guests, this perk has the effect of freezing off-site visitors out of the most popular restaurants at the most popular times.

Length-of-Stay Passes

These tickets, which can be tailored to fit the length of your stay, offer you unlimited access to the major and minor parks and are slightly cheaper than comparable multiday passes.

Transportation

On-site guests have unlimited use of the monorails, buses, and boats of the Disney World transportation system, which is your best bet for getting to the major parks. The buses for the on-site hotels, for example, can deliver riders right to the Magic Kingdom gates, eliminating the need to take a ferryboat or monorail from the Ticket and Transportation Center (TTC)—and cutting at least 15 minutes off the commute.

Using Disney transportation can save you money, since many families staying on-site don't rent a car. Round-trip cab or shuttle transportation from the airport to the on-site hotels runs around $60 to $70 for a family of four. Compare that to the average $300 rate for weekly car rental—which you may need if staying off-site—and the result is real savings.

Use of Other On-Site Hotel Facilities

If you want to use the child-care or sporting facilities of other Disney hotels or dine at their restaurants, you'll receive preferential treatment over off-site visitors. (Of course, each hotel, reasonably enough, allows its own guests first shot at its services.) This means that even if you're staying at the midpriced Dixie Landings, you can use the kids' club at the Polynesian or take a tennis lesson at the Grand Floridian.

Charging Privileges

If you're staying on-site, everyone in your party will be issued a resort ID the day you arrive. The ID allows you to charge tickets, souvenirs, and food at sit-down restaurants—either at the hotels or within the parks—to your hotel room. (The small vendors selling things like ice cream or bottled water still require cash.) It's certainly better not to have to carry huge amounts of cash all the time, especially at the pools, water parks, and marinas.

It's up to you whether or not your older kids have charging privileges. It makes it easier to send Johnny to the snack bar for a round of Cokes, but if you do opt to give the minors charging privileges, be sure to impress upon them that these IDs work like credit cards; they are not an open invitation for the kids to ingratiate themselves with the gang in the arcade by ordering pizza for everyone, purchasing all seven dwarfs from the hotel gift shop, or, heaven forbid, obtaining cash advances.

Helpful Hint

If an ID with charging privileges is lost, it should be reported to the front desk immediately to avoid unauthorized charges.

Family Atmosphere

All the on-site hotels are designed with families in mind—the ambience is casual, security is very tight, and there are always other kids around to play with. The on-site hotels have laundry facilities, generally located near the pools and arcades so that you can run a load while the youngsters play; there is late-night pizza delivery to your room, or you can visit fast-food courts; and if there is not a child-care facility at your particular hotel, Guest Services can help you arrange for an in-room sitter. The emphasis at the Disney hotels is on making life more convenient for parents.

Cool Themes

All the on-site hotels have a theme that is carried out in megadetail. At the Polynesian, you're always greeted by the staff with "Aloha," jazz music plays all day at Port Orleans, and the dressers in rooms at All-Star Sports look like gym lockers. This makes staying at an on-site hotel almost as exciting for kids as being inside the parks.

In fact, because the on-site hotels are so unspeakably cool, it can be fun to just visit other hotels when you need an afternoon break from touring. Many families told us that they ate meals at several different on-site hotels during their visit; the restaurants carry out the themes too, so if three days at the Polynesian have left you burned out on pineapple juice, go Mexican at Coronado Springs.

Rating the On-Site Disney Hotels

Not content with merely dominating the entertainment market, the Walt Disney Company has begun turning its attention to lodging the 10 million visitors who stream into Orlando each year. Orlando has more than 100,000 hotel rooms, and an increasing percentage of these rooms are Disney-owned—that is, on-site.

The majority of the new hotels added by Disney fall into the budget and midpriced categories. Until now, cost has been the primary reason for visitors to stay off-site; with the explosion in on-site budget and midpriced resorts, Disney is work-

Best On-Site Choices at a Glance

BEST MAGIC KINGDOM RESORT: WILDERNESS LODGE

This resort has just knocked off the longtime champ, the Polynesian. The Wilderness Lodge has a lot of repeat business; once families stay here, they report that they have no interest in going anywhere else.

BEST EPCOT RESORT: THE BEACH CLUB

You like Epcot? It's a stroll away— and the pool is to die for.

BEST MODERATELY PRICED RESORT: PORT ORLEANS

The best of both worlds—all the charm and intimacy of a full-priced hotel at a reduced cost.

BEST BUDGET RESORT: ALL-STAR SPORTS, MUSIC, AND MOVIES

The All-Star Sports, Music, and Movies have the distinction of being both the winner and the only entry in the category—but they're still worth mentioning because of strong reader support.

BEST VILLA: BOARDWALK VILLAS

A great location, tons of eateries, and lively nightlife just outside your door.

ing to eliminate even that objection. Each time Disney opens a new resort, your options increase.

And the need to make decisions multiplies as well. All this expansion means that even if a family has decided to stay on-site, they still face a bewildering number of choices. Does the convenience of being on the monorail line justify the increase in price? Do you want to stay amid turn-of-the-century Victorian splendor, or is a fort more your style? Is it important to be near swimming, golf courses, stables, and other sporting activities, or do you plan to spend most of your time in the parks? As with all of Disney World, making the best choice hinges on your awareness of what your family really wants.

Definition of Star Ratings for Hotels

★★★ This resort was a favorite among families surveyed and offers solid value for the money.

★★ Surveyed families were satisfied with the service and amenities at this property and felt they got what they paid for.

★ This resort is either more adult-oriented, with fewer amenities designed to appeal to families, or is more expensive than you'd expect considering the location or level of service.

On-Site Luxury Hotels

Luxury hotels are actually full-scale resorts, with fine dining, amenities such as health clubs and spas, and a variety of sporting options. You can have valet parking, bell service, room service, and other perks that make the mechanics of checking in and out much easier. There's a price attached—the Disney luxury hotels cost, on average, twice as much a night as the midpriced hotels. Luxury hotels include the BoardWalk, Yacht and Beach Club, Contemporary, Grand Floridian, Polynesian, Swan, Dolphin, Wilderness Lodge, and Animal Kingdom Lodge.

On-Site Midpriced and Budget Hotels

"Midpriced" is something of a misnomer because both the price and the quality are higher than for a typical chain hotel in Orlando. You'll pay about $30 more a night than you would at a comparable off-site hotel, but you get a mood that's pure Disney. As you sip a drink and watch your kids zoom down the tongue of the beloved sea serpent slide at the Port Orleans pool, you certainly won't feel like you're slumming. The hotels are well maintained and landscaped, with gobs of atmosphere thrown in to carry their motifs to the nth degree. Resorts that fall into the midpriced description include the Caribbean Beach, Port Orleans, Dixie Landings, and Coronado Springs Resorts.

The budget hotels are the All-Star Resorts—3 mega hotels, including All-Star Music, All-Star Sports, and All-Star Movies.

It's worth noting that the budget and midpriced hotels don't run with quite the legendary efficiency of the more expensive resorts. I recently endured a 40-minute check-in procedure at All-Star Sports, something that would be unheard of at the Grand Floridian. A woman behind me was grousing that there was no freebie Mickey Mouse lotion in her room like they had at the Yacht Club. But these minor inconveniences pale when you consider that most of the on-site benefits—easy transportation to the parks, help with tickets and reservations, the Early Entry perk—are just as available to those paying $74 a night at the All-Star Resorts as to those paying $374 at the BoardWalk. And, hey, the maids still leave your kids' stuffed animals in the window to greet them in the evening, so who can complain?

Villa-Style Accommodations

Larger families or those who would like to prepare their own meals may want to rent a villa. Resorts included in this category are the BoardWalk Villas, Disney's Old Key West, and the Disney Institute Villas.

On-Site Camping

If you want to stay on-site but can't afford one of the resorts, camping at the Fort Wilderness Campground may be your best option.

Magic Kingdom Hotels

If you'll be spending most of your time at the Magic Kingdom—and you're willing to spend the bucks—consider one of these resorts.

The Polynesian Resort
★★★
407-824-2000

Designed to emulate an island village, the Polynesian is relaxed and casual. The main desk, as well as most of the restaurants and shops, is in the Great Ceremonial House, along with orchids, parrots, and fountains. Guests stay in one of the 863 rooms in the sprawling "long houses."

Proximity to the Magic Kingdom	Excellent, via direct monorail, launch, or ferryboat
Proximity to Epcot	Good, via monorail with one change at the TTC
Proximity to MGM	Fair, via bus
Proximity to the Animal Kingdom	Fair, via bus

Pluses

+ The Polynesian offers the most options for transport to the Magic Kingdom. You're on the monorail line but also within walking distance of the ferryboats, and launches leave from the docks regularly. Your best route to the Magic Kingdom depends on the location of your room. Near the lagoon? Take the launch. Near the Great Ceremonial House? The monorail is faster. On the beach? Walk to the ferryboat.

+ A private beach, with an attractive pool and several boating options, is available. Like the beach at the Grand Floridian, the Polynesian beach has canvas shells that provide shade for napping babies and toddlers digging in the sand.

+ The Neverland Club is the best on-site child care in Walt Disney World.

Minuses

– Without a discount, expect to pay $279 to $425 a night.

– Like the Contemporary, it's an older resort.

Overall Grade: ★★★ The Polynesian enjoys a loyal repeat clientele, and that says it all.

The Wilderness Lodge	★★★ 407-824-3200

Disney opened the Wilderness Lodge near the campgrounds of Fort Wilderness in 1994. At about $185 to $250 a night, the rustic-looking, western-spirited resort is aimed at filling the gap between the midpriced and luxury hotels.

As is typical with the newer resorts, the theme of Wilderness Lodge extends into every aspect of the hotel's design—the pool begins indoors as a hot spring and then flows into a meandering creek, culminating with a waterfall into the rocky caverns of the outdoor pool. The awe-inspiring lobby, which looks like a Lincoln log project run amok, centers on an 82-foot fireplace that blazes all year round. The quilted bedspreads and Indian wallpaper in the guest rooms, the staff dressed like park rangers, and even the stick ponies children ride to their tables in the Whispering Canyon Cafe—all combine to evoke the feel of a National Park Service lodge built a hundred years ago.

When you check in, you're given a brochure on Wilderness Lodge lore, which will help you find the 100 animals hidden in the lobby, many of them carved into totems or branded into chandeliers. And you'll learn that "it took over 2 billion years to build the fireplace," because the rock represents strata from all the layers of the Grand Canyon.

Proximity to the Magic Kingdom	Good, via launch
Proximity to Epcot	Fair, via bus
Proximity to MGM	Fair, via bus
Proximity to the Animal Kingdom	Fair, via bus

Pluses

+ The lodge is heavily themed. The pool area is especially dramatic.

+ You are close to River Country and have all the down-home fun of Fort Wilderness without having to camp.

+ On-site child care.

+ Tons of happy quasi-campers here. The Wilderness Lodge enjoys a loyal repeat business.

Minuses

− At $185 to $250 a night, it's still not cheap.

− This is the only Magic Kingdom resort without monorail access to the Kingdom. The boat takes slightly longer.

− The rooms sleep only four people (the other full-priced resorts sleep five).

Overall Grade: ★★★

Fort Wilderness Campground

★★
407-824-2900

A resort unto itself, Fort Wilderness offers campsites for tents and RVs as well as air-conditioned trailers for rent. The wide-open spaces, perfect for volleyball, biking, and hiking, are a relief for families with kids old enough to explore on their own.

Proximity to the Magic Kingdom	Good, via bus or launch
Proximity to Epcot	Fair, directly via bus, or via bus to the TTC, where you can change to the monorail
Proximity to MGM	Fair, via bus
Proximity to the Animal Kingdom	Fair, via bus

Pluses

+ Fort Wilderness offers a huge variety of activities for kids, such as hayrides, horseback and pony riding, and a petting farm with pigs, goats, and geese.

+ Proximity to River Country and the Hoop-Dee-Doo Musical Revue.

+ Hookups and tent sites are as low as $36 a night. The trailers rent for about $229 a night but sleep six people and offer full kitchens.

+ Groceries are available at the on-site trading post.

+ Daily maid service is free in the rental trailers.

Minuses

− Camping may not seem like a vacation to you.

− A large number of people are sharing relatively few facilities, and the pools and beach can get very crowded.

- Some families have reported the rental trailers are quite shabby and not up to Disney standards. One woman wrote that the first time she entered her rental trailer, the doorknob fell off in her hand!

- The place is so spread out that it requires its own in-resort bus system to get guests from one area to another. You can rent golf carts or bikes, but make no mistake: Fort Wilderness is large and hard to navigate.

Overall Grade: ★★ If you like to camp and are willing to put up with a little inconvenience for great savings, this is a good option.

The Grand Floridian
★★
407-824-3000

Modeled after the famed Florida beach resorts of the 1800s and possibly the prettiest of all Disney hotels, the Grand Floridian has 900 rooms ensconced among its gabled roofs, soaring ceilings, and broad white verandas.

Proximity to the Magic Kingdom	Excellent, via direct monorail or launch
Proximity to Epcot	Good, via monorail with a change at the TTC
Proximity to MGM	Fair, via bus
Proximity to Animal Kingdom	Fair, via bus

Pluses

+ Convenient location on the monorail line.

+ A private beach on the Seven Seas Lagoon and numerous boating options.

+ On-site child-care center.

+ Phenomenal dining. Citricos and Victoria and Albert's are among the finest restaurants in all of Disney World. If you have the kids along, check out 1900 Park Fare, which serves a buffet with the characters.

+ On-site health club.

+ Exceptionally lovely rooms. The Grand Floridian is a favorite with honeymooners and others seeking a romantic ambience. (It's within sight of Disney's wedding chapel.)

Minuses

– Extremely pricey, with rooms from $304 to $515 a night.

– The elegance puts off some families who feel funny trooping past a grand piano in dripping bathing suits.

Overall Grade: ★★ Expensive but luxurious.

The Contemporary Resort   ★★
407-824-1000

You'll either love or hate the Contemporary, which has 1,050 rooms surrounding a mammoth high-tech lobby full of shops and restaurants. This place is always hopping.

Proximity to the Magic Kingdom	Excellent, via direct monorail
Proximity to Epcot	Good, via monorail with a change at the TTC
Proximity to MGM	Fair, via bus
Proximity to the Animal Kingdom	Fair, via bus

Pluses

+ Located on the monorail line.

+ Fairly easy to book, and discounts are available.

+ Disney movies are shown nightly, and the Contemporary is also home to the Fiesta Fun Center, a giant arcade.

+ The standard water sports are available, along with tennis and a spa.

+ The California Grille is one of Walt Disney World's premier restaurants.

Minuses

– It's loud, with a big-city feel that is exactly what many families come to Florida to escape. "Like sleeping in the middle of Space Mountain," wrote one mother. Note: The Garden Wings are both quieter and cheaper than the main building.

– Like the other hotels on the monorail line, the Contemporary is expensive. Expect to pay $219 to $295 a night.

Overall Grade: ★★ Convenient and lively. Perhaps a little too lively.

Epcot Hotels

The Epcot resorts share their own "backdoor" entrance into Epcot's World Showcase. Trams, water taxis, and walkways link the resorts to Epcot, where guests can enter the park, buy tickets, get maps, and rent strollers from the World Traveler shop. The World Showcase does not open until 11 A.M., so buses transport Epcot resort guests directly to Future World.

The Disney Yacht and Beach Clubs	★★★ 407-934-7000

Designed to resemble a turn-of-the-century Nantucket seaside resort, the Yacht and Beach Clubs are situated on a 25-acre freshwater lake. The Yacht Club, with 635 rooms, is the more elegant of the two, but the sunny gingham-and-wicker-filled Beach Club, with 580 rooms, is equally charming. The Yacht and Beach Clubs hit the perfect balance for families with young kids in tow—homey, lovely, and not one bit fancy.

Proximity to the Magic Kingdom	Fair, via bus
Proximity to Epcot	Excellent, via a short stroll over a bridge
Proximity to MGM	Excellent, via water taxi
Proximity to the Animal Kingdom	Fair, via bus

Pluses

+ Stormalong Bay, the water recreation area that separates the two resorts, is like a private water park. The sand-bottomed "bay" contains pools of varying depths, water-slides, and a wrecked ship for atmosphere. It's especially fun to climb the shipwreck nearly to the top of its rigging and then zoom through a long tube into the middle of the pool. In fact, the water areas at the Yacht and Beach Clubs are so nice you'll have no trouble convincing the kids to return "home" for a dip in lieu of a more time-consuming trek to Typhoon Lagoon or Blizzard Beach.

+ The Yacht and Beach Clubs are literally on the doorstep of the Epcot World Showcase and an easy boat commute to MGM as well.

+ The Sandcastle Club offers on-site child care for children ages 3 to 12.

+ Disney characters are on hand for breakfast at the Cape May Cafe in the Beach Club.

+ The two resorts share an on-site health club.

+ Bayside Marina offers paddleboats, pontoons, and Toobies—small motorized bumper boats that can be rented for $10 for a half-hour.

Minuses

− Rates run $269 to $430 a night, but discounts do apply in the off-season.

Overall Grade: ★★★ These hotels enjoy a large repeat business from satisfied families. If your kids like hanging out at the pool, and you all like Epcot, try the Yacht or Beach Club on your next trip down.

The BoardWalk Inn

★★★
407-939-5100

The BoardWalk Inn and the BoardWalk Villas form the hub of a large complex with convention space, four restaurants, the ESPN sports club, as well as a dance and comedy club. The mood? Turn-of-the-century Atlantic City. Cheery, attractive rooms are clustered above an old-fashioned boardwalk, and the action on the waterfront goes on until late at night.

In fact, some readers have written in to claim that the BoardWalk is a far more affordable version of Pleasure Island. The two nightclubs, Atlantic Dance and Jellyrolls, charge a slight cover during the on-season, but even with this you'll be paying far less than the $18 admission fee to Pleasure Island.

The midway-style games, carnival barkers, and arcades can keep older kids busy. A fun extra is renting a surrey bike ($10.75 for a half-hour) and taking the whole gang for a loop around the lagoon. (You'll be gasping for air by the time you pass the Yacht Club.) The BoardWalk area is stunningly beautiful at night.

Proximity to the Magic Kingdom   Fair, via bus
Proximity to Epcot   Excellent, via a short stroll
Proximity to MGM   Excellent, via water taxi
Proximity to the Animal Kingdom   Fair, via bus

Pluses

+ Great location for both Epcot and MGM.

+ A far, far wider selection of restaurants and entertainment than at the other resorts.

+ The resort is relatively new and looks it. The rooms are spacious, modern, and attractive.

+ On-site health club.

+ An excellent selection of water activities—and surrey bike rental is awesome.

+ You'll have no trouble keeping older kids entertained here—although you may go broke in the process.

+ On-site kids' club.

Minuses

− Expensive, at $269 to $360 a night.

− May be too lively and hopping for families with very young kids.

Overall Grade: ★★★ You'll feel like you're right in the middle of the action—because you are.

BoardWalk Villas

★★
407-939-5100

The villa side of the BoardWalk complex offers the same lively activities and great restaurant selection—as well as more room upstairs. Many of the suites have whirlpool tubs, and the mini-kitchens are well stocked. Villa units are a bit more expensive than the regular rooms.

Proximity to the Magic Kingdom	Fair, via bus
Proximity to Epcot	Excellent, via a short stroll
Proximity to MGM	Excellent, via water taxi
Proximity to the Animal Kingdom	Fair, via bus

Pluses

+ Lots of space for large families.

+ Food can be prepared in the room—saving you money.

+ Great location for both Epcot and MGM.

+ A far, far wider selection of restaurants and entertainment than at the other resorts.

+ On-site health club.

+ An excellent selection of water activities.

+ Proximity to the ESPN Sports Club.

+ Plenty of activities to keep older kids entertained.

+ On-site kids' club.

Minuses

– Expensive, at $269 to $579 a night.

– May be too lively and hopping for families with very young kids.

Overall Grade: ★★ New, fresh, and fun—and a great option if you have a large family and need the space of a villa.

Caribbean Beach Resort

★★
407-934-3400

This family-priced 2,112-room resort is located on 200 acres with a private lake and white-sand beaches. Each section of this mammoth hotel is painted a different tropical color and named after a different Caribbean island. Each "island" has its own shuttle-bus stop, private beach, and pool. The rooms, although small, are attractively decorated.

Proximity to the Magic Kingdom	Fair, via bus
Proximity to Epcot	Fair, via bus
Proximity to MGM	Fair, via bus
Proximity to the Animal Kingdom	Fair, via bus

Pluses

+ The price is right, at $124 to $169 a night.

+ Parrot Cay, a manmade island with a playground, climbing fort, and small aviary, is fun for young kids.

+ The standard selection of watercraft.

+ Fast food, as well as a full-service restaurant, is available in the plaza called Old Port Royale.

Minuses

− Although the buses are regular, they're not as swift as the water taxis or monorails. Expect a longer commute time.

− The place is huge. It may be a major hike from your hotel room to the food plaza or marina. If you have young kids, bring your own stroller.

− No on-site child care.

Overall Grade: ★★ Solid value for the money.

The Disney Swan and Disney Dolphin ★ 407-934-3000

This convention/resort complex is connected to Epcot and MGM by water taxi and bridges. The Swan and Dolphin are "twin" hotels (like the nearby Yacht and Beach Clubs), which means that although they have separate check-ins (and are in fact owned by separate companies), the resorts are alike in architecture and mood. Both the Swan and the Dolphin have an emphatically sophisticated feel; but since their openings, both have also made great strides to become more family-oriented and offer amenities directed toward the parents of young children.

Proximity to the Magic Kingdom	Fair, via bus
Proximity to Epcot	Excellent, via tram or water taxi
Proximity to MGM	Excellent, via water taxi
Proximity to the Animal Kingdom	Fair, via bus

Pluses

+ Disney is aggressively going after the convention trade with the Swan and Dolphin. If a working parent is lucky, he or she can score a free family vacation here.

+ Camp Swan and Camp Dolphin offer excellent on-site child care. Planned activities range from tennis programs to craft classes, are geared for kids as young as 3, and are reasonably priced.

+ The new, expanded beach area offers a playground, kiddie pools, waterslides, and a small marina with paddleboats.

+ Bike rentals, tennis courts, and health clubs are also available.

Minuses

- Expensive, at $265 to $410 a night.

- Although considered on-site, these hotels are not owned by Disney and have less of a Disney feel. It's an intangible, but you notice the difference immediately.

- Because of the proximity to Epcot and MGM and the fact that they're gunning for the convention trade, these are adult-oriented resorts, with a citified atmosphere.

Overall Grade: ★ A great place to go if the company is picking up the tab. Otherwise, try the Yacht and Beach Clubs first.

Downtown Disney Hotels

Port Orleans and Dixie Landings	★★★ 407-934-5000

These hotels are both based on an Old South theme; they offer unbeatable amenities and ambience for the price. Port Orleans transports guests to the heart of the French Quarter, with manicured gardens, wrought-iron railings, and streets with names like Rue d'Baga. The Mardi Gras mood extends to the pool area, dubbed the "Doubloon Lagoon," where alligators play jazz while King Triton sits atop the waterslide regally surveying his domain.

Dixie Landings is a bit more down-home than Port Orleans, with a steamboat-shaped lobby, general stores run by gingham-clad girls in braids, and "Ol' Man Island"—a swimming area based on the Disney film *Song of the South*. A bit schizophrenic in architecture, with white-columned buildings encircling fishing holes and cotton mills, Dixie Landings manages to mix in a variety of Southern clichés without losing its ditzy charm. If Huck Finn ever married Scarlett O'Hara, this is where they'd come on their honeymoon.

Comparatively speaking, Port Orleans is only half the size of Dixie Landings—which is the major reason it gets our nod as the best. At Port Orleans the odds are that you'll be close to the pool, lobby, food court, and shuttle bus station; at Dixie Landings, getting around is more of a headache. Both resorts have a fast-food court, a sit-down restaurant, and a bar that offers live entertainment. The food court at Dixie Landings is more complete, but the sit-down restaurant at Port Orleans is quieter and more relaxing. If you're in a rush, the Creole munchies in the Port Orleans bar and the Cajun ones at the Dixie Landings bar make an adequate meal.

Proximity to the Magic Kingdom	Fair, via bus
Proximity to Epcot	Fair, via bus
Proximity to MGM	Fair, via bus
Proximity to the Animal Kingdom	Fair, via bus

Pluses

+ Great pools (especially at Port Orleans), which can easily keep the kids entertained for an afternoon.

+ So cleverly designed and beautifully maintained that you won't believe you're staying on-site for half the price of the other resorts. (Rooms are $124 to $169.)

+ Both hotels have marinas with the standard selection of watercraft as well as bike rentals.

+ The Sassagoula Steamboat offers both resorts easy water access to Downtown Disney and Pleasure Island.

Minuses

– Unless you drive your own car, you are dependent on buses for transport to the major and minor parks, which means a slightly longer commuting time. The fact that the two resorts share buses slows you down a bit.

– No on-site child care.

Overall Grade: ★★★ You get a good deal here in more ways than one.

Disney's Old Key West ★★
407-827-7700

Designed to be sold as time-shares, the villas of Old Key West (formerly known as the Vacation Club) are available for nightly rentals. You'll get all the standard amenities of a Disney resort—plus a lot more room.

Proximity to the Magic Kingdom	Fair, via bus
Proximity to Epcot	Fair, via bus
Proximity to MGM	Fair, via bus
Proximity to the Animal Kingdom	Fair, via bus

Pluses

+ If you have more than two children and need to spread out, or if you'd like a kitchen where you can prepare your own meals, Old Key West is a good on-site option.

+ Tennis, pools, a cute sand play area with a permanent castle, and a marina are on-site. There's an arcade, fitness room, and movies for rental.

+ Prices run from $234 for a studio with a kitchenette to $1,155 for a three-bedroom Grand Villa, which could easily accommodate 12 people. A roomy two-bedroom villa with full kitchen is about $455, which compares with a room at the Grand Floridian or Yacht Club. If you're willing to swap proximity to the parks for more space and the chance to cook your own meals, Old Key West may be just what you need.

Minuses

– Still much pricier than off-site villas such as Embassy Suites.

– Quieter, with less going on than at the resorts.

– No child-care options.

Overall Grade: ★★

Disney Institute Villas

★
800-496-6337

Designed for families—large families—these villas are far from the maddening crowd, tucked behind Downtown Disney. Formerly known as the Disney Village Resort Villas, the resort offers one-, two-, and three-room villas. Many of the guests are taking classes at the Disney Institute or are golfers looking for action on the nearby courses.

Proximity to the Magic Kingdom	Fair, via bus
Proximity to Epcot	Fair, via bus
Proximity to MGM	Fair, via bus
Proximity to the Animal Kingdom	Fair, via bus

Pluses

+ Proximity to Downtown Disney and Pleasure Island.

+ Proximity to golf.

+ You have a choice of one-, two-, or three-bedroom villas.

+ Best choice for those traveling with a huge brood, such as a family reunion; several villas easily sleep up to 12 people. Some of the villas are designed like treehouses, while others have lofts and skylights.

+ As well as great access to golf, you'll find tennis, boating, biking, and six small swimming pools.

+ Proximity to all the activities of the Disney Institute, including the huge health club—by far the best in all of Disney World, if not Florida.

Minuses

− You're a fairly long way from the theme parks, even by bus.

− Buses have to snake through a spread-out complex, with lots of pickup points. It can add up to a pretty long commute.

− There's only one restaurant, although if you're cooking in your villa a lot, this may not be a problem. You also have access to plenty of eateries at the nearby Downtown Disney.

− The villas, although recently refurbished, are much older than those at Old Key West or the BoardWalk. The architecture is very low key, and the resort is not as thematic as the other on-site hotels.

− It's quite expensive, with villas ranging from $204 to $1,300 a night. Average villas run about $359, and far cheaper suites can be found off-site.

− Guests of the Disney Institute get first crack at the villas. If the Institute isn't full, other people are welcome to rent the villas—but you may feel like a stranger at someone else's party.

Overall Grade: ★ Lots of space, but you have to rely on buses or your own car to get to where the action is.

Animal Kingdom Hotels

All-Star Sports, All-Star Music, ★★ *and All-Star Movies Resorts* 407-939-5000/939-6000

The All-Star Resorts have rapidly built such a loyal following that, despite having nearly 6,000 rooms, they fill up quickly. There are three reasons for the resorts' success—price, price, and price. The All-Star Resorts make staying on-site possible for families who previously could only dream of such a splurge.

All-Star Sports contains five sections—tennis, football, surfing, basketball, and baseball—with the decor themed appropriately. At the Music Resort, you can choose between jazz, rock 'n' roll, country, calypso, and Broadway tunes. All-Star Movies offers *The Love Bug, Toy Story, Fantasia, 101 Dalmatians,* and *The Mighty Ducks.*

The in-your-face graphics of the brightly colored buildings and the resorts' general zaniness appeal to kids. There are giant tennis ball cans and cowboy boots, a walk-through jukebox, and footballs the size of houses. At the calypso pool in All-Star Music, the buildings are lime green and punctuated with maracas; pitcher Goofy throws water in the diamond-shaped baseball pool at All-Star Sports and stands as goalie at the hockey rink of the Mighty Ducks pool at All-Star Movies. Palm trees are set to tip off before a gargantuan backboard in the basketball section of All-Star Sports, Mickey conducts sprays of water in the Fantasia pool of All-Star Movies, and show tunes play all day under the marquee on the streets of the Broadway district. It's budget, but it ain't boring.

Proximity to the Magic Kingdom	Fair, via bus
Proximity to Epcot	Fair, via bus
Proximity to MGM	Fair, via bus
Proximity to the Animal Kingdom	Good, via a short bus ride

Pluses

+ In a word, cost. Rooms start at $74 during the off-season.

+ All-Star Resorts offers an affordable option for families with a disabled member. For $89 a night you can have a slightly larger ground-floor suite with roll-in showers.

+ The shuttle buses are a good transportation option, considering the price. When you get into this price range at the off-site hotels, you often have to pay for a shuttle. They run every 15 minutes, and service is prompt.

+ Proximity to Blizzard Beach and the Animal Kingdom.

+ The food court, although crowded, provides a fair selection.

Minuses

- Food options are limited. Fast-food courts only, with no restaurants or indoor bars.

- Sports options are limited; swimming is about it.

- The rooms are very small; they sleep four, but you'll be bunched.

- By breaking each resort into five separate sections, Disney is striving to eliminate that sleeping-in-the-middle-of-Penn-Station feel. But there's no way around the fact that it takes more effort to get around a huge hotel than a small one.

– Longer check-in than is typical for Disney resorts.

Overall Grade: ★★ Lots of bang for the buck here.

Coronado Springs Resort	★★ 407-939-1000

Disney's first moderately priced convention hotel has a Mexican theme, with Spanish tiled roofs, adobe walls, and a pool area that is dominated by an imposing Mayan temple. The rooms are scattered around a 15-acre lake and a series of rocky streams. Most of the action centers on the 95,000-square-foot convention space, but the resort is open to regular vacationers as well.

Proximity to the Magic Kingdom	Fair, via bus
Proximity to Epcot	Fair, via bus
Proximity to MGM	Fair, via bus
Proximity to the Animal Kingdom	Good, via a short bus ride

Pluses

+ Dramatic pool area with waterslide, arcade, bar and fast-food stand, and a themed playground. The Dig Site is the heart of all the resort action.

+ Marina with standard boat and bike rentals.

+ On-site health club—a rarity in this price range.

+ An elegant New World Cuisine restaurant called the Maya Grill. Be sure to ask to see the desserts.

+ Close to the Animal Kingdom and Blizzard Beach.

Minuses

— Coronado Springs is designed as a convention hotel, meaning that you have more businesspeople and fewer families than is typical for a Disney resort. You might actually hear cursing by the pool here.

— The food court is far too small to accommodate nearly 2,000 rooms. Some families have reported that they had to leave the resort to get a quick breakfast during peak hours.

— The resort is quite spread out, even by Disney standards. If you're in one of the more far-flung rooms, you may face a 15-minute walk to the pool area and food court. Definitely bring strollers for little ones and rent bikes for the older kids or have them bring their in-line skates.

Overall Grade: ★★ The price is right, and the resort is gaining in popularity.

Disney's Animal Kingdom Lodge   Coming Soon

The Animal Kingdom Lodge, located just southwest of the Animal Kingdom theme park, is set to open in Spring 2001.

The Animal Kingdom Lodge will offer the same dramatic theming as the Wilderness Lodge (they have the same designer) but with a safari twist; the crescent design allows many of the rooms a direct view of the resort's 30-acre private savanna where over 100 animals will live. Besides the chance to see an impala from your bedroom window, expect a flowing swimming pool, a marketplace-themed food court and shopping area, a Simba's Clubhouse play area for the kids, and a multicultural restaurant combining the flavors of Malaysian, Indian, Chinese, and French cuisines.

Prices have not yet been set, but the 1,307-room resort will likely fall into the luxury price range, and offer bus service to all Disney parks. For details, call 407-W-DISNEY.

Disney Village Hotels

The Disney Village Hotels include the Buena Vista Palace, the Grosvenor, Doubletree Suites, the Hilton, the Hotel Royal Plaza, the Courtyard by Marriott, and the Travelodge Hotel.

Because they're neither owned by Disney nor built on Disney property, the Disney Village Hotels are somewhat of a hybrid between the on-site and off-site lodgings. Located just across the road from the Downtown Disney Marketplace, these hotels are also considered to be "official" Disney World hotels, meaning they run frequent shuttles to all Disney theme parks and offer price breaks on admission tickets. Nonetheless, I have trouble recommending the Village Hotels with a clear conscience. They're quite expensive for what you get, and less pricey accommodations are available just a couple of minutes away on Exit 27. If you do opt for a Village Hotel, consider the Hilton, which has a kids' club.

Proximity to the Magic Kingdom:	Fair, via bus
Proximity to Epcot:	Fair, via bus
Proximity to MGM:	Fair, via bus
Proximity to the Animal Kingdom:	Fair, via bus
Proximity to Downtown Disney:	Excellent, via a short walk

Great Off-Site Hotels for Families

Although on-site resorts offer proximity to Disney World parks and plenty of perks, there are deals to be had at off-site hotels too.

Delta Orlando Resort ★★
407-351-3340

Located just across from Universal Orlando and the new Islands of Adventure, the Delta Orlando offers resort-style amenities at budget prices. Wally's Kids Club, named after resort mascot Wally Gator, provides daily activities for children 4 to 12 from 10 A.M. to 6 P.M.

In addition to scavenger hunts, pool games, and crafts, special activities are highlighted on a regular basis: There may be a cooking lesson with the resort chef (the kids return wearing chef hats and clutching sacks of chocolate cookies that they made themselves), a scuba demonstration in the pool, a tennis clinic, or a magic class taught by a professional magician. There's a small fee (usually around $6) for these special activities. On Thursday, Friday, and Saturday nights there's a themed Kids' Night Out featuring dinner, games, and movies for a price of $20 for the first child, $15 for each sibling.

Action centers on the Oasis, a recreation area in the center of the resort with an enormous pool, three hot tubs and saunas, two kiddie pools, a small miniature golf course, volleyball, and two playgrounds. Parents can relax and let the kids explore.

All in all, the Delta is a clear winner in its price range. Rates are $59 to $99. Call 800-776-3358 or 407-351-3340.

Embassy Suites Resort Lake Buena Vista ★★
407-239-1144

This resort, with a dramatic coral stucco exterior and open-air atrium decorated in Caribbean shades of teal and purple, offers dramatically good deals for families. The 280 suites can sleep up to six people comfortably and offer kitchens with microwaves, fridges, and coffeemakers. A full range of sporting activities—an indoor-outdoor pool, tennis, basketball, volleyball, shuffle-board, and a jogging trail with exercise stations—are close at hand, and the resort offers several significant freebies to guests: shuttle service to the Disney parks, drinks at the manager's daily cocktail party from 5:30 to 7:30 P.M., and a bountiful breakfast buffet. (What many hotels advertise as a free breakfast often turns out to be a paper cup of orange juice and a wrapped roll, but this spread features a fruit bar, sausage, bacon, eggs, pan-cakes, French toast, and made-to-order omelettes.)

The Crazy Cat Kids' Club cranks up from 4:30 to 10:30 P.M. for kids 3 to 12; cost is $8 for dinner, $6 to make a craft. Beeper service is provided for parents, and the kids' club has plenty of Nintendo games, a video wall with five separate TV sets, a crawl castle, and a small ball pit.

At $129 to $249 for a suite, and so many perks included in the price, the Embassy Suites offers decent value and a great location just off Exit 27 on I-4, a mere 10-minute ride from the Disney parks. Call 800-EMBASSY or 407-239-1144.

The Holiday Inn *Sunspree Resort*	★★ 800-Holiday/407-239-4500

As you walk through the Sunspree, it's immediately evident that children aren't just tolerated here—they're welcomed guests. Located less than two miles from the Disney gates, the Holiday Inn Sunspree offers mini-kitchens with refrigerator, microwave, and coffeemaker in every room. It's a nice option for families who don't need a full suite (and don't want to pay suite prices) but would like to save a few bucks by eating cereal and sandwiches in their room. The Sunspree offers a food court where kids eat free.

Camp Holiday posts daily activities, such as kids' karaoke and the kids' kazoo band, and winners of coloring and essay contests are prominently displayed in the hall. Many of the rooms have VCRs, and a wide selection of movies is available for rent. There's also a small theater where kiddie movies play all day long, and kids can play virtual reality games and surf the Internet in the Cyber Arcade. You'll find few conventioneers or business travelers at the Holiday Inn Sunspree—the clientele is overwhelmingly families.

Each day from 8 to 12 P.M. Camp Holiday activities are provided for kids 3 to 12 at Max's Magic Castle. Hotel mascot Max the Raccoon and his friends supervise Bingo games, magic shows, and movies. Beepers are available for rental, which adds to parental peace of mind; daytime child care is also available on-site. Max will also come to your room to tuck tired toddlers in after a tough day in the parks.

For a special treat, the Holiday Inn Sunspree offers Kidsuites—a special block of themed rooms, each done up like a child's fantasies come to life. Kids can sleep, for example, in a western jailhouse, a fort, a castle, a space capsule, or an igloo. (Parents sleep in a separate area attached to the Kidsuites, which offers a little privacy.) Or perhaps it would be more accurate to say they can try to sleep—these rooms are so cool they can whip kids into a total frenzy.

Rates for the Sunspree are $109 to $149 per night. Kidsuites are $39 extra. Call 800-HOLIDAY or 407-239-4500.

The Hyatt Regency Grand Cypress Resort ★★   407-239-1234

The Grand Cypress isn't a hotel; it's an event. Elegant and lushly landscaped, with 750 rooms and an enormous pool and grotto area with waterfalls and caves, golf courses, lakes, and riding trails, you could spend a vacation here without ever leaving your hotel. Because it is flanked by a golf course and an equestrian center, you seem far from the Orlando frenzy—but in reality Disney World is only three miles away. The Grand Cypress is home to Camp Hyatt and a child-care center that plans summertime activities for children ages 3 to 12, at a cost of $6.50 an hour. Evening child care is available for a rate of $6.00 an hour with a $3 add-on for each additional child. The Camp Hyatt program is $18 a half-day per child (9 A.M. to noon) and $42 per child for a whole day (9 A.M. to 4 P.M.).

The Grand Cypress also boasts five restaurants—including Hemingway's, a Key West–style getaway perched dramatically atop the resort waterfall—and a stellar Sunday brunch that's widely conceded to be the best in town, even by the staffs at other hotels.

Rates are $295 to $540. Call 800-233-1234 for reservations and 407-239-1234 for information about Camp Hyatt.

Hilton Disney Village ★   800-782-4414/407-827-4000

Conveniently located with shuttle service to area attractions, the Hilton has the additional boon of a kids' club, called Vacation Station, for kids ages 4 to 12. It's open from 5 P.M. until midnight with a charge of $6 an hour; there are price breaks for families. Kids can eat dinner at the hotel while their parents are out on the town. (The Hilton is a mere stroll away from Downtown Disney.) There's a playroom, large-screen TV with Disney movies, Sega games, and a variety of arts and crafts.

How to Find an Affordable Off-Site Hotel

Unless you are familiar with the specific hotel, your best bet is to choose a reliable chain like Days Inn or Quality Inn and then look for a location off I-4, preferably at either Exit 25 or Exit 27, the two exits that flank Disney, or on International Drive.

Here's the scoop on three main off-site areas that tourists frequent: Exits 25 and 27 off I-4 and International Drive. Both Exit 27 and Exit 25 are within a 10-minute drive of the theme parks. Exit 27 backs up to the hotels of the Disney Village Hotel Plaza, and any number of upscale eateries and hotels are nearby, mixed in with

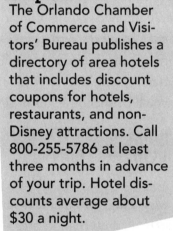

Helpful Hint
The Orlando Chamber of Commerce and Visitors' Bureau publishes a directory of area hotels that includes discount coupons for hotels, restaurants, and non-Disney attractions. Call 800-255-5786 at least three months in advance of your trip. Hotel discounts average about $30 a night.

the Days Inns and fast-food places. The Hyatt Regency Grand Cypress, Embassy Suites Lake Buena Vista, and Holiday Inn Sunspree are all on Exit 27. This area has undergone major expansion in the last few years. On Palm Parkway, just off Exit 27, there are several new suite hotels, including Homewood Suites and Sierra Suites, as well as a recently opened Hampton Inn and Courtyard by Marriott. As chain hotels go, these are all fresh and bright.

Exit 25 (also known as U.S. 192) is a bit seedier and boasts outlets and gift shops instead of fancy restaurants and resorts, but hotels there run about $30 a night cheaper than at a comparable hotel on Exit 27. And make no mistake—this is as close as you will get to WDW for less than $100 a night.

International Drive is farther out, about 20 minutes from the theme parks, but it is modern and well kept, the sort of place where you'll find the most beautifully landscaped Pizza Hut in existence. International Drive boasts every chain restaurant you've ever heard of, as well as a funky Ripley's Believe It or Not, which appears to be sinking into the ground. You'll find ice skating, miniature golf, shopping and entertainment complexes, and a three-story McDonald's. International Drive is the conduit that runs between Sea World, Universal Orlando, and Wet 'n Wild, and is your most central location if you'll be spending lots of time at these three parks.

Things to Ask When Booking an Off-Site Hotel

If you decide to stay off-site, you should be aware that there is a wide range of amenities and perks among the hundreds of hotels in the Orlando area. To make sure you're getting top value for your dollar, take nothing for granted. Some $250-a-

Helpful Hint

One note of caution: An extremely cheap hotel rate, say $50 or less, generally means that the hotel is located in a less desirable part of town than those I've listed—in regard to both theme park proximity and general security. Unless you are personally familiar with the location and quality of the hotel, proceed with caution.

night hotels charge you for shuttle service to the parks; some $75 ones do not. Some hotels count 11-year-olds as adults, and others consider 19-year-olds to be children. Some relatively inexpensive resorts have full-fledged kids' clubs; some larger and far more costly ones are geared to convention and business travel and don't even have an arcade. The moral is: Always ask.

The following questions should help you ferret out the best deal.

@ *Does the hotel provide in-room babysitters? What are their qualifications? What's the cost? How far in advance should I reserve a sitter? Do you have on-site child care?*

Several of the larger hotels have their own version of a kids' club, a drop-off child-care center with planned activities for the youngsters.

@ *Does the hotel provide bus service to the Magic Kingdom, Epcot, Animal Kingdom, and MGM? The minor parks? How often? How early—and how late—do the buses run? Is there any charge? Are the buses express, or do they stop and pick up riders at other hotels?*

Careful here. Often small off-site hotels share shuttles, which means lots of stops and a long commute time.

@ *Do kids stay free? Up to what age?*

This can be vitally important. On-site Disney hotels allow kids under 18 to lodge free with parents. The policy at off-site hotels varies.

@ *Does the hotel provide a free buffet breakfast?*

@ *What fast-food or family-style restaurants are nearby?*

@ *Do you have any suites with kitchens?*

No one would suggest you should spend a vacation cooking. But many families report that doing the cereal and juice thing in their rooms saved them plenty of money.

Money-Saving Tip
Some hotels, such as the Holiday Inn Sunspree, have mini-kitchens with small refrigerators and microwaves—all you need for simple meals. And they don't cost any more than a regular room.

@ *Does the hotel provide airport pickup?*
Most off-sites can at least direct you to a shuttle service.

@ *Is there a laundry facility on the premises?*

@ *Can I buy tickets to area attractions through the hotel's Guest Services desk? Are the tickets discounted?*
Many Orlando hotels offer discounts to Universal Orlando, Sea World, and area dinner shows. Not only do you save money, but you also save the time you'd otherwise spend waiting in line. Use caution, however, if the off-site hotels try to sell you Disney tickets. They're only slightly cheaper than the regular-price passes you'd buy at the theme park gates, and they may limit your access to the minor parks.

CHAPTER

3

Once You
Get There

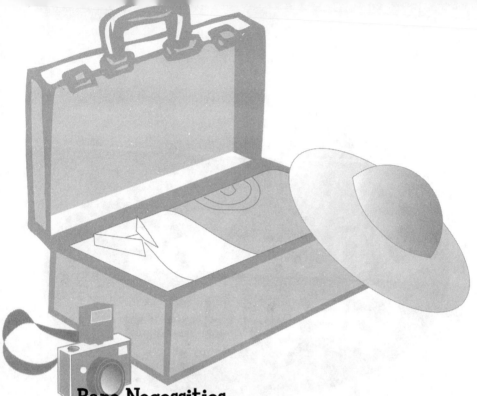

Bare Necessities:
Strollers, Babies, and First Aid

Now on to some of the more practical information. Whether you're pregnant, traveling with a baby, or nursing a sore ankle, Disney World is prepared to accommodate your needs.

Strollers

- All kids under 3 need a stroller, for napping and waiting in line as well as riding.

- For kids 3 to 6, the general rule is this: Strollers are a must at Epcot, nice in the Magic Kingdom, and not really needed at the Animal Kingdom or MGM, where the parks are smaller and a lot of time is spent in sit-down shows.

- Strollers rent for $6 a day, so if you'll need one every day, consider bringing your own from home. But if you have an older child who will need a stroller only at Epcot, rental isn't a bad option.

@ Tie something like a bandanna or a balloon to your stroller to mark it and reduce the chance it'll be swiped while you're inside Peter Pan's Flight. As one mother observed, "Otherwise honest people seem to think nothing about stealing a stroller but stop when they see they might be taking a personal possession as well."

Money-Saving Tip

If you plan to spend time at more than one park, you don't have to pay for a stroller twice: Keep your receipt and show it for a new stroller when you arrive at the next park.

@ Stroller stolen anyway? In the Magic Kingdom, check in at the Trading Post in Frontierland or Tinkerbell's Treasures in Fantasyland. At Epcot, you can get a new stroller at the World Traveler shop located between France and the United Kingdom. Try Oscar's Super Service at MGM and Garden Gate Gifts in the Oasis at the Animal Kingdom. So long as you've kept your receipt, there's no charge for a replacement stroller.

@ If at 8 A.M. your 5-year-old swears she doesn't need a stroller but at noon she collapses in a heap halfway around Epcot's World Showcase, head for the World Traveler shop between France and the United Kingdom. The World Traveler is also the place to rent a stroller if you're coming from the Swan, Dolphin, BoardWalk, or Yacht and Beach Clubs and thus using the "backdoor" entrance.

❷ Likewise, if you're staying at one of the more sprawling resorts, like the All-Star Sports, Music, and Movies, Caribbean Beach, Coronado Springs, Dixie Landings, or Fort Wilderness resorts, bring a stroller from home. It's likely to be quite a trek from your room to the pool or shuttle-bus stop.

Baby Services

Rockers, bottle warmers, high chairs, and changing tables are all found at the Baby Services centers; diapers, formula, and jars of baby food are also for sale. The centers are an absolute haven for families traveling with a very young child. (One mother reported that the attendant on duty was even able to diagnose a suspicious-looking rash on her toddler as a reaction to too much citrus juice, evidently a common Florida malady. She later took the child to a doctor and learned the attendant had been right on the money.)

In the Magic Kingdom, Baby Services is beside the Crystal Palace at the end of Main Street. It's inside the Guest Services building at MGM, in Safari Village at the Animal Kingdom, and near the Odyssey Restaurant at Epcot.

Diapers are available at the larger shops, but they're behind the counter, so you'll have to ask. Changing tables are available in most women's restrooms and now—finally—some men's as well. You can always use the Baby Services centers to change infants, and there are potty-chairs for toddlers as well.

Nursing Moms

Disney World is so casual and family-oriented that you shouldn't feel self-conscious about discreetly nursing in the theaters or restaurants. Some shows, such as the Hall of Presi-

dents in the Magic Kingdom or Impressions de France in Epcot, are dark, quiet, and ideal for nursing.

If you're too modest for these methods or if your baby is easily disturbed, try the rockers in the Baby Services centers.

First Aid

Next to the Magic Kingdom's Crystal Palace is the first-aid clinic, staffed by two nurses. Epcot has a first-aid clinic located beside the Odyssey Restaurant, the MGM clinic is in the Guest Services center, and the Animal Kingdom clinic is in Safari Village near the shop called Creature Comforts.

Although most patients suffer from minor problems such as sunburn, motion sickness, and boo-boos, the center is also equipped for major emergencies and, when necessary, ambulance service to an area hospital.

Helpful Hint

It's worth remembering that any medical problem that could occur at home could also occur in the midst of a vacation. I've received letters from people who have broken bones, fainted from the heat, and come down with chicken pox while in Orlando. Their general advice to others is to seek medical help the minute you suspect there may be a problem. Waiting only makes the solution more painful and more expensive.

Should you suffer a medical emergency, take comfort in the fact that the Disney people have received ringing endorsements for their response in times of crisis. One mother who developed an eye infection from a scratched cornea reported that the nurse at the Epcot first-aid clinic, immediately recognizing the severity of the problem, arranged for her transport to Sand Lake Hospital so she could see an ophthalmologist. "We only had a long weekend," she writes, "and I would have felt horrible if the kids spent it in a hospital waiting room. But as it was, the nurse handled everything, and my husband and children were able to remain in the park while I was treated. My husband kept phoning in to the nurse for updates, and I met up with them back at Epcot a couple of hours later, looking like Long John Silver."

Another mother writes, "When our 8-year-old son developed a (repeat) ear infection in the middle of the Magic Kingdom, we went to the first-aid clinic. There, a sweet nurse gently examined him, contacted his doctor back in Ohio to get his regular prescription, and gave him Tylenol for immediate relief. By the time we arrived back at our rooms at Port Orleans, the prescription was there, and by the next morning Nicky was back on his feet and ready to go."

A woman who suffered a miscarriage while staying at an on-site hotel also offered the highest praise to the staff there, both for their swift medical response and for their emotional support.

General First-Aid Tips

- If someone begins to feel ill or suffers an injury in the parks, head straight for the first-aid clinic. If the people there can't fix it, they'll find someone who can.

- Likewise, all on-site hotels and most off-site hotels have physicians on call 24 hours a day. Contact Guest Services or call 407-396-1195 between 8 A.M. and 10 P.M. for in-room health care. Turner Drugs in Orlando (407-828-8125) will deliver to any on-site hotel room (and many off-site ones) 24 hours a day. There's a $5 charge for delivery, with a surcharge between 10 P.M. and 8 A.M.

@ For minor health problems, visit the Medi-Clinic at the intersection of I-4 and Route 192 or the Lake Buena Vista Clinic, which will pick you up at your hotel room between 8 A.M. and 8 P.M. For more serious illnesses or injuries, head for the emergency room at Sand Lake Hospital.

@ Of course, no matter where you're staying, in a true emergency you should call 911.

Things You Don't Want to Think About

Rain

Go anyway. Short of an all-out hurricane, Disney attractions are open as usual and crowds will be thinner. If you get caught in one of those afternoon cloudbursts so common in Florida summers, rain ponchos are available for about $5 in most of the larger shops. Although hardly high fashion, they're better (and safer) than trying to maneuver an umbrella through crowds while pushing a stroller.

Lost Kids

Obviously, your best bet is not to get separated in the first place. Savvy families have standard meeting spots.

If you do get separated and your kids are too young to understand the idea of a meeting place, act fast. Lost-kid logs are kept at the Baby Services centers at the major parks. More im-

Insider's Secret

Everyone designates Cinderella Castle or Spaceship Earth as a meeting place, which is one reason those places are always mobbed. Plan to catch up with your crowd at a more out-of-the-way locale such as the flower stall on Main Street or the gardens beside the Canada pavilion.

Helpful Hint
Most important, be sure your kids know what to do if they get separated from you.

portant, Disney employees are well briefed about what to do if they encounter a lost child, so the odds are good that if your child has been wandering around alone for more than a couple of minutes, he has been intercepted by a Disney employee and is on his way to Baby Services.

In real emergencies—if the child is very young or is handicapped or if you're afraid she's been nabbed—all-points bulletins are put out among employees. So if you lose a child, don't spend a half-hour wandering around. Contact the nearest Disney employee and let the system take it from there.

Helpful Hint
The one glitch in the system is that, sometimes, lost kids are so interested in what's going on around them that they don't look lost, and thus no Disney employee intercepts them. It's worth taking a couple of minutes to explain to young children that if they get separated from Mom and Dad, they should tell someone wearing a Disney name tag. The Disney employee can call the child's name in to Baby Services, and, assuming you've contacted Baby Services to report the child as missing, the attendant there can tell you where the child is.

Closed Attractions

Because Disney World is open 365 days a year, there is no downtime for refurbishing and repairing rides. Thus, at any given time, as many as four attractions throughout Disney

World may be closed for repairs. If an attraction your family eagerly anticipated is closed, it can be heartbreaking. Call 407-824-4321 before you leave home to find out which attractions are scheduled to be shut down for maintenance during the week you're visiting. That way, if Space Mountain or Star Tours is closed, at least you'll know before you get to the gate.

There's still a slight chance that a ride will be malfunctioning and temporarily closed when you visit, but the Disney people are so vigilant about repairs that this happens very, very rarely. (The one exception to this is Test Track at Epcot; its opening was delayed for some time, and it closes for servicing more often than any other Disney attraction.)

Auto Breakdowns

If you return to the parking lot at the end of the day to find your battery dead or your tire flat, walk back to the nearest tram stop. The roads at Disney World are patrolled continuously by security staff who can call for help. Twelve thousand visitors locked their keys in their car at Disney World last year, so the security people are used to it.

A full-service gas station is located near the toll plaza at the Magic Kingdom entrance. Although prices are high, the station does provide towing and minor repairs in an emergency. If the car can't be swiftly repaired, don't despair. The

Insider's Secret

By far the most common problem is forgetting where you parked. Be sure to write down your row number as you leave your car in the morning. Although Pluto 47 seems easy to remember now, you may not be able to retrieve that information 12 brain-numbing hours later.

day isn't lost. Disney World personnel will chauffeur you to any of the theme parks or back to your hotel.

Running Out of Money

The Sun Bank, which has branches all around Disney World, gives cash advances on MasterCard and Visa, provides refunds for lost American Express or Bank of America travelers checks, and exchanges foreign currency for dollars. Guest Services at some hotels will give you cash advances on credit cards as well.

Crime

Use common sense, especially in trying to avoid the most common crime: theft. Make use of the lockers so that you won't have to carry valuables or new purchases around the parks or take cameras and camcorders onto the rides with you, and be extra cautious at the water parks, where you may be tempted to leave your wallet in your lounge chair while riding the waves. It's far better to either wear one of those waterproof waist pouches in the water or rent a locker, returning to it whenever you need money. The locker keys are on elasticized cords that slip around your wrist, so there's no hassle in hanging on to them.

Don't let paranoia ruin your trip—statistically, Orlando is a pretty safe town—but do keep your wits about you, making sure that hotel doors are bolted, that rental cars are locked, and that you stick to major roads while exploring.

Saving Time

- Prepare as much as you can before you leave home. You should purchase theme park tickets, reserve rental cars, and book shows or special dinners long before you pull

out of your own driveway. Every call you make now is a line you won't have to stand in later.

- Visit the most popular attractions before 11 A.M. or after 6 P.M.

- Eat lunch either at 11 A.M. or after 2 P.M. This system will have you eating while everyone else is in line for the rides and riding while everyone else is eating.

- It also saves time—and money—to make lunch your big meal of the day. Most families opt to eat a large breakfast and large dinner and snack at lunch; go against the crowds by eating your big meal in early afternoon, when the parks are too hot and crowded for effective touring anyway.

- Split up. Mom can make the dinner reservations while Dad rents the strollers. Mom can take the 9-year-old to Space Mountain while Dad and the 4-year-old try out the Tomorrowland Speedway. Security in Disney World is very tight, so preteens and teens can tour on their own, meeting up with the rest of the family periodically.

- Be aware that once you cross the Florida state line, there is an inverse relationship between time and money. You have to be willing to spend one in order to save the other. One family proudly listed their cost-saving measures, such as staying 30 miles outside of Orlando and cooking every meal themselves. They concluded by

Time-Saving Tip
If you have three days or fewer to tour, it is imperative that you go during the off-season. You can see in three days in November what would take six days to see in July.

stating that it took them six days to tour the major parks, something most families can manage comfortably in four days. Considering the high cost of admissions, it's doubtful that they saved very much money at all—and they certainly wasted time.

@ Don't feel you have to do it all. If you study this guide and your maps before you go, you'll realize that not every ride or show will be equally attractive to your family. The world won't come to an end if you skip a few pavilions.

@ The full-service restaurants within the theme parks can be slow. If you're on a tight touring schedule, stick to fast food or sidewalk vendors and order a pizza at night when you get back to your hotel room.

Saving Money

Saving money at Disney World is somewhat of an oxymoron, but there are ways to minimize the damage.

@ Purchase a Magic Kingdom Club Gold Card. A two-year membership qualifies you for savings of up to 20 percent at Disney hotels during certain seasons of the year, discounts on theme park tickets, meals, merchandise, and a host of other benefits.

@ If the cost of flying the whole family down and then renting a car is prohibitive, consider renting a van in your hometown and driving to Orlando.

@ Eat as many meals as possible outside the parks. If you have a suite, fixing simple meals there is clearly your most economical option. Many Orlando hotels offer free breakfasts to guests, and there are numerous fast-food and family chain restaurants along International Drive and the I-4 exits.

@ If you'd like to try some of the nicer Epcot restaurants, book them for lunch, when prices are considerably lower than for dinner. And remember that restaurant portions are huge, even with kiddie meals. Consider letting two family members share an entrée.

@ Children's value meals run about $3 at the fast-food places and $4 at the sit-down restaurants. Kids sometimes eat free at certain establishments; signs are prominently posted announcing the restaurants that offer this deal.

@ Purchase film, blank videotapes, diapers, and sunscreen at home before you come. These things are all available in the parks, but you'll pay dearly for the convenience.

Money-Saving Tip

Except for maybe an autograph book and a T-shirt, hold off on souvenir purchases until the last day. By then the kids will really know what they want and you won't waste money on impulse buys.

@ The All-Star Resorts, Caribbean Beach Resort, Port Orleans, Dixie Landings, Coronado Springs, and Fort Wilderness Campground provide your most economical on-site lodging. (Note: The All-Star Resorts fill up fast, so call at least eight months in advance if you want to stay at an on-site budget hotel.) Off-site, there are several Comfort Inns and Days Inns along I-4 and International Drive.

@ If you're driving to Orlando and not arriving until afternoon or evening, don't reserve your on-site room until

the second day of your visit. It's silly to pay for a whole day of Grand Floridian amenities if you'll be checking in at 10 P.M. Instead, stop your first night at a budget hotel, rise early and check out the next morning, and then go straight to your on-site hotel. They'll let you unload your bags, pick up your tickets and resort ID, and go on to the theme parks.

@ If you move from park to park in your car, save your parking receipt so you'll have to pay the $6 fee only once. (There's no parking charge for on-site visitors.) Likewise, be sure to save stroller receipts.

@ If you plan to try any of the minor parks such as Typhoon Lagoon, Blizzard Beach, or Pleasure Island, buy a Park Hopper Plus pass. Without it, you'll pay separately for each minor park, which can add up very fast. Some families reported that they went to one of the water parks several times during their Disney World stay—a treat that is easy with a Park Hopper Plus pass but totally unfeasible otherwise.

@ Call the Orlando Visitors Bureau at 800-255-5786 before you leave home and request a Magic Kingdom Club Card, which entitles you to savings at restaurants, area attractions, and many off-site hotels. The Bureau will also send you a Vacation Planner booklet, with lots of discount coupons for off-site hotels, restaurants, and dinner shows.

Money-Saving Tip

If you belong to the Entertainment Club, stay at one of the hotels listed in the back of your coupon book; they offer 50 percent price breaks to members.

◉ The dinner shows are expensive, costing a family of four about $130, and even a character breakfast can set you back $50 or more. If the budget is tight, skip these extras and concentrate on ways to meet the characters inside the parks.

◉ Employees of many of the companies that have exhibits inside Disney World, such as Kodak and GM, are entitled to discounts and benefits similar to those of Magic Kingdom Club cardholders. (Employees of the federal government also qualify for these price breaks.) Most companies don't publicize this benefit, but if your employer sponsors an exhibit inside Disney World, contact your employee benefits office well before you leave home and see if any discounts are offered on park admissions or on-site lodging. (Note: Sometimes employees can enter an attraction through the private lounge and ride without having to get into the line at all. This can be a big bonus if you're a GM employee who wants to ride Test Track.)

Money-Saving Tip
On-site hotels offer a deal where you buy a souvenir beverage mug the first day of your trip and get free refills for the remainder of your stay. Since drinks at Disney World are very expensive, this little perk can save you at least $20.

◉ Disney park admission prices are spiraling out of control, with four substantial increases in the last two years; buy your tickets when you make your hotel reservations, and you'll be protected in case Disney decides it's time for another increase.

Meeting the Disney Characters

Meeting the characters is a major objective for some families and a nice diversion for all. If your children are young, prepare them for the fact that the characters are much, much larger than they appear on TV and often overwhelming in person. I once visited Disney World with a 20-month-old whose happy babble of "my Mickey, my Mickey" turned into a wary "no Mickey, no Mickey" the minute she entered the Magic Kingdom gate and saw that the mouse in question was a good 6 feet tall. Kaitlyn's reaction is not unusual; many kids panic when they first see the characters, and pushing them forward only makes matters worse. The characters are trained to be sensitive and sensible (in some cases more so than the parents) and will always wait for the child to approach them. Schedule a character breakfast on the last morning of your visit; by then cautious youngsters have usually warmed up.

Many kids enjoy getting character autographs, and an autograph book can become a much-cherished souvenir on your return home. You might also want to prepare the kids for the fact that the characters don't talk. As many as 30 young people in Mickey suits (mostly women, because the suits are pretty small) might be dispensed around Disney World on a busy day, and they can't all be gifted with that familiar squeaky voice. So the characters communicate, and pretty effectively, through body language.

Also be aware that because of the construction of their costumes, the characters can't always see what's beneath them too clearly. Donald and Daisy, for example, have a hard time looking over their bills, and small children standing close by may be ignored. If it appears this is happening, lift your child to the character's eye level.

Times and places for meeting the characters are listed on the theme park maps that you are given as you enter the parks; each park also has a chalkboard indicating when the characters appear. Meeting the characters in the theme park is free, but it can get pretty wild. If you want to be assured of a good picture, either head for Mickey's Toontown Fair, which has a crowd control system (that is, a line), or schedule a character breakfast.

Disney Photo Ops

You can rent 35-millimeter cameras at any of the Kodak Camera Centers for a nominal fee. Film and two-hour photo developing are widely available throughout Disney World. Needless to say, the prices of both are higher than at home, but it's good to know you can get more film fast if you go into a photo frenzy.

The employees at the Camera Centers are generally knowledgeable about photography and are a good source of advice if you've borrowed a big-deal camera from Aunt Lizzie and can't figure out how to advance the film.

For those postcard-perfect shots, Kodak has well-marked Photo Spot locations through all the major theme parks.

Helpful Hint

Camcorders can be a hassle to carry on the rides, but it's way too risky to leave them in strollers while you're inside the attractions. Consider taking your camcorder with you on only one day, preferably the last day of your trip, when you're revisiting favorite attractions—that way you'll leave with a "Disney World Greatest Hits" tape.

Camcorder Taping Tips

- ℮ If you do plan to take your camcorder with you frequently, make use of the lockers located near the main gates of all three parks. Lockers can be especially helpful if you'll be riding Space Mountain and Big Thunder Mountain, where you'll risk jarring the machine, or Splash Mountain, where there's a very good chance it'll get wet. Never take a camcorder on Kali River Rapids in the Animal Kingdom.

- ℮ Don't pan and zoom too much because sudden camera moves disorient the viewer. If you're filming the kids, say, on the teacups, use the wide-angle setting and keep the camera stationary. Attempting to track them in close-ups as they spin past is too tough for anyone but a pro.

Insider's Secret
Remember to ask each time you board the monorail if the driver's cab is vacant. Sooner or later you'll get the chance to ride up front, and one bonus is the chance to film panoramic views of the parks as you enter.

- ℮ If you're using vocal commentary such as "We're in Frontierland now, looking toward Big Thunder Mountain Railroad," be sure to speak loudly. The background noise of the parks will muffle your words.

- ℮ Camcorder filming is allowed inside many attractions, even many of those where flash photography is forbidden.

- ℮ Film events such as parades, character shows, and theater-style attractions—for example, the Country Bear Jam-

boree or the Indiana Jones Epic Stunt Spectacular. These are especially fun to watch once you're home.

Best Souvenirs

For serious shopping, head to World of Disney at the Downtown Disney Marketplace, which has a little bit of everything. But if you're looking for a slightly unusual souvenir, consider the following:

- Boldly colored T-shirts featuring the flags of Epcot countries, available at Disney Traders, near the mouth of the World Showcase Lagoon.

- Autograph books, which can be purchased nearly anywhere on the first day of your trip. The signatures of the more obscure characters like Hades or the Queen of Hearts are especially prized.

- Passports, purchased from vendors all around Epcot. Collecting a stamp and greeting from every country in the World Showcase is a good way to keep very young kids interested in this admittedly rather adult section of Epcot.

- Characters in vehicles, purchased at the small trinket shops near the stroller rental stands. Mickey rides a moveable crane, Minnie a pink roadster, Donald a locomotive, and so on; these figures are the perfect size for a toddler's chubby fist. At $3 each, they're one of the few souvenir bargains to be found at Disney World.

- Disney watches, with an outstanding selection to be found at Uptown Jewelers on Main Street in the Magic Kingdom. Check out the Goofy watch—it runs backward.

- A piñata from the Mexican pavilion at Epcot.

- Character Christmas ornaments, found at It's a Wonderful Shop at MGM, Ye Olde Christmas Shoppe in the Magic Kingdom, and Days of Christmas in the Downtown Disney Marketplace.

- Planet Hollywood T-shirts, available in a separate shop downstairs from the restaurant. T-shirts from the nearby House of Blues and Bongo's Cuban Cafe are nifty too.

- Also at MGM, old movie posters and other campy knickknacks from Hollywood's golden era are sold at Sid Cahuenga's One-of-a-Kind.

- Character cookie cutters and presses that stamp Mickey's visage onto toast and pancakes are at Yankee Trader in Liberty Square in the Magic Kingdom. A Disney-themed breakfast on your first Saturday home is a nice way to fight those post-trip blues.

- There's a cool Hollywood Tower Hotel gift shop complete with bathrobes, towels, ashtrays, and "I survived" T-shirts as you exit the Twilight Zone Tower of Terror.

- Get character-themed athletic gear at Team Mickey in the Downtown Disney Marketplace. You'll find some items here that you won't see anywhere else—such as Mickey golf balls, softballs, basketballs, and Little Mermaid ballet tights.

- All the on-site hotels have their own T-shirts, a nice variation from the shirts you see in the parks.

- Animal Kingdom T-shirts are also unique. Try the Outpost near the entrance or the larger Island Mercantile in Safari Village. Stuffed versions of the characters in safari

gear are especially adorable. Eeyore's carrying the tent on his back!

@ And, of course, mouse ears are sort of retro-chic. Get your name stitched on at the Chapeau in the Magic Kingdom.

Special Tips for Extra-Crowded Times

If your schedule is such that you simply have to go Easter week or in the dead of summer, the following tips will make the trip more manageable.

Time-Saving Tip

Stay on-site. You'll have the advantage of the Early Entry mornings, and you won't have to hassle with the traffic jams that paralyze Orlando during the on-season. It's also very helpful to be able to arrange priority seating at restaurants in advance. If you're visiting at a busy time and haven't arranged priority seating in advance, room service is a good option. Order a late afternoon "dinner" and rest while you eat.

@ Allow an extra day—or two. First of all, you won't be able to see as much in a single day as you would if you were going at a less crowded time. Second, you'll tire more easily when the crowds are thick, and you'll need longer rest periods to recuperate. Many families schedule an entire day off from touring in the middle of their week, which is really helpful when you're going in the busy season.

@ Stay on-site. The parks can actually close to day visitors during extra-crowded times, but on-site guests are always admitted.

🎟 Use the FASTPASS System, which is explained on pages 127–128.

🎟 Read the sections on each park and choose the two or three things you most want to see. Focus on them and be aware that when you're touring at a crowded time, you probably won't get to "see it all." Just make sure that what you do see is the best.

Insider's Secret
You must be at the parks when they open. By 10 A.M. you'll face hour-long waits at many rides, and the parks may even close to arriving guests.

Special Tips for Big Families

If you're down at Disney World with a really big brood, the following tips—all offered by family reunion veterans—might make things a little less hectic.

🎟 Staying on-site makes splitting up much easier because you can rely on the Disney World transportation system instead of the family car. This is especially vital if there is wide variation in the age, stamina, or risk tolerance of the family members.

🎟 Best on-site options for large families include the trailers at Fort Wilderness Campground and the Old Key West, Disney Institute, and BoardWalk Villas.

🎟 Rent a pager at Guest Services in the major theme parks or through Guest Services at your hotel. Because big groups tend to scatter, a pager can be invaluable for get-

ting everyone reassembled when it's time to eat or head for home. Lacking this, you can also leave messages for each other at Guest Services.

@ Have everyone wear the same color T-shirt or hat each day. A tour guide operator passed along this tip, which makes it much easier to spot "your people" in a sea of faces.

Money-Saving Tip
If the adults plan to head out for a night, an in-room sitter is generally less expensive than drop-off child care when more than three kids are involved.

Special Tips for Grandparents

Many grandparents travel to Disney World with their grand-kids, and although Orlando truly can be the ultimate multi-generational destination, a few pointers may make the trip go more smoothly.

@ If at all possible, stay on-site. It's easier to return to your hotel for rests, and you skip the hassles of commuting.

@ Be sure to alternate shows and other attractions that allow you to rest with more active touring.

@ A day at the Disney Institute can be a great way to break up the more active touring. Some classes are for adults, others for kids, but the class times are set up in a way that makes it easy to drop the grandkids at Broadway Bound and then head off for a cooking or photography course of your own.

@ If you have back or joint problems or are easily tired, rent a wheelchair. All the theme parks offer wheelchair rental

from the same spot that rents strollers, located near the main entrance. If your grandchildren are old enough to enjoy pushing you, go the conventional wheelchair route; if not, arrive early enough to guarantee the availability of an electric cart. One huge boon of wheelchair rental is that you and your entire party board rides at a completely different entrance from the ordinary queue, and this line is invariably shorter. For this reason, many young and able-bodied people rent a wheelchair and take advantage of the wheelchair-boarding zones to cut down on their time waiting in line. This is obviously unethical, and a little scam most often played by teenagers, but there is no reason for an older person not to take advantage of the rental wheelchairs, especially at Epcot. Just be sure to get a copy of the *Guidebook for Disabled Visitors,* which is generally available at the place where you rent your wheelchair. Or you can order one by calling 407-824-4321 at least three weeks before your trip to Disney World. The guidebook gives information on how each ride should be boarded.

@ Avoid the summer at all costs. Not only are the crowds worse, but Florida heat and humidity can also be hard on senior citizens.

Special Tips for Pregnant Guests

I've personally toured Disney World twice while pregnant and not only lived to tell the tale but honestly enjoyed both trips. However, a few precautions are in order.

@ Make regular meal stops. Instead of buying a sandwich from a vendor, get out of the sun and off your feet at a sit-down restaurant.

Helpful Hint

Standing stock-still can be much more tiring than walking when you're pregnant, so let your husband stand in line for rides. You and the kids can join him just as he's about to enter the final turn of the line.

- If you aren't accustomed to walking five or six miles a day—an average Disney World trek—begin getting in shape at home. By taking 30- to 40-minute walks, beginning a couple of months before your trip, you'll be less likely to get sore or poop out early once you're at Disney World.

- Dehydration is a real danger. Drink lots of fluids and keep a juicebox in your tote bag for emergencies.

- This is definitely an occasion when it's worth the money to stay on-site. Return to your room in midafternoon to put up your feet.

- If staying on-site isn't feasible, the Baby Services centers have rockers and are a good place for mothers-to-be to take a break. And the parks are full of benches—sit when you can.

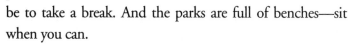

Helpful Hint

Most important of all, check out restroom locations in advance.

- Once you're inside the holding area for theater-style attractions, such as the Country Bear Jamboree or Universe of Energy, find a bench and sit down. If the benches are taken, sit on the floor near the wall and don't stand up when the Disney attendant gets on the loudspeaker and asks everyone to move into the theater; all

the people in the holding area will be admitted into the theater, so it's pointless to get up now and join the mob at the turnstiles. Let everyone else go ahead and then amble through. (This is a good strategy for anyone who is utterly exhausted, pregnant or not.)

Special Tips for Disabled Guests

@ Wheelchairs can be rented at any stroller-rental booth, and most attractions are accessible by wheelchair. Attendants will be happy to help guests with special needs board and disembark from rides; guests in wheelchairs are boarded through their own gates and are often able to avoid waiting in lines altogether.

If someone in your party is in a wheelchair, be sure to request a copy of the *Guidebook for Disabled Visitors* either when you order your tickets in advance or at the wheelchair-rental booth. It's a specific guide to how each ride should be boarded.

@ A tip from frequent visitors: If you're traveling with someone in a wheelchair, it's emphatically worth the money to stay on-site. Disney does an excellent job of offering disabled guests a number of transportation options. The ferry and monorail are wheelchair accessible, but, if needed, you can request a van with a motorized platform. The resorts offer rooms with specially equipped bathrooms and extra-large doors; life jackets for the handicapped are available at resort pools and water parks. The Polynesian gets high marks from readers with special needs, but for those seeking a less expensive option, the All-Star Resorts have several rooms

especially designed to meet the needs of the disabled for $84 a night.

@ Portable tape players and cassettes for sight-impaired guests are available, as are TDDs for the hearing-impaired. Check with Guest Services in the theme parks.

Deaf guests can call Florida Relay Services at 800-955-8771.

@ All on-site hotels are equipped to refrigerate insulin.

Finally, not a tip but a word of reassurance: If you're traveling with someone who has a chronic health problem or disability, rest assured that Disney World cast members will help you in any way they can. Because Disney World is frequently visited by children sponsored by the Make-a-Wish Foundation and other programs like it, the personnel at Disney World are accustomed to dealing with a wide variety of challenges and have proven themselves able to accommodate visitors who are quite seriously ill. The key is to make everyone at both your hotel and within the theme parks aware of your presence and the possibility that you'll need special assistance.

Touring Tips and Plans

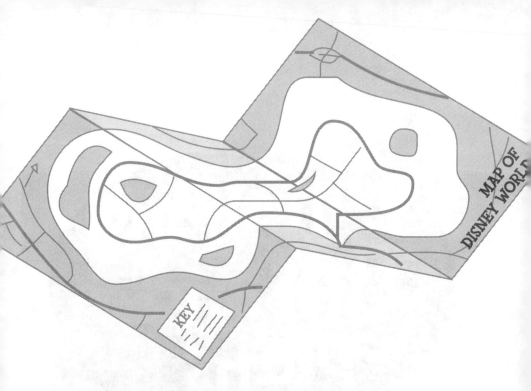

KEY

General Disney World Touring Tips

The size of Disney World is often a shock to first-time visitors, many of whom arrive with vague notions that they can walk from Epcot to the Magic Kingdom or even that they are separate sections of the same theme park. There is also some confusion over the names: Some people use "Walt Disney World" and "Magic Kingdom" synonymously, whereas in reality the Magic Kingdom is a relatively small part of the much larger Disney World complex. There's more to this place than Cinderella Castle and Space Mountain.

Thus, an understanding of the Disney World layout and transportation system is vital because you'll be covering many miles in the course of your touring. Despite the distances involved, the tips in this chapter encourage you to visit more than one park a day, allowing you to follow a morning of bodysurfing at Typhoon Lagoon with an afternoon show at MGM. The best way to avoid overstimulation and burnout is to work a variety of experiences—some active, some passive, some educational, some silly—into each day.

- For families with kids, it is especially important to avoid the exhaustion that comes with just trying to get there. If you're staying off-site, it can take a full two hours from the moment you leave your hotel to the moment where you board your first ride, which is enough to shatter the equanimity of even the most well-behaved kid. Your kids have been waiting for this vacation a long time, and now they've been flying and riding a long time: You owe it to them to get into the parks quickly.

> **Insider's Secret**
> Come early! If you only follow one tip from this whole book, make this the one. By beating the crowds, not only can you visit attractions in quick succession but you also avoid the parking and transportation nightmares that occur when the parks fill to peak capacity around 11 A.M.

- Every touring guide to Disney World tells people to come early, and in the 10 years since I've written my first edition, I've noticed that the mornings have become a bit more crowded, especially with the advent of the Early Entry mornings for on-site guests. But the majority of the people touring Disney World on any given day still arrive between 10 and 11 A.M., proudly announcing that this is their vacation, and they'll sleep in if they want. (These same people seem to take a strange inverse pride in bragging about how long they stood in line and how little they saw.) Arriving early is like exercising regularly; everyone knows you should do it, but most people don't. So if your 4-year-old wants to take three Dumbo flights back-to-back or your 10-year-old is determined to tackle every coaster in the Magic Kingdom, your best plan is still to get there early.

@ On the evening you arrive, call 824-4321 or check with your hotel to confirm the opening time of the theme park you plan to visit the next day. If you learn, for example, that the Magic Kingdom is scheduled to open at 9 A.M., be at the gate by 8:30. Frequently the gates open a half-hour early, and you can head toward the most popular attractions while the other 50,000 poor saps are still out on I-4.

Insider's Secret
What if everyone comes early? They won't.

@ Even if the park doesn't open ahead of the stated time, guests are frequently ushered into one section early. This means you can get maps and entertainment schedules before you enter the body of the park and have breakfast if you order something simple and eat fast.

@ In the Magic Kingdom, visitors are usually allowed to travel the length of Main Street before the park actually opens. You can window-shop or grab a muffin at the Main Street Bakery and still be at the ropes blocking the end of Main Street by 8:50 A.M., when the ropes usually drop. Similarly, at MGM visitors are often allowed onto Hollywood Boulevard to browse the shops and nibble a bite at Starring Rolls before the main park opens.

Insider's Secret

If you have young kids and a special early morning showing of Voyage of the Little Mermaid is scheduled at MGM, you should go there first. Older kids? Try the Twilight Zone Tower of Terror first, then the Rock 'n' Roller Coaster, and then head for Voyage of the Little Mermaid.

@ At Epcot, there are even more advantages to an early arrival. Spaceship Earth (a.k.a. the Big Ball) stands silent and empty at the day's beginning. A family can get strollers, ride Spaceship Earth, make dinner reservations at the WorldKey Information System beside the Big Ball, and have a quick breakfast—all before the park officially opens.

@ Eat at "off" times. Some families eat lightly at breakfast, have an early lunch around 11 A.M. and supper at 5 P.M. Others eat a huge breakfast and have a late lunch around 3 P.M., then a final meal after the parks close. If you tour late and you're really bushed, all on-site hotels and many off-site hotels have in-room pizza delivery service.

Helpful Hint

Plan to see the most popular attractions either early in the day, late at night, or during a time when a big event siphons off other potential riders (such as the 3 P.M. parade in the Magic Kingdom).

@ Be aware that kids usually want to revisit their favorite attractions. (My daughter insisted on riding Dumbo every single day the first time we visited Disney World, something I hadn't foreseen and that radically restructured our touring plans.) Parents who overschedule to the point where there is no time to revisit favorites risk a mutiny.

One way to handle this is to leave the entire last day of your trip free as a "greatest hits" day, so that you can go back to all your favorites one more time. If you feel like lugging the camcorder around only once, make this the day.

@ Use the touring plan to cut down on arguments and debates. It's a hapless parent indeed who sits down at breakfast and asks, "What do you want to do today?" Three kids will have three different answers, and the indecision and bickering waste valuable time.

@ When making plans, keep the size of the parks in mind. MGM is small and can be crisscrossed to take in various shows. Likewise, the Animal Kingdom can be easily toured in four to five hours. The Magic Kingdom has more attractions and more crowd density, slowing you down; while some cutting back and forth is possible, you'll probably want to tour one "land" fairly thoroughly before heading to another. Epcot is so enormous you're almost forced to visit attractions in geographic sequence or you will spend all your time and energy in transit.

@ If you're going to be at the Magic Kingdom for two days or longer, plan to visit the most popular attractions on different days. Many families arrive at the Magic Kingdom determined to take in Space Mountain, Splash Mountain, Big Thunder Mountain, Alien Encounter, and Pirates of the Caribbean their first day—and then wind up spending hours in line. Better to try to see a

Time-Saving Tip

If you leave a park and plan to return to either that park or another, save your stroller receipt and have your hand stamped. You won't have to pay a new stroller deposit at the new park if you can show a receipt, and you can enter the new park swiftly by showing your stamped hand and ticket. Don't worry if you're leaving to swim; the hand stamps are waterproof, although sunscreen can smear them.

couple of the biggies during the first hour after the park opens. After that, move on to less popular attractions, saving the other biggies for subsequent mornings.

@ If you're staying off-site and using your own car to visit more than one park in a day, save your parking receipt so you won't have to pay the fee more than once. Disney resort guests don't have to pay to park; just show the attendant your resort ID.

@ Try park-hopping. Many families with a multiday pass figure: We'll spend Monday at the Magic Kingdom, Tuesday at MGM, Wednesday at Blizzard Beach, Thursday at Epcot, and Friday in the Animal Kingdom. Sounds logical, but a day at the Magic Kingdom is too much riding, 12 hours at Epcot is too much walking, the Animal Kingdom simply doesn't require that much time, a whole day at MGM is too much sitting, and anyone who stays at Blizzard Beach from dusk to dawn will wind up waterlogged. It's especially essential to take Epcot in small doses; if you do all the Future World attractions at once, the Audio-Animatronics will run together in the kids' heads, they'll likely get antsy, and any educational potential will be lost.

❧ If you're trying to predict how crowded a ride or show will be, four factors come into effect:

The newness of the attraction: In general, the newer it is, the hotter it is, particularly if it's a thrill ride like Test Track or Rock 'n' Roller Coaster.

The quality of the attraction: Space Mountain, the Voyage of the Little Mermaid, IllumiNations, and other Disney "classics" will be mobbed five years from now.

Speed of loading: Continuous-loading attractions such as Pirates of the Caribbean, It's a Small World, Spaceship Earth, and the Great Movie Ride can move thousands of riders through in an hour. The lines at the start-and-stop rides such as Dumbo, Astro Orbiter, and the Mad Tea Party move much more slowly.

Capacity: Movies like *O Canada!* at Epcot and *MuppetVision 4-D* in MGM, and shows like the Country Bear Jamboree in the Magic Kingdom can seat large crowds at once. Lines form and then disappear rapidly as hundreds of people enter the theater. For this reason, theater-style attractions are good choices in the afternoon, when the park is crowded.

❧ Take some time to familiarize yourself with the sprawling WDW transportation system.

If you're staying on-site, you'll be able to take a direct bus, boat, or monorail to any of the four major theme parks; there is bus service to the minor parks, but it isn't always direct. If you're going to Typhoon Lagoon, for example, you may have to make a stop at Downtown Disney as well.

Off-site visitors can drive directly to Epcot, MGM, the Animal Kingdom, or any of the minor parks, all of which have their own parking lots and shuttle trams. But the parking lot for the Magic King-

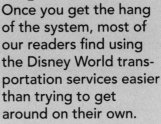

Helpful Hint
Once you get the hang of the system, most of our readers find using the Disney World transportation services easier than trying to get around on their own.

dom is so far from the actual park that off-site visitors will have to park, catch the tram, and then go through the TTC in order to catch a monorail or ferryboat to get to the Magic Kingdom. (This is why we recommend that off-site visitors allow 45 minutes to get to the Magic Kingdom, even if their hotel is close to the park.)

Trying to get from one on-site hotel to another? Use the nearest theme park as your transfer station. If you're staying at Dixie Landings and trying to get to your dinner reservations at the Grand Floridian, for example, take the bus to MGM and then get on a Grand Floridian bus.

It may sound overwhelming, but everything is very well marked, you're given a transportation guide when you check into your hotel, and there are always plenty of Disney employees on hand to answer your questions.

🌀 If you'll be at Disney World for more than four days, consider planning a "day off" in the middle of your vacation. Families sometimes feel so compelled to do it all that they come back from their trip exhausted and irritable. But a day in the middle of the trip devoted to sleeping in, hanging around the hotel pool, taking in a character breakfast, visiting the other hotels, or shopping can make all the difference. You'll start the next day refreshed and energized.

@ You need a strategy for closing time. Except for the Animal Kingdom, the major parks all have nighttime extravaganzas that result in huge logjams as nearly every guest in the park assembles for the show and then all mob the exits en masse when it's over. Your best bet is to be either in the front of the crowd or at the back. If you'd like to clear out fast at the Magic Kingdom, ask an attendant which direction the parade will be coming from and aim to be at the beginning of the route. Once the parade is over, push your stroller out of the way (trying to get back your $1 deposit will just trap you in a line) and head for the exits. At Epcot? Watch from the Mexico or Canada Pavilion if you're leaving by the main gate or by the bridge between France and the United Kingdom if you're leaving by the back door. If you're watching Fantasmic! at MGM, arrive early enough to be in the top row of the Mickey section, which is nearest the main exit.

If you can't be among the first people to leave the park, be among the last. Shop or snack and let the bulk of the crowd pass you. Only when the streets have cleared should you head for the exits.

Use Your Time Wisely

This boils down to one thing: Avoid the lines. The following biggie attractions can draw long lines early and do stay crowded all day.

Head for the most crowded attractions first. On Early Entry days, it is especially essential that you go directly to any

Must-See List for WDW

AT THE MAGIC KINGDOM
Big Thunder Mountain
Dumbo
Space Mountain
Splash Mountain

AT EPCOT
Honey, I Shrunk the Audience
Test Track

AT ANIMAL KINGDOM
It's Tough to Be a Bug
Kilimanjaro Safaris
Lion King Show

AT MGM
Star Tours
Twilight Zone Tower of Terror
Rock 'n' Roller Coaster
Voyage of the Little Mermaid
Fantasmic!

biggies that open early. In the Magic Kingdom, this means you should head straight for Space Mountain. Even with the surge of Early Entry people, the lines will still be half as long as they will be later in the day. At MGM, you can ride the Rock 'n' Roller Coaster and the Tower of Terror with minimal waits in the morning; some thrill junkies ride these two over and over, knowing how hard it can be to get back on later in the day.

If your kids are too young to be drawn to the coasters and other biggie rides, you should still try to see certain attractions first. In the Magic Kingdom, Dumbo, the Mad Tea Party, and Goofy's Barnstormer are slow-loading, low-capacity rides capable of producing hour-long lines by midafternoon. These attractions take about 15 to 30 riders at a time, in contrast to a theater-style attraction such as the Legend of the Lion King Show or the Country Bear Jamboree, which can let in several hundred people at a clip. Ride the rides first; save the shows for later.

Insider's Secret

Obviously, you won't be able to see all the biggies in the first hour the park is open. If you encounter a wait longer than 30 minutes, move on. The Magic Kingdom and MGM parades draw big crowds, making it easier to sneak onto rides then, and many attractions empty out just before the park's closing time. Or you can try the ride again on a subsequent morning.

Be Willing to Split Up

By this point in the planning process, it is probably beginning to dawn on you that every single member of the family expects something slightly different from this vacation. If you want to maximize your use of an Early Entry morning, one parent can take the kid who likes scary rides to Space Mountain and Alien Encounter while the other parent takes the less bold child to Fantasyland. When the rest of the park opens, link up and head together to the Haunted Mansion or Splash Mountain.

Discuss which attractions you'll enjoy as a family; some rides, shows, and parades will be a blast for everyone. And the underlying rule is that you have respect for each other's priority choices, participating cheerfully even if it might not have been your first choice.

But if an attraction holds appeal for only one or two family members, there's no need to drag the whole crew along. A 13-year-old boy on It's a Small World is not a pretty sight. Teenagers, in fact, often like to split off from the family for an hour or two and hang out in Innoventions or the arcades or simply ride a favorite over and over. Security in the Disney parks is so tight that this is an option worth considering. Just make sure to have a clearly designated meeting time and place.

FASTPASS

Last year, Walt Disney World introduced the FASTPASS system, which is designed to reduce the time theme park guests spend waiting in line during peak seasons. Attractions presently offering the FASTPASS option include Splash Mountain and Space Mountain in the Magic Kingdom; Countdown to Extinction, Kilimanjaro Safaris, and Kali River Rapids at the Animal Kingdom; Test Track at Epcot; Tower of Terror and the Rock 'n' Roller Coaster at Disney-MGM Studios.

Here's how it works: You enter the gate and head toward a popular attraction. There, digital clocks show the estimated wait time and the return time for FASTPASS, usually a one-hour time-slot. Let's say you enter the Animal Kingdom gates

Insider's Secret
During the on-season, FASTPASS is also available for Buzz Lightyear, Jungle Cruise, and Winnie the Pooh in the Magic Kingdom, *Honey I Shrunk the Audience* at Epcot, and Star Tours, Voyage of the Little Mermaid, and Indiana Jones at MGM Studios.

at 10 A.M. and find that a long line has already formed for Kilimanjaro Safaris, and the return time is 12:30 to 1:30 P.M. If you opt to get a FASTPASS, insert your theme park ticket into the designated turnstile. You'll get the original ticket back, as well as the FASTPASS. Then go on to tour the rest of the Animal Kingdom, and when you return to Kilimanjaro Safaris at 12:30 you'll be allowed to enter through the FAST-PASS turnstile, and proceed directly to the attraction boarding area. The waits with FASTPASS average 10–15 minutes, a vast improvement over the 90 minute waits that big attractions often post during peak times.

In order to let as many guests as possible take advantage of the system, only one FASTPASS per ticket can be issued at a time.

Touring Tips for Visitors Staying On-Site

@ By far the greatest advantage to staying at one of the hotels found within Disney World is the easy commute to the theme parks. Visitors with small kids can return to their hotels in midafternoon and then reenter the parks about 5 or 6 P.M. Remember the mantra: Come early, stay late, and take a break in the middle of the day.

If you arrive early, you'll have been touring for five or six hours by 1 P.M. and will be more than ready for a rest. Have a late lunch either at one of the theme park restaurants, which are cheaper and easier to get into at midday, or back at your hotel. Once "home," nap or take a dip in the pool.

@ Take advantage of Early Entry mornings. If Epcot is the featured park on Tuesday, go to Epcot on Tuesday. By getting in the park an hour and a half ahead of the stated

Insider's Secret

In the off-season, the Magic Kingdom, MGM, and Animal Kingdom sometimes close at 6 P.M., but Epcot stays open later, even during the least crowded weeks of the year. The solution? Spend mornings at one of the parks that closes early, return to your hotel for a break, and then spend late afternoons and evenings at Epcot. Not only does this buy you more hours per day in the theme parks, but many of the best places for dinner are at Epcot anyway.

time, you can easily ride the most popular attractions before the crowds arrive. During Christmas week, my family was able to ride six rides in the Fantasyland and Tomorrowland sections of the Magic Kingdom during our first hour. Later in the day we noticed that some of those same rides were posting 90-minute waits.

Since the program has been in effect, however, many families have pointed out that the designated park for that day draws a disproportionate number of visitors, who come early and stay all day. The solution is to park-hop. If the park of the day is the Magic Kingdom, and it's mobbed by midmorning, take the monorail over to Epcot.

Touring Tips for Visitors Staying Off-Site

@ Time your commute. If you can make it from your hotel to the theme park gates within 30 minutes, it may still be worth your while to return to your hotel for a midday break. This is a distinct possibility for guests of the hotels at the Disney Village Hotel Plaza and some I-4 establishments. If your hotel is farther out, it's doubtful you'll want to make the drive four times a day.

@ If it isn't feasible to return to your hotel, find afternoon resting places within the parks. (See "Afternoon Resting Places" in the discussion of each theme park.) Sometimes kids aren't so much tired as full of pent-up energy. If you suspect that's the case, take preschoolers to the Toontown playground in the Magic Kingdom or let older kids run free among the forts and backwoods paths of Tom Sawyer Island. The Honey, I Shrunk the Kids Adventure Zone at MGM and the Boneyard at the Animal Kingdom are also perfect for burning off excess energy.

@ If you're willing to leave the parks in the middle of the afternoon, you have even more options. Cool off in the 24-screen movie theater in Downtown Disney or at a water park. River Country is an easy commute from the Magic Kingdom since it runs its own launch. If you stash your bathing suits in one of the lockers under the railroad station in the Magic Kingdom, you can retrieve them around lunchtime and go straight to River Country without having to return to your car.

The hotel restaurants in the Magic Kingdom resorts are never crowded at lunch, and the dining is much more leisurely than in the parks. An early dinner (around 5 P.M.) can also effectively break up a summer day, when you may be staying at the park until midnight.

@ If you'll be touring all day, get strollers for all preschool-age kids. Few 5-year-olds can walk through a 14-hour day.

@ Visit one of the parks not featured as the Early Entry park for the on-site guests. (You can find out which park is featured which day by calling 824-4321.)

@ If you have any kind of multiday ticket, you can use Disney World transportation to move from park to park or to a Disney resort.

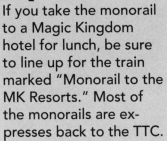

Helpful Hint

If you take the monorail to a Magic Kingdom hotel for lunch, be sure to line up for the train marked "Monorail to the MK Resorts." Most of the monorails are expresses back to the TTC.

How to Customize a Touring Plan

Get Some General Information

In creating a personalized touring plan, your first step is to request maps and transportation information at the time you make your hotel reservations. Familiarize yourself with the overall map of Disney World and the maps of the major theme parks so you can arrive in Orlando with some sense of the proximity and location of major attractions. Getting to Big Thunder Mountain Railroad early is considerably easier if you know where Big Thunder Mountain Railroad is.

Also request the projected park hours for the week you'll be visiting. There's no point in planning a fun-filled night at the Magic Kingdom if you're going on a day when it closes at 6 P.M.

Ask Yourself Some Basic Questions

Consider how long you'll want to stay at each park. If your kids are under 10, you'll probably want to spend more time in the Magic Kingdom and MGM than at Epcot. Older kids? Plan to divide your time fairly equally among the major parks, but save more time for the water parks and Downtown Disney.

The time of year you're visiting is a factor too; even though you may be able to tour MGM thoroughly on a single day in October, it will take you twice as long to see the same number of attractions in July. Likewise, in the summer the combination of the crowds, the heat, and extended park hours means you'll need to build in more downtime, such as afternoons by the resort pool.

Helpful Hint
If you're traveling in the off-season, when the Magic Kingdom, MGM, and the Animal Kingdom all close early, Epcot becomes almost by default "the evening park."

If you're traveling in the on-season, when all the major parks run extended hours, spend at least one evening in each major park so that you can enjoy the closing shows and parades.

Set Your Priorities

Next, poll your family on which attractions they most want to see and build these priorities into the plan. I'd let each family member choose three "must-sees" per park. For example, at MGM, 10-year-old Jeremy wants to ride the Twilight Zone Tower of Terror and Star Tours and see the Indiana Jones Epic Stunt Spectacular. His 6-year-old sister, Elyce, chooses *Muppet-Vision 4-D* and the Beauty and the Beast Show and wants to meet the characters at one of the greeting times. Mom thinks the Prime Time Cafe sounds like a hoot, wants to ride the Great Movie Ride, and agrees that the Indiana Jones show sounds great. Dad is all over the Tower of Terror thing, likes the Muppets too, and thinks the Animation Tour sounds interesting.

The key is to build these nine things into the touring plan first; make sure that you do them if you do nothing else.

With any luck you'll have a bit of overlap on the must-sees and thus time to do other things. So go on and create a "would be nice" list too—shows and attractions that you'd enjoy even if they aren't top priorities. If you manage to work in a few of these, so much the better.

Cut Some Deals

Building each family member's must-sees into the touring plan has many advantages: You're seeing the best of the best, you've broken out of that "gotta do it all" compulsion, and the kids feel that they are being listened to and made full partners in the vacation planning.

But there's another huge advantage: A customized touring plan minimizes whining and fights. Your 12-year-old is more apt to bear a character breakfast with good grace if she knows that you'll be spending the afternoon at Blizzard Beach, one of her top choices. Kids understand fair. They might fidget a bit in Chefs de France, but if you've already covered Test Track, Innoventions, and *Honey, I Shrunk the Audience*, you're perfectly justified in saying, "This is Mom's first choice at Epcot, so be quiet and eat your croquette de boeuf."

Break Up the Days

Next, divide each day of your visit into three components: morning, afternoon, and evening. It isn't necessary that you specify where you'll be every hour—that's too confining—but you need some sense of how you'll break up the day.

Pencil in things that have to be done at a certain time: You have a character breakfast scheduled for Tuesday morning, for example, or you must be in the Magic Kingdom on Friday night because that's the only time the evening parade will be running during your visit, or you've arranged priority seating at the Living Seas pavilion for noon on Thursday.

If you're staying on-site, use the Early Entry schedule to help you choose which park you'll visit on which day, with an understanding that you may not remain in that park for the whole day.

If you're traveling during the on-season, the final product will look something like this:

Monday
Morning: Magic Kingdom
Afternoon: Rest by hotel pool
Evening: Epcot

Tuesday
Morning and afternoon:
   Animal Kingdom
Night: Downtown Disney

Wednesday
Morning: MGM
Afternoon: Blizzard Beach
Evening: Magic Kingdom

Thursday
Morning: Epcot
Afternoon: Rest by pool
Night: MGM

If you're traveling during the off-season, it may look more like this:

Monday
Morning and afternoon:
   Magic Kingdom
Evening: Epcot

Tuesday
Morning and afternoon:
   Animal Kingdom
Evening: Dinner show

Wednesday
Morning and afternoon: MGM
Evening: Epcot

Thursday
Morning: Typhoon Lagoon
Afternoon: Rest at hotel
Night: Downtown Disney

Friday
Morning: MGM
Afternoon and evening:
   Magic Kingdom

Favorite Preschool Attractions

The following attractions received the highest approval rating from kids ages 2 to 5.

IN THE MAGIC KINGDOM

It's a Small World

Peter Pan's Flight

Legend of the Lion King

The Many Adventures of Winnie the Pooh

Cinderella's Golden Carrousel

Dumbo

Mad Tea Party

Goofy's Barnstormer

Donald's boat; Minnie and Mickey's houses in Toontown

Tomorrowland Speedway

Buzz Lightyear's Space Ranger Spin

Jungle Cruise

Country Bear Jamboree

The parades

IN THE ANIMAL KINGDOM

Kali River Rapids

Festival of the Lion King

It's Tough to Be a Bug

AT MGM

Muppet Vision 4-D

Honey, I Shrunk the Kids play area

Voyage of the Little Mermaid

And, whatever you do, save time to meet the characters. It's a major thrill for kids this age.

Favorite Preteen and Teen Attractions

The following attractions received the highest approval rating from the Disney World visitors we surveyed, ages 11 to 16.

IN THE MAGIC KINGDOM

Space Mountain

Splash Mountain

Alien Encounter

Big Thunder Mountain Railroad

Mad Tea Party

Haunted Mansion

AT EPCOT

Test Track

Honey, I Shrunk the Audience

Body Wars

IllumiNations

The American Adventure

Innoventions

AT MGM

The Twilight Zone Tower of Terror

Star Tours

Indiana Jones Epic Stunt Spectacular

Rock 'n' Roller Coaster

Favorite Preteen and Teen Attractions (continued)

IN THE ANIMAL KINGDOM

Kilimanjaro Safaris

Countdown to Extinction

It's Tough to Be a Bug

IN THE REST OF THE WORLD

Blizzard Beach

Typhoon Lagoon

Water Sprites (the rental speedboats at Downtown Disney and on-site hotels)

Planet Hollywood

DisneyQuest (the arcade at West Side in Downtown Disney)

CHAPTER
5
The Magic
Kingdom

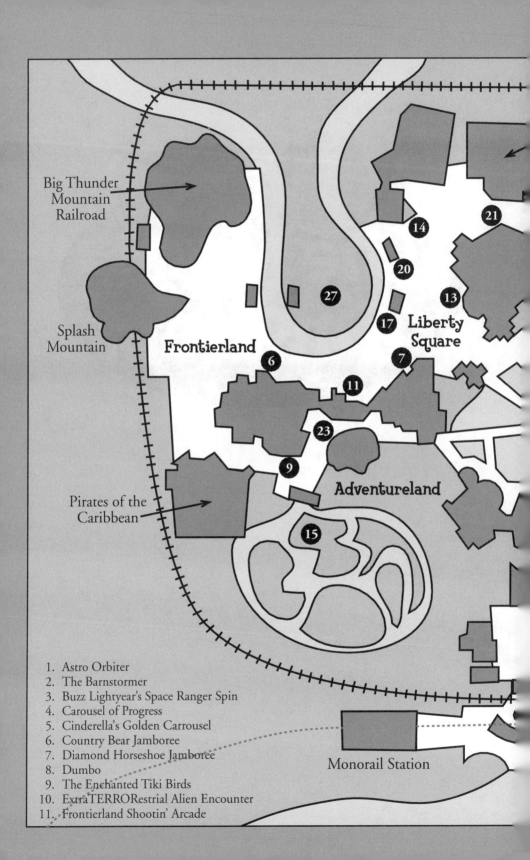

Big Thunder
Mountain
Railroad

Splash
Mountain

Frontierland

Liberty
Square

Adventureland

Pirates of the
Caribbean

Monorail Station

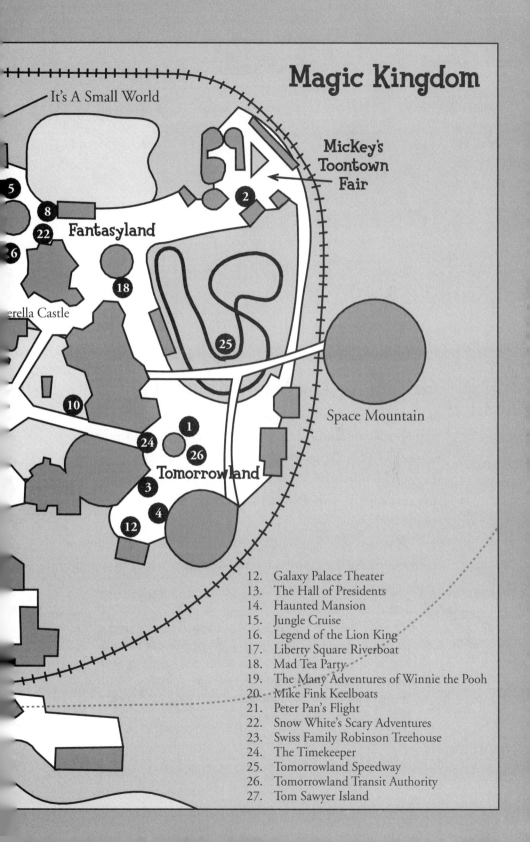

Magic Kingdom

It's A Small World

Mickey's
Toontown
Fair

Fantasyland

erella Castle

Space Mountain

Tomorrowland

Getting to the Magic Kingdom

If you're staying off-site, prepare for a complicated journey. Either drive or take a shuttle to the Ticket and Transportation Center (TTC). From the TTC, you can cross the Seven Seas Lagoon by ferryboat or monorail. As you enter the front gates, the turnstiles to the right are usually less crowded than those to the left.

If you're staying on-site, getting to the Magic Kingdom is a lot easier. At the Contemporary Resort, you can bypass the

Insider's Secret

Make it a habit each time you board the monorail to ask if the driver's cab is vacant; people who'd like to ride up front wait in a special holding area. Because monorails run every three minutes during the peak times, you shouldn't have to wait long, and the view is spectacular.

TTC and take the monorail directly to the Magic Kingdom. Likewise, if you're staying at the Grand Floridian, the monorail will have you at the Magic Kingdom within minutes. Or you can take the launch from the marina dock.

Guests at the Polynesian Resort have the most choices of all: the launch, the monorail, or the ferryboat. If your room is on the lagoon, walk to the ferryboat. If you're in one of the buildings near the Great Ceremonial House, the monorail is a better bet. If your room is close to the pool, take the launch.

Guests at Disney hotels that are not on the monorail line can take shuttle buses that deliver them directly to the Magic Kingdom, bypassing the TTC. This saves you at least 10 minutes of commuting, more during the morning rush hour

From Fort Wilderness Campground or Wilderness Lodge, take the launch.

Getting Around the Magic Kingdom

The Disney World Railroad, which leaves from the main gate with stops near Splash Mountain in Frontierland and Toontown, can save you a bit of time and effort if you happen to hit it right. Don't think, however, that catching the train to Splash Mountain in the morning is your fastest way there. The Railroad Station is busy in the morning, and you may have to wait for a second or third train; by that time, you could have walked. If you're arriving in the afternoon or some other time when the station is less crowded, the odds are you can catch the next train. This may save you a few steps, especially if you're headed toward Toontown.

Be prepared to make frequent rest stops while touring the Magic Kingdom. You won't walk as much as you do in

Helpful Hint

Walking is by far the fastest means of transport in the Magic Kingdom. The trolleys, vintage cars, and horse-drawn carriages are fun, but think of them as pleasant rides, not as a serious means of getting around the park.

Epcot, but you're likely to spend more time waiting in lines. Standing still is ultimately harder on the feet—and the nerves—than walking.

Tips for Your First Hour in the Magic Kingdom

@ On-site guests can enter the Magic Kingdom one hour early on Monday, Thursday, and Saturday. Usually only Tomorrowland and Fantasyland are open; go to Space Mountain first if your kids are old enough to handle it. Younger kids? Start out in Fantasyland on Dumbo.

Off-site guests or anyone visiting on a morning which is not an early entry morning, should be through the gates 30 minutes earlier than the stated opening time, 45 minutes if you plan to have breakfast on Main Street. Get strollers and pick up a map and entertainment schedule at City Hall.

@ Be at the end of Main Street at least 10 minutes before the stated opening time. If your kids are up for it, head for Splash Mountain when the ropes drop, then to Big Thunder Mountain Railroad, then across to Space Mountain. (For Splash Mountain, line up at the bridge to Adventureland; for your shortest shot to Big Thunder

Mountain Railroad, head toward the walkway marked "Liberty Square/Frontierland.")

ℚ If there's a gap in the ages of your children and the 9-year-old is ready for the coasters but the 4-year-old isn't, split up. Mom can take one child, Dad the other, and you can meet up again in an hour.

Main Street Touring Tips

ℚ Although you might want to spend a few minutes mingling with the characters who greet you as you enter, don't stop to check out the shops or minor attractions of Main Street in the morning; you need to hurry on to the big rides.

ℚ Return to Main Street to shop in midafternoon. Especially worthwhile are Disney Clothiers, Uptown Jewelers, and the Emporium. Main Street is also a good place for lunch.

Insider's Secret

After shopping, either stow your purchases in the lockers beneath the Railroad Station or, if you're a guest at a Disney resort, have them sent directly to your hotel room. If you're not planning to see the parade, be sure to be off Main Street by 2:30 P.M. After that, it's a mob scene.

ℚ A fun diversion for kids is having their bangs trimmed amid the old-fashioned splendor of the Harmony Barber Shop beside the flower market on Main Street. The barbers are jovial, even by Disney employee standards, and happy to explain the history of the moustache cups, shaving mugs, and other tonsorial paraphernalia. Many families wait to have their baby's first trim on Main Street; Dean, one of the longtime barbers, has a scrapbook of first-haircut photos.

◉ If you're touring the Magic Kingdom late and your party splits up, make sure you choose a spot on Main Street as your meeting place. Disney employees clear people out of the other sections of the park promptly at closing time, but Main Street stays open up to an hour after the rides shut down and is the best place to reassemble the family before heading for the parking lot.

◉ A blackboard posted at the end of Main Street provides up-to-date information about the approximate waiting times at Magic Kingdom rides, as well as all show times and where to meet the characters. Consult it whenever you're unsure about what to do next.

Fantasyland

Fantasyland, located directly behind Cinderella Castle, is the land with most of the kiddie rides. It's the most congested section of the Magic Kingdom.

Fantasyland Touring Tips

◉ Wait times for Dumbo are always two or three times longer than for other Fantasyland rides. Go there first.

◉ Visit Fantasyland either before 11 A.M., after 7 P.M., or during the 3 P.M. parade.

◉ Don't eat or shop in Fantasyland. Similar food and toys can be found elsewhere in far less crowded areas of the Magic Kingdom.

The Magic Kingdom Don't-Miss List

IF YOUR KIDS ARE 7 OR OLDER:

Space Mountain

Splash Mountain

Pirates of the Caribbean

Big Thunder Mountain Railroad

Haunted Mansion

Legend of the Lion King

The parades

Buzz Lightyear's Space Ranger Spin

Any Fantasyland rides that catch their fancy

IF YOUR KIDS ARE UNDER 7:

Dumbo

Mad Tea Party

It's a Small World

Peter Pan's Flight

The Many Adventures of Winnie the Pooh

Toontown, especially Goofy's Barnstormer

Pirates of the Caribbean

Country Bear Jamboree

Legend of the Lion King

The parades

Splash Mountain, if they pass the height requirement

Big Thunder Mountain Railroad,
if they pass the height requirement

Buzz Lightyear's Space Ranger Spin

Quick Guide to Magic

Attraction	Location	Height Requirement
Astro Orbiter	Tomorrowland	None
Big Thunder Mountain Railroad	Frontierland	40 inches
Buzz Lightyear's Space Ranger Spin	Tomorrowland	None
Carousel of Progress	Tomorrowland	None
Cinderella's Golden Carrousel	Fantasyland	None
Country Bear Jamboree	Frontierland	None
Diamond Horseshoe Jamboree	Frontierland	None
Dumbo	Fantasyland	None
The Enchanted Tiki Birds	Adventureland	None
ExtraTERRORestrial Alien Encounter	Tomorrowland	44 inches
Frontierland Shootin' Arcade	Frontierland	None
Galaxy Palace Theater	Tomorrowland	None
Goofy's Barnstormer	Toontown	None
The Hall of Presidents	Liberty Square	None
The Haunted Mansion	Liberty Square	None
It's a Small World	Fantasyland	None
Jungle Cruise	Adventureland	None
Legend of the Lion King	Fantasyland	None
Liberty Square Riverboat	Liberty Square	None

Scare Factor

0 = Unlikely to scare any child of any age.

! = Has dark or loud elements; might rattle some toddlers.

!! = A couple of gotcha! moments; should be fine for school-age kids.

!!! = You need to be pretty big and pretty brave to handle this ride.

Speed of Line	Duration of Ride/Show	Scare Factor	
Slow	2 min.	!	7 and up
Moderate	3 min.	!!	5 and up
Fast	6 min.	0	3 and up
Fast	22 min.	0	10 and up
Slow	2 min.	0	2 and up
Moderate	15 min.	0	All
Fast	30 min.	0	All
Slow	1.5 min.	0	All
Fast	20 min.	0	All
Fast	20 min.	!!!	10 and up
Slow	n/a	0	7 and up
Fast	30 min.	0	All
Fast	20 min.	0	10 and up
Slow	1 min.	!	5 and up
Slow	9 min.	!!	7 and up
Fast	11 min.	0	All
Slow	10 min.	0	All
Moderate	25 min.	!	3 and up
Fast	15 min.	0	All

(continues)

Quick Guide to Magic

Attraction	Location	Height Requirement
Mad Tea Party	Fantasyland	None
The Many Adventures of Winnie the Pooh	Fantasyland	None
Mike Fink Keelboats	Liberty Square	None
Peter Pan's Flight	Fantasyland	None
Pirates of the Caribbean	Adventureland	None
Skyway to Fantasyland	Tomorrowland	None
Skyway to Tomorrowland	Fantasyland	None
Snow White's Scary Adventures	Fantasyland	None
Space Mountain	Tomorrowland	44 inches
Splash Mountain	Frontierland	40 inches
Swiss Family Robinson Treehouse*	Adventureland	None
The Timekeeper	Tomorrowland	None
Tomorrowland Speedway	Tomorrowland	None
Tomorrowland Transit Authority	Tomorrowland	None
Tom Sawyer Island	Frontierland	None

* According to WDW, this ride will soon be redesigned to become Tarzan's Treehouse.

Scare Factor

0 = Unlikely to scare any child of any age.
! = Has dark or loud elements; might rattle some toddlers.
!! = A couple of gotcha! moments; should be fine for school-age kids.
!!! = You need to be pretty big and pretty brave to handle this ride.

Kingdom Attractions

Speed of Line	Duration of Ride/Show	Scare Factor	Age Range
Slow	2 min.	0	4 and up
Moderate	5 min.	0	All
Slow	15 min.	0	All
Moderate	3 min.	0	All
Fast	8 min.	!	6 and up
Moderate	5 min.	0	3 and up
Moderate	5 min.	0	3 and up
Slow	2.5 min.	!	5 and up
Moderate	3 min.	!!!	7 and up
Moderate	10 min.	!	5 and up
Slow	20 min.	0	4 and up
Fast	20 min.	0	3 and up
Slow	5 min.	0	2 and up
Fast	10 min.	0	All
Slow	n/a	0	4 and up

🅔 Park your strollers in one spot and walk from ride to ride. Fantasyland is geographically small, so this is easier than constantly loading and reloading the kids, only to push them a few steps.

Helpful Hint

Stay alert. Because the kiddie rides tempt them to wander off, this is the most likely spot in all of Disney World to lose your child.

Fantasyland Attractions

It's a Small World

During this 11-minute boat ride, dolls representing children of all nations greet you with a song so infectious you'll be humming it at bedtime. The ride loads steadily, so the lines move fast, making this a good choice for afternoon. And it's one of the best attractions to film with a camcorder.

Helpful Hint

It's a Small World, although beloved by preschoolers, can be torture for older siblings. One family's 10-year-old wrote in that Disney should offer an "I Survived It's a Small World" T-shirt similar to those they sell outside Alien Encounter or the Twilight Zone Tower of Terror.

Peter Pan's Flight

Tinkerbell flutters overhead as you board miniature pirate ships and sail above Nana's doghouse, the sparkling night streets of London, the Indian camp, and Captain Hook's cove.

Of all the Magic Kingdom attractions, this one is most true to the movie that inspired it.

Legend of the Lion King

This show is a huge hit with kids, combining complex human-controlled puppets, live action, special effects, and music to retell Simba's familiar story.

The show runs every 30 minutes, and 480 people are seated at once, meaning that even if the afternoon line looks discouraging, you should still queue up—or at least let one parent be the Line King while the other takes the kids for a drink or potty break.

The Scare Factor
Legend of the Lion King is a bit dark and loud in the beginning, but most kids are familiar with the story and take it in stride.

The Many Adventures of Winnie the Pooh

The upbeat ride follows Pooh and friends through a "blustery" day, meaning your honey pot–shaped car will swirl and jostle a bit. Designed specially for younger kids, the ride is gentle and fine for any age. Pooh's Thoughtful Shop, located at the exit, has great souvenirs for Pooh fans. (And the shop smells like honey!)

Cinderella's Golden Carrousel

Seventy-two white horses prance while a pipe organ toots out "Chim-Chim-Cheree" and other Disney classics. The Carrousel is gorgeous at night, and benches nearby let Mom and Dad take a breather.

Snow White's Scary Adventures

Don't expect to see much of the dwarfs. This ride focuses on the part of the movie where Snow White is fleeing the witch.

You ride mining cars through the dark, and the Wicked Witch appears several times quite suddenly.

The Scare Factor

It's hard to know exactly who this ride was designed for—it's boring for kids over 6 and unnerving for preschoolers. If you look at the sign, you'll see where they slipped the word "Scary" between "Snow White" and "Adventures." Another sign warns you that the witch is inside. In short, although the special effects are very simple, the mood of the ride is foreboding enough to give toddlers the willies.

Skyway to Tomorrowland

This overhead cable car offers good views, especially at night. Skippable in the daylight, unless you're enchanted by the sight of rooftops.

Dumbo

This happy little elephant has become the center of some controversy: Is he worth the wait or not? Although the lines do indeed move slowly, making a one-hour wait possible for a 90-second ride, there's something special about this attraction. It's frequently featured in the ads, so it has become an integral part of our collective Disney consciousness.

If you visit this ride first thing in the morning, you can cut the wait down, perhaps to only a few minutes. The height of your Dumbo flight can be controlled by a joystick, making the ride appropriate for any age.

Mad Tea Party

Spinning pastel cups, propelled by their riders, swirl around the Soused Mouse, who periodically pops out of the teapot.

Because you largely control how fast your teacup spins, this ride can be enjoyed by people of all ages.

Time-Saving Tip
Rider volume ebbs and flows at Mad Tea Party. If the line looks too daunting, grab a drink or make a bathroom stop. By the time you emerge, the crowd may have dispersed.

Ariel's Grotto Playground
A small play area with squirting fountains, the grotto is a good place for toddlers and preschoolers to cool off on a hot afternoon. Go inside the cave to meet Ariel and get her autograph only if the line is short; some parents report waiting up to 30 minutes for an autograph, far too long for a single character.

Mickey's Toontown Fair

Mickey's Toontown Fair (most often referred to as just "Toontown") makes you feel as if you are immersed in a giant cartoon. There is a lively, campy county fair theme and attractions designed to appeal primarily to the 2- to 8-year-old set.

Toontown is full of great photo ops, such as the bright blue car outside Pete's Garage or Minnie's House, where the oven bakes a cake before your eyes and kids can make popcorn pop by pushing a microwave button. Donald's boat, the Miss Daisy, is a great play area with squirting fountains, making Toontown a good choice after you've finished Fantasyland and the kids just want to run and play for a while.

Toontown is also the best place in the park to meet the characters: After you tour Mickey's House and meet him in the tent behind it, enter the main tent called Toontown Hall of Fame. You'll see three separate lines marked something like "Mickey's Pals," "The Hundred Acre Wood," "Forest Friends,"

"Villains," or "Princesses." At least four characters will be waiting in each room. There is plenty of time for photos and autographs, and because guests are admitted 15 at a time, young children can visit the characters without being trampled or mobbed. After you've visited one group, you can always rejoin the line and visit another.

The centerpiece of Toontown is a zippy little roller coaster called Goofy's Barnstormer, which takes you on a wild trip through Wise Acre Farm with you-know-who as the pilot. The ride lasts only 50 seconds, so the line moves fast, and this is the sort of ride many kids insist on doing again and again.

The Scare Factor

Goofy's Barnstormer is a good choice for kids not quite up to Splash Mountain or Space Mountain; the thrills are there, but the ride is so short that you barely get out one good scream before it's over. You can see the whole path of the ride from the ground, so if you have any doubts, watch the Barnstormer make a couple of trips and then decide.

Toontown Touring Tips

Like Fantasyland, Toontown can become unbearably crowded in midafternoon. By early evening, however, the crowds thin. If you've missed Goofy's Barnstormer in the morning, check back in the evening, when waits are minimal.

Helpful Hint

Donald's boat is a great place to cool off—and get soaked—on a summer afternoon.

Insider's Secret

The very best time to visit Mickey and the other Toon-town characters is Sunday morning, when your kids are apt to be well rested and the crowds are light.

Tomorrowland

After years of trying to constantly update Tomorrowland and keep it fresh, the Disney imagineers have decided to go with a '50s sci-fi look that reflects "the future that never was." In this Tomorrowland the mood is decidedly campy—as evidenced by the robot paperboy hawking tomorrow's news and the street sweepers on rollerblades.

Tomorrowland Touring Tips

@ If you don't plan to ride Space Mountain or see Alien Encounter, save Tomorrowland for afternoons, when the park is at its most crowded. Several Tomorrowland attractions, such as Timekeeper and Carousel of Progress, are high capacity and relatively easy to get into even in the most packed part of the day.

Insider's Secret

If you plan to ride Space Mountain, make a beeline for it immediately on entering the park gates. After 9:30 A.M. there are substantial lines. By midmorning, Alien Encounter also has lines.

@ Tomorrowland has its own tip board across from Alien Encounter, and it lists approximate wait times for rides.

Check the tip board if you're headed for Space Mountain; if the wait is longer than 40 minutes, come back another time.

@ There's an arcade across from Space Mountain that is a good place for the less adventurous members of your party to wait while the coaster warriors tackle Space Mountain.

Time-Saving Tip

Looking for fast food during peak dining hours? Tomorrowland food stands are rarely as busy as those in other lands. Cosmic Ray's Starlight Cafe, the largest fast-food place in the Magic Kingdom, can move you in and out fast.

Tomorrowland Attractions

Space Mountain

This three-minute roller-coaster ride through inky darkness is one of the few scream-rippers in the Magic Kingdom. The cars move at 28 miles per hour, a fairly tame pace compared to that of the monster coasters at some theme parks, but the entire ride takes place inside, and it's impossible to anticipate the

The Scare Factor

Children under 7 must be 44 inches tall and have an adult present to ride. Children under 3 and pregnant women are prohibited. Some kids 3 to 7 liked the ride, but most surveyed found it far too scary. Kids in the 7 to 11 age-group in general give a thumbs-up, and teens adore Space Mountain.

turns and dips in the blackness, which adds considerably to the thrill.

Tomorrowland Speedway
These tiny sports cars circle a nifty-looking racetrack, and although the

Insider's Secret
Ride in the morning and then get a FASTPASS so you can return later and ride with a minimal wait.

ride isn't anything unusual, kids under 11 rated it highly, perhaps because even young drivers can steer the cars themselves. (If Jennifer's legs are too short to reach the gas pedal, Mom or Dad can handle the floor pedals while she steers.) Kids 52 inches and taller can drive solo.

Helpful Hint
Try to persuade your child not to rush through Tomorrowland Speedway; loading and unloading the race cars takes time, and you may as well drive slowly rather than sit for five minutes in the pit waiting to be unloaded.

Galaxy Palace Theater
This large outdoor theater hosts a variety of shows during the on-season, including a character show in midafternoon. Check your entertainment schedule or the blackboard at the end of Main Street for details.

Because the theater is so huge, you can almost always be seated if you arrive 10 to 15 minutes before show time.

Skyway to Fantasyland
This attraction offers pretty views at night, but by the time you wait in line to board you could have walked.

Buzz Lightyear's Space Ranger Spin

This ride is an "interactive fantasy in which riders help Buzz save the world's supply of batteries." More specifically, the ride transports guests into the heart of a video game where they pass through various scenes, shooting at targets. (Hint: You get more points for hitting distant or moving targets, so don't spend all your time taking cheap shots.) Your car keeps your score, and at the end you learn whether you're a Space Ace or a lowly trainee. Buzz is addictive, but at least the line moves fast. Hardly any kid will let you do it just once.

Astro Orbiter

A circular thrill ride—sort of a Dumbo on steroids—Astro Orbiter is a bit too much for preschoolers and a bit too little for teens. Like Dumbo, it loads slowly; if you wait to ride at night, the crowds are lighter and the astro-ambience is even more convincing.

The Scare Factor

Astro Orbiter is a good choice for those in the 7 to 11 range who are not quite up to Space Mountain. But this is not, repeat not, a good choice for anyone prone to vertigo or motion sickness.

Timekeeper

In this Circlevision 360 film, Jules Verne and H. G. Wells take the audience from nineteenth-century Paris into the future. The voices of Robin Williams and Rhea Perlman, your time-travel pilot and navigator, add to the fun.

The show is well done, but guests stand throughout the presentation. Strollers are not allowed inside the theater, which means babies and toddlers have to be held during the show, and preschoolers often need to be lifted up to have a prayer of seeing the show—a drawback that eliminates it for many families.

Lines disappear every 20 minutes, allowing 1,000 people at a time to enter, making *Timekeeper* a good choice for the most crowded times of the afternoon.

Tomorrowland Transit Authority

This little tram circles Tomorrowland and provides fun views, including a glimpse inside Space Mountain. The ride is never crowded, and often the attendant will let you stay on for another ride. The rocking of the train has lulled more than one cranky toddler into a nap.

Carousel of Progress

This is another fairly long show (22 minutes), another high-capacity attraction, and thus another good choice for the crowded times of the afternoon. Kids under 10, however, may be bored by this salute to the uses of electricity, especially once they've seen the more high-tech presentations of Epcot. (Due to be closed and revamped in 2001.)

ExtraTERRORestrial Alien Encounter

Alien Encounter opened three years ago amid considerable controversy. The original version was dubbed too tame, but the second manifestation is so terrifying that people are often literally screaming so loud they can't hear the story.

Alien Encounter is about a time-travel experiment that runs amok, "releasing" an alien into your theater. Although you never totally see the beast, you see flashes of parts of his body and hear him rattling around above your head and behind you. Like Epcot's *Honey, I Shrunk the Audience,* some of the special effects are tactile; the shoulder harness gives the sensation that the monster is just behind you, slipping around your shoulders and down your back. The danger is mostly implied because the imagineers working on the attraction theorized that the mind can conjure up far worse things than they could ever create. At one point in the presentation, when the tactile and aural effects are at their peak, you sit in total darkness for more than a minute.

Helpful Hint

Alien Encounter has a surprisingly small sign and is not that easy to find. It's directly across from *Timekeeper* as you enter Tomorrowland via the Main Street bridge.

Kids must be 44 inches to enter. The preshow is misleading; the main show is far scarier. I'd send a parent through first to preview the experience before going in with kids under 10.

The Scare Factor

I've received more negative mail on Alien Encounter than on any other attraction at Disney World, most of it indicating that the show is far, far too intense for children under 10. One mother pointed out that the shoulder harness not only gave her 8-year-old the sense he was strapped down but also prevented her from putting her arm around him or comforting him when he panicked. "There is fun scary and scary scary," one 7-year-old wrote. "Alien Encounter is scary scary."

Adventureland, Frontierland, and Liberty Square Touring Tips

⚲ If you have two days to spend touring the Magic Kingdom, begin your second day in Frontierland, at Splash Mountain. Move on to Big Thunder Mountain Railroad, then the Haunted Mansion in Liberty Square. All three attractions are relatively easy to board before 10 A.M., and you can return to ride less crowded Liberty Square and Frontierland attractions later in the day.

Because most visitors tour the lands in a clockwise or counterclockwise fashion, these three lands reach peak capacity around noon and stay crowded until around 4:30 P.M., when the people lined up to watch the 3 P.M. parade finally disperse. So if you miss Splash Mountain, the Haunted Mansion, or Big Thunder Mountain Railroad in the morning, wait until evening to revisit them.

✆ Should you, despite your best intentions, wind up in one of these three sections in midafternoon, you'll find a bit of breathing space on Tom Sawyer Island, with the Enchanted Tiki Birds, in the Hall of Presidents, or among the shops in the shady Adventureland Pavilion. Surprisingly, Pirates of the Caribbean isn't that difficult to board in midafternoon. The lines look terrible, but at least you wait inside, and this is one of the fastest-loading attractions in Disney World.

Time-Saving Tip

Everyone dashes to Splash Mountain the minute the ropes drop in the morning, and on very busy days this means the line may be massive within minutes after the park opens. If you hustle straight to Frontierland and arrive only to find yourself facing a wait longer than 30 minutes, move on to Big Thunder Mountain Railroad; check Splash Mountain again immediately afterward, and you may find that the initial surge of people has moved through and the line is a bit shorter.

Adventureland

Thematically the most bizarre of all the lands—sort of a Bourbon Street meets Trinidad by way of the Congo—Adventureland still manages to convey an exotic mood.

Adventureland Attractions

Jungle Cruise

You'll meet up with headhunters, hyenas, water-spewing elephants, and other varieties of frankly fake wildlife on this 10-minute boat ride. What distinguishes this attraction is the amusing patter of the tour guides—these young adventurers in pith helmets are unsung heroes of Disney casting genius.

The cruise is not at all scary and is fine for any age, but the lines move with agonizing slowness. If you decide to take the cruise, go in the morning—or during the 3 P.M. parade.

The Enchanted Tiki Birds

These singing/talking birds, and the singing/talking flowers and statues around them, represent Disney's first attempt at the Audio-Animatronics that are now such an integral part of Epcot magic. The 1998 addition of Iago from *Aladdin* and Zazu from *The Lion King* as the new co-owners added a much-needed shot in the arm to this rather tired old attraction. The music is livelier and kids enjoy seeing their favorite birds. Note: Stick around for Iago's stream of insults as you exit the theater. It's the funniest part of the show.

Swiss Family Robinson Treehouse

There's a real split of opinion here—some visitors love this replica of the ultimate treehouse, while others rate it as dull. Kids who have seen the movie tend to like it a lot more.

Helpful Hint

One word of warning: This is a tough attraction to tour with toddlers. Lugging a 2-year-old through the exhibit is tiring, but the real problem is that the bamboo and rigging look so enticing that kids want to climb on their own and at their own pace. This may not sit well with the 800 people in line behind you. Note: At Disneyland, this attraction was transformed into Tarzan's Treehouse. A similar change may be coming at Walt Disney World.

Pirates of the Caribbean

This ride inspires great loyalty, and a significant number of guests of all ages name it as their favorite in all the Magic Kingdom. Your boat goes over a small waterfall, and the pirates are remarkably lifelike, right down to the hair on their legs. The theme song is positively infectious, and young buccaneers can stop off at the Pieces O' Eight gift shop on the way out for plastic weaponry.

The Scare Factor

The queue, which winds through a dark, drafty dungeon, scares more kids than the ride does. Unfortunately, the scariest elements of the ride occur in the first three minutes; there are gunshots, skeletons, cannons, and one segment where you go through about a minute of shadowy darkness; by the time you get to the mangy-looking and politically incorrect buccaneers, the mood is up-tempo, as evidenced by the cheerful theme song. Fine for most kids over 6, unless they're afraid of the dark.

Frontierland

Kids love the rough-and-tumble, Wild West feel of Frontierland, which is home to several of the Magic Kingdom's most popular attractions.

Frontierland Attractions

Big Thunder Mountain Railroad

A roller coaster disguised as a runaway mine train, Big Thunder Mountain is considerably less scary than Space Mountain, but almost as popular. The glory of the ride is in the setting. You zoom through a deserted mining town. If you're wondering if the coaster may be too much for your kids, be advised that Big Thunder Mountain is more in the rattle-back-and-forth than in the lose-your-stomach-as-you-plunge genre.

The Scare Factor

Almost any child over 7 should be able to handle the dips and twists, and many preschoolers adore the ride as well. Children under 7 must ride with an adult, and no one under 40 inches tall is allowed to board. If you're debating which of the three mountains—Space, Splash, or Big Thunder—is most suitable for a kid who has never ridden a coaster, Big Thunder is your best bet.

Splash Mountain

Based on *Song of the South* and inhabited by Brer Rabbit, Brer Bear, Brer Fox, and the other characters from that film, Splash Mountain takes riders on a watery, winding journey through swamps and bayous, culminating in a 40-mile-an-hour drop over a five-story waterfall. "Zip-A-Dee-Doo-Dah," perhaps the most hummable of all Disney theme songs, fills the air, making the ride both charming and exhilarating—truly the best of both worlds.

Splash Mountain can get very crowded; ride early in the morning or in the last hour before closing. Also, you can get really soaked, which is great fun at noon in June, less of a thrill at 9 A.M. in January. Some people bring big black plastic garbage bags to use as ponchos and then discard them after the ride.

The Scare Factor

The intensity of that last drop, which momentarily gives you the feeling that you're coming out of your seat, along with the 40-inch height requirement, eliminates some preschoolers. If your kids are unsure about Splash Mountain, watch a few cars make the final drop before you decide. Our mail indicates that most kids over 5 love the ride.

Diamond Horseshoe Jamboree

You can buy sandwiches, snacks, and drinks during this 30-minute saloon show, which is full of hokey humor and lively dance. Some of the puns will go over the heads of younger children, but the material is delivered in such a broad style that kids find themselves laughing even when they're not quite sure why. Audience "volunteers" are often dragged into the action.

Money-Saving Tip

The Jamboree is a great place to get off your feet for a midday break, almost like a free dinner show. In fact, the Jamboree is a good alternative to the Hoop-Dee-Doo Revue at Fort Wilderness for families on a budget.

Frontierland Shootin' Arcade

Bring your quarters. This is a pretty standard shooting gallery
but a good place for the kids to kill a few minutes while adults
wait in line at the Country Bear Jamboree.

Country Bear Jamboree

Younger kids fall for the funny, furry Audio-Animatronic crit-
ters featured in this 15-minute show. From the coy Teddi
Barra to the incomparable Big Al, from Bubbles, Bunny, and
Beulah (a sort of combination of the Andrews Sisters and the
Beach Boys) to Melvin the Moosehead, each face is distinctive
and lovable.

The Jamboree seats large numbers of guests at a time, so
you can slip in easily in the evening or during the 3 P.M. parade. (But don't, for heaven's sake, try to get in just after the
parade when thousands of tourists suddenly find themselves
on the streets of Frontierland with nothing to do.) Kids 9 and
up rate the bears as hokey; if there's a split in your children's
ages, one parent can take little kids to the Jamboree while the
other rides nearby Splash Mountain with the older ones.

A different but equally charming show runs at Christmas.

Tom Sawyer Island

A getaway playground full of caves, bridges, forts, and wind-
mills, Tom Sawyer Island is a good destination when the kids
become too rambunctious to handle. Adults can sip a lemonade at Aunt Polly's Dockside Inn, the island's fast-food restaurant, while the kids run free.

The big drawback is that the island is accessible only by
raft, which means you often have to wait to get there and wait
to get back. If your kids are under 5, don't bother making the
trip. The terrain is too widespread for preschoolers to play
without supervision, and young kids can better blow off steam

in Toontown. Likewise, there is little on the island for adults and teenagers to do. But if your kids are 5 to 9 and beginning to get a little squirrelly, stop off at Tom Sawyer's Island, where such behavior is not only acceptable—it's de rigueur.

Liberty Square

Walk on a few feet from Frontierland and you'll find yourself transported back another hundred years to colonial America, strolling the cobblestone streets of Liberty Square.

Liberty Square Attractions

Liberty Square Riverboat

The second tier of this paddlewheel riverboat offers outstanding views of Liberty Square and Frontierland, but, as with the other Rivers of America crafts, board only if you have time to kill and the boat is in the dock. The one exception? Periodically the characters, dressed in Dixieland Band costumes, take the ride with you. That makes it much more fun.

There are some seats, but most riders stand.

The Hall of Presidents

This attraction may remind you that one of the villains in the movie *The Stepford Wives* was a Disney imagineer. The Hall of Presidents is indeed a Stepford version of the presidency, with eerily lifelike and quietly dignified chief executives, each responding to his name in the roll

Time-Saving Tip
The theater holds up to 700 people, which means that lines disappear every 25 minutes. Ask one of the attendants at the lobby doors how long it is before the next show and amble in about 10 minutes before show time.

call with a nod or tilting of the head. In the background, other presidents fidget and whisper. Bill Clinton made his debut in 1994, and Maya Angelou narrates the show.

The presidential roll call and the film that precedes it will probably bore most kids under 10. Older children will find the 20-minute presentation educational. Babies and toddlers consider the Hall a fine place to nap. A good choice for the afternoon.

Mike Fink Keelboats

These small boats, usually operative only during the on-season, follow the same route as the canoes and riverboat. But the riverboat holds more people per trip, so if time is limited, take that. A good choice for afternoon.

The Haunted Mansion

More apt to elicit a giggle than a scream, the Mansion is full of clever special effects—at one point a ghost "hitchhikes" a ride in your own "doom buggy." The cast members, who dress as morticians and never smile, add to the fun with such instructions as "Drag your wretched bodies to the dead center of the room." The mansion is full of "in" jokes. For example, the tombstones outside name the imagineers who designed the ride. And take a glance at the pet cemetery as you leave.

The Mansion draws long lines in the afternoons; try to see it midmorning, or—if you have the courage—it's fun to tour at night.

The Scare Factor

A significant number of kids 7 to 11 listed the Haunted Mansion as one of their three favorite attractions, but a few mothers of children under 7 reported that their kids were frightened by the darkness. Fine for most kids over 7; the ride is richly atmospheric, but the spooks are played for laughs.

Full-Service Restaurants in the Magic Kingdom

Let's face it, no one goes to the Magic Kingdom expecting haute cuisine. The sit-down restaurants here are geared toward serving recognizable favorites such as salads, burgers, and fried chicken, and getting people in and out reasonably fast. For greater variety, look to Epcot; and for more creative presentation, try MGM.

Notable Fast-Food Restaurants in the Magic Kingdom

In general, the overcrowded fast-food places in Fantasyland should be avoided completely, as should the Adventureland Veranda, where you wait far too long for mediocre Chinese food. You'll have better luck at the places listed below.

- The Mile Long Bar in Frontierland is a good place for tame Tex-Mex, and lines move more swiftly than those at the Pecos Bill Cafe next door.

- Cosmic Ray's Starlight Cafe in Tomorrowland is by far the fastest of the fast-food places.

- Try a citrus swirl at the Sunshine Tree Terrace in Adventureland. Like Sleepy Hollow, this snack shop is tucked out of the way with its own quiet courtyard.

- If you're headed for Tom Sawyer's Island anyway, stop off at Aunt Polly's, which offers all the necessary ingredients for an impromptu picnic—sandwiches, chicken, ice cream, apple pie, and lemonade.

- Families who demand healthy snacks should drop by the Liberty Square Market, where fresh fruits and juices are available.

Quick Guide to Full-in the Magic

Restaurant	Description
Cinderella's Royal Table	She'll greet you at the door
Crystal Palace	Winnie the Pooh characters visit
Liberty Tree Tavern	All-American cuisine
The Plaza Restaurant	Good for lunch
Tony's Town Square Cafe	Great choice for families with toddlers

For descriptions of ratings, prices, priority seating, and suitability for kids, see pages 316–317.

Afternoon Resting Places

- The Disney World Railroad (you can rest while you ride)
- The small park across from Sleepy Hollow in Liberty Square
- The Diamond Horseshoe Jamboree
- The Hall of Presidents
- Legend of the Lion King
- Galaxy Palace

Service Restaurants Kingdom

Rating	Price	Priority Seating	Suitability	Details on
★★	$$$	Necessary	High	Page 329
★★	$$	Recommended	High	Page 331
★★	$$	Recommended	High	Page 336
★★	$$	Recommended	High	Page 340
★★	$$	Recommended	High	Page 342

@ Country Bear Jamboree

@ The Enchanted Tiki Birds

@ Tom Sawyer Island

@ Guests with a Park Hopper Plus pass can take the launch marked "Campground and Discovery Island" to either River Country or Discovery Island. If it's hot, bring your suits along or wear them under your clothes. An hour or two in River Country can cool you off and revive your spirits.

> ## Helpful Hint
> If you want a leisurely, quiet lunch, take the resort monorail to one of the Magic Kingdom hotels. The coffee shops and restaurants are rarely crowded in the middle of the day.

Best Vantage Points for Watching the Parades

The Magic Kingdom has two basic parades—the 3 P.M. parade that runs daily and the nighttime parade that runs nightly in the on-season and periodically during the off-season. In summer and on crowded days, the evening parade often runs twice, once from Main Street to Frontierland and then from Frontierland back to Main Street. If you're visiting during the on-season, ask an attendant what direction the parade will be coming from and try to be near the beginning of the route; those near the end of the route will have to wait an additional twenty minutes before they see their first float.

One good location is at the very beginning of Main Street, along the hub in front of the Railroad Station. (The parade usually begins here, emerging from behind City Hall.) You do lose the vantage point of the floats coming down Main Street, but it's worth it not to have to fight the crowds.

The crowds grow less manageable as you proceed down Main Street and are at their worst in front of Cinderella Castle. In fact, if you find yourself behind four layers of people on Main Street, send one of your party toward the entrance gate to check out the situation at the hub; you may find there's still curb space there when the rest of the route is mobbed.

If you find yourself deep in the bowels of the theme park at parade time, don't try to fight your way up Main Street to the hub—you'll never make it. Instead, go to the end of the route in Frontierland. The crowds here are thinner than in front of the Cinderella Castle or in Liberty Square.

Best Restroom Locations in the Magic Kingdom

By "best" I mean least crowded. You can get in and out of these rather quickly.

- Behind the Enchanted Grove snack bar near the Mad Tea Party.

- In the passageway between Adventureland and Frontierland. This one draws traffic but is so huge that you never have to wait long.

- Near the Skyway to Fantasyland in Tomorrowland.

- If you're in the Baby Services center for other reasons, make a pit stop.

- The sit-down restaurants have their own restrooms, which are rarely crowded.

Insider's Secret
As you leave Pirates of the Caribbean, make a stop at the restroom located at the back of the market stalls. This one is so secluded that I didn't find it until my seventeenth fact-finding trip to Disney World.

Tips for Your Last Hour in the Magic Kingdom

⊜ Some rides—most notably Big Thunder Mountain Railroad, Cinderella's Carrousel, Astro Orbiter, Dumbo, Splash Mountain, and the Skyway between Tomorrowland and Fantasyland—are particularly beautiful at night.

⊜ If you're visiting on an evening when a parade is scheduled, ask an attendant which direction it will be coming from. If it begins on Main Street, move as far as possible up Main Street and stake your curb space near the hub. Make a final potty run before the parade starts so you'll be ready to make a fast exit once the final float rolls by. If you're on Main Street near the hub, you may want to go ahead and turn in your rental stroller. If you're farther back, just park the stroller out of the way and hoof it. Pushing a stroller down Main Street in the crush of departing people is at best difficult and sometimes impossible.

Helpful Hint

If you've missed any of the biggie rides earlier in the day, return in the last hour; lines are shorter just before closing, especially in Frontierland.

⊜ If the parade is coming from Frontierland, line up in front of the Country Bear Jamboree. But don't try to exit the park just behind the parade; people will still be waiting to watch it on Main Street, and the entire park bottlenecks there, causing frightening crowds. Instead, stop for a snack or do a bit of window shopping and aim to leave after the main surge of people has exited the park.

The rides stop running at the official closing time, but Main Street stays open up to an hour longer.

Tips for Leaving the Magic Kingdom

@ Upon leaving at the end of the day, visitors staying off-site should pause for a second as they exit the gates. If a ferryboat is in the dock to your far left, that's your fastest route back to the TTC. If there's no boat in sight, queue up for the monorail that runs directly back to the TTC.

@ Guests at the Contemporary Resort should take the resort monorail. Guests at Wilderness Lodge or Fort Wilderness should take the hotel launch. Guests staying at the Polynesian Resort or the Grand Floridian should glance down at the launch dock, which is straight ahead as you exit the Magic Kingdom gates. If a launch is in sight, take it back to your hotel; otherwise head for the resort monorail.

@ Guests at the other Disney hotels should return to the shuttle bus station.

CHAPTER

6

Epcot Center

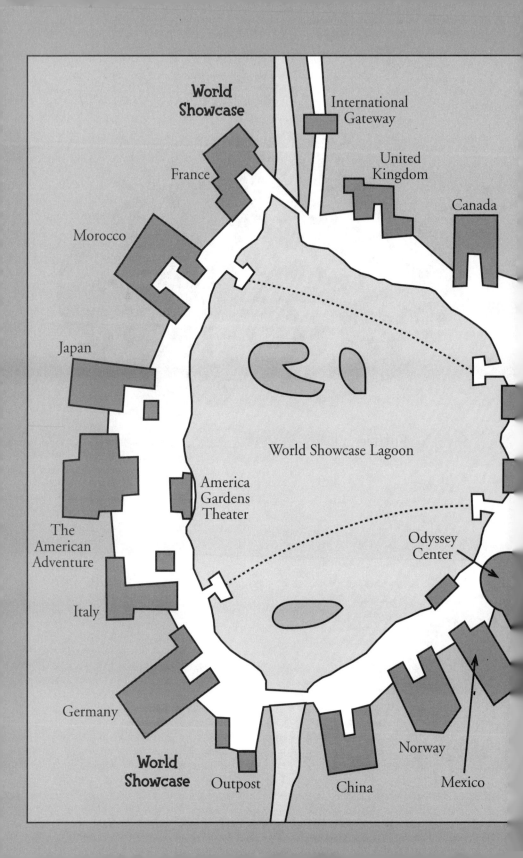

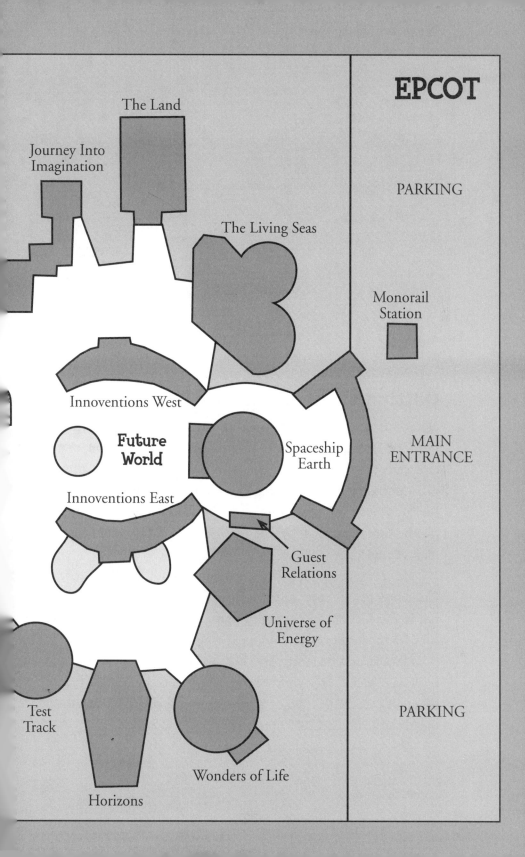

Getting to Epcot

Many off-site hotels and most on-site hotels offer shuttle buses to Epcot, but Epcot is easy to reach by car. If you arrive early in the morning, you can park very close to the main entrance gate and forgo the tram ride. If you arrive a bit later, however, the trams do run quickly and efficiently. Just be sure to write down the number of the row where you parked your car.

If you're staying at the Polynesian, Grand Floridian, or Contemporary Resort, your fastest route is to take the monorail to the Ticket and Transportation Center (TTC) and then transfer to the Epcot monorail. The Swan, the Dolphin, the BoardWalk, and the Yacht and Beach Clubs are connected to a special "backdoor" World Showcase entrance by bridge. Either take the shuttle tram or a water taxi or, if you're staying at the Yacht or Beach Club, simply walk over the bridge.

Getting Around Epcot

As any Disneyphile can tell you, Epcot is an acronym for the Experimental Prototype Community of Tomorrow. But as one of the players at the Comedy Warehouse on Pleasure Island suggests, maybe Epcot really stands for Every Person Comes Out Tired.

Epcot is indeed sprawling—more than twice the size of the Magic Kingdom—but the FriendShips that crisscross the World Showcase Lagoon and the double-decker buses that encircle the lagoon should be viewed as fun rides, not transportation. Your fastest means of getting around is walking.

Tips for Your First Hour at Epcot

- On-site guests can enter Epcot one hour early on Tuesday and Friday. If you're touring Epcot on an Early Entry morning, only four attractions—usually Spaceship Earth, the Living Seas, Living with the Land, and Journey into Imagination—are open. Ride Spaceship Earth first and then go to the Journey into Imagination pavilion and see *Honey, I Shrunk the Audience.* A line for Test Track may be forming before the ropes that allow you into that section of the park are actually dropped. If the posted wait time is less than 40 minutes, line up now.

- As soon as you enter the main gate, veer left to rent a stroller. Then, assuming it's operative, ride Spaceship Earth.

- Pick up a map/entertainment schedule. If you haven't arranged priority seating, enter the WorldKey Information System and do that now.

- If you have time before the rest of the park opens, browse through Innoventions. It's probably a mistake to let the kids at the games—once they start, it will be hard to get them out—but scope out the exhibits you'd like to return to later.

@ After the ropes are dropped and you're allowed to enter the body of the park, veer sharply left and ride Test Track first, then Body Wars in the Wonders of Life pavilion.

@ After Body Wars, leave the Wonders of Life pavilion—knowing you can always return for the films and interactive exhibits later—and head for the first showing of *Honey, I Shrunk the Audience.* If Test Track and Body Wars are too wild for you, go to *Honey, I Shrunk the Audience* first.

Epcot Touring Tips

@ Take Epcot in small doses if your kids are young; three to four hours at a time is enough.

@ Visit newer attractions such as *Honey, I Shrunk the Audience* and Test Track first thing in the morning.

@ Test Track is prone to technical problems and has been operative at times and not at others. Check the Epcot tip board between Communicore East and West to make sure it's running before you sprint over there.

@ In the off-season, Epcot hours are often staggered. Future World is generally open from 9 A.M. to 7 P.M. and the World Showcase from 11 A.M. to 9 P.M.

@ You can avoid crowds by touring Future World until midmorning and then drifting toward the World Showcase in the afternoon, where you can escape to the films and indoor exhibits during the hottest and busiest times.

Time-Saving Tip

Avoid the high-capacity shows such as Universe of Energy or *O Canada!* in the morning. Your time is better spent moving among the continuous-loading attractions such as Body Wars, Test Track, the Land, the Living Seas, and Journey into Your Imagination. With the exception of *Honey, I Shrunk the Audience,* save the theater-style attractions until afternoon.

@ Then, after an early dinner, head back into Future World. It's easier to ride anything there, even Test Track, if you wait after 8 P.M. when people begin to gather for Illumi-Nations.

@ If you are touring off-season and plan to spend mornings in the other parks and evenings at Epcot,

Helpful Hint

Touring Epcot is easier if you zig when everyone else zags. During the summer and other busy times, Future World stays crowded from mid-morning until late afternoon and then empties as people head toward their dinner reservations in the World Showcase.

make your dinner priority seating times as early as possible, leaving yourself several hours to tour after dinner.

@ Another alternative: If your children have had a good afternoon nap and can keep going until 10 P.M., make your dinner reservations very late. The restaurants accept their final seating just before the park shuts down, and all the transportation stays operative for at least 90 minutes after the official park closing time. Eating late buys you maximum hours in the park, assuming your kids can handle the schedule—and assuming you're seeing Illumi-Nations on another night.

@ Upon entering a World Showcase pavilion that has a show or film—France, Canada, America, or China—ask the attendant how long you have until the show begins. If your wait is 10 minutes or less, queue up. If the wait is longer, browse the shops of the pavilion until about 10 minutes before show time. The World Showcase theaters are so large that even people near the back of the line will be seated.

Insider's Secret

Most people circle the World Showcase Lagoon in a clockwise fashion, beginning with Mexico. You'll make better time if you move counterclockwise, beginning with Canada.

@ Innoventions and the interactive exhibits in the Wonders of Life, Journey into Imagination, and Spaceship Earth pavilions are very worthwhile—and a nice break from

Helpful Hint

If you miss the chance to exit before the IllumiNa-tions crowd or you've opted to stay for the show, don't join in the throngs that mob the exit turn-stiles and shuttle buses just after the show has ended. Pick up dessert before the show and then, after IllumiNations, find a table, sit down, relax, and let the crowds pass you by. The trams and monorails will still be running long after you finish your snack, and the lines waiting for them will be far shorter.

The Epcot Don't Miss List

Spaceship Earth

Cranium Command in the Wonders of Life pavilion

Test Track

Honey, I Shrunk the Audience

The American Adventure in the America pavilion

IllumiNations

Innoventions

The Epcot Worth-Your-While List

Universe of Energy

Body Wars in the Wonders of Life pavilion

The Living Seas

The Making of Me in the Wonders of Life pavilion

Living with the Land and
Food Rocks in the Land pavilion

Horizons

Journey into Imagination

Wonders of China in the China pavilion

O Canada! in the Canada pavilion

Maelstrom in the Norway pavilion

Impressions de France in the France pavilion

Quick Guide to

Attraction	Location	Height Requirement
The American Adventure	World Showcase	None
Body Wars	Future World	None
Circle of Life	Future World	None
Cranium Command	Future World	None
El Rio del Tiempo	World Showcase	None
Food Rocks	Future World	None
Honey, I Shrunk the Audience	Future World	None
Horizons*	Future World	
Image Works	Future World	None
Impressions de France	World Showcase	None
Innoventions	Future World	None
Journey into Your Imagination	Future World	None
The Living Seas	Future World	None
Living with the Land	Future World	None
Maelstrom	World Showcase	None
The Making of Me	Future World	None
O Canada!	World Showcase	None
Spaceship Earth	Future World	None
Test Track	Future World	40 inches
Universe of Energy	Future World	None
Wonders of China	World Showcase	None

*Being redone; no information available as we go to press.

Scare Factor

0 = Unlikely to scare any child of any age.
! = Has dark or loud elements; might rattle some toddlers.
!! = A couple of gotcha! moments; should be fine for school-age kids.
!!! = You need to be pretty big and pretty brave to handle this ride.

Epcot Attractions

Speed of Line	Duration of Ride/Show	Scare Factor	Age Range
Fast	30 min.	0	All
Fast	5 min.	!!	6 and up
Fast	20 min.	0	All
Fast	20 min.	0	6 and up
Fast	9 min.	0	All
Fast	15 min.	0	All
Fast	25 min.	0	5 and up
Fast	n/a	0	All
Fast	20 min.	0	10 and up
n/a	n/a	0	3 and up
Fast	13 min.	!	3 and up
Mod	8 min.	0	All
Fast	10 min.	0	All
Fast	15 min.	!	4 and up
Slow	15 min.	0	4 and up
Fast	20 min.	0	10 and up
Moderate	15 min.	0	All
Slow	25 min.	!!!	7 and up
Slow	30 min.	!	3 and up
Fast	20 min.	0	10 and up

the enforced passivity of all the rides. But ride the rides first and save the interactive games for midafternoon or early evening.

@ If you're not staying for IllumiNations, begin moving toward the exit gates while the show is in progress.

Future World

Future World comprises nine large pavilions, each containing at least one major attraction, and is very much like a permanent World's Fair, mixing educational opportunities with pure entertainment. Most visitors are drawn first to the rides with their spectacular special effects, but don't miss Innoventions and the chance to play with the smaller, interactive exhibits. Many of these encourage young visitors to learn while doing, and stopping to try them out helps kids avoid what one mother termed "Audio-Animatronics overload."

Sensitive to complaints that Epcot "was boring" and "never changed," Disney has made efforts to render Future World more appealing to kids. Three pavilions—Horizons, Test Track, and Universe of Energy—have undergone substantial alterations to make the preshows and technical presentations shorter and the special effects zippier. And Innoventions is constantly changing, with new exhibits moving in and out on a regular basis.

Future World Attractions

Spaceship Earth

Whatever their age, few travelers can remain blasé at the sight of Spaceship Earth, the most photographed and readily recognizable symbol of Epcot.

The ride inside, which coils toward the top of the 17-story geosphere, traces developments in communication from cave drawings to computers. The voice of Jeremy Irons croons in your ear as you climb past scenes of Egyptian temples, the Gutenberg press, and a performance of *Oedipus Rex*. Even preschoolers rated Spaceship Earth highly, probably due to the excitement of actually entering the "Big Ball" and the impressive finale, which flashes a planetarium sky above you as you swirl backward down through the darkness.

Helpful Hint
If you can't ride Spaceship Earth early in the morning, save it for evening.

The Living Seas

The Living Seas pavilion features a saltwater aquarium so enormous that Spaceship Earth could float inside it. You begin with a short film that discusses the critical role of the ocean as a source of energy, and then swiftly move on to board a gondola that takes you through an underwater viewing tunnel. More than 200 varieties of marine life, including stingrays, dolphins, barracuda, and sharks, swim above you. Unfortunately, the gondola ride is so brief that there's not much time to look.

The most enjoyable part of the attraction comes after you disembark at Seabase Alpha. You can remain here as long as you choose, wandering through two levels of

Time-Saving Tip
If you plan to devote a day to Sea World while in Orlando, you'll find much of the same stuff there, so hold your time at the Living Seas pavilion to a minimum.

observation tanks that allow you to view the fish and the human divers at close quarters. (A new program allows adult visitors to suit up and enter the tank with a guide for $150. Call 407-WDW-TOUR for details.)

The Land

This cheerful pavilion, sponsored by Nestlé and devoted to the subject of food production and the environment, is home to three separate attractions as well as a rotating restaurant and fast-food court. Because there are so many places to eat here, the Land is crowded from 11 A.M. to 2 P.M., when everyone heads in for lunch.

@ Living with the Land. Visitors travel by boat past scenes of various farming environments, ending with a peek at fish farming, drip irrigation, and other innovative agricultural technologies. Perhaps because there are few special effects, this attraction is less interesting to preschoolers. But, as is the case in all of Future World, the presentation moves swiftly. In short, this won't be your children's favorite attraction, but they won't complain either. (Hour-long guided tours of the greenhouse are also available, at a price of $6 for adults, $4 for kids. Ask a host for details.)

@ *Circle of Life.* This film, in the Harvest Theatre, graphically illustrates how we interact—both positively and negatively—with our environment. Two years ago *Circle of Life* was revamped to make it more appealing to kids, with Pumba, Timon, and Simba from *The Lion King* as the new stars; the resulting film is both educational and entertaining. It's a good choice for afternoon.

@ *Food Rocks.* A funny 15-minute show featuring famous rock 'n' roll stars masquerading as foods, *Food Rocks* is another good choice for afternoon. The Peach Boys sing about "good nutrition," while an eggplant is dubbed "Neil Moussaka," and the Refrigerator Police oversee "every bite you take."

Journey into Your Imagination

In 1999 Disney revamped Journey into Imagination into Journey into Your Imagination.

The premise is that riders are volunteers at the Imagination Institute's Open House, taking part in a series of perceptional experiments on how color, dimension, gravity, illusion, and sound affect the human imagination. Your host is the energetic but somewhat pompous Dr. Nigel Channing, played by Eric Idle, in a reprise of his *Honey, I Shrunk the Audience* role. Figment, the flying purple dragon from the original Journey into Imagination, is still on hand to help, albeit in a much reduced capacity. The kids I know really miss him.

Once loaded into your vehicle, you'll pass before the Imagination Scanner, which reveals cobwebs and "Vacancy" signs. "Perfect subjects," Dr. Channing enthuses, but you won't stay blank for long, because your senses are getting ready to be challenged to the max. Is that a train coming toward you in the dark? Is the butterfly cage empty or full? Don't answer too fast—your perception may change within seconds. In the gravity lab,

Helpful Hint
As you leave the Journey Into Your Imagination pavilion, take time to check out Splashtacular, a fun fountain show that gives kids the chance to get wet.

water from a leaky tub drips up, and later you'll learn that each sound has its own color. After a series of such sensory-jolting exercises, the Imagination Scanner reveals your mind is now so full that you literally blow the machine.

Then it's on to ImageWorks, Kodak's "What If?" lab, with interactive exhibits where you can distort your facial image, produce sounds by stepping on pictures of lightning and lions, and picture yourself skydiving high above Cinderella Castle. The most popular experiment is "What If I Could Become Something Else?" which allows you to transfer your own face onto a koala, sunflower, or dozens of other images . . . and then e-mail the results home to yourself and three friends free of charge. It's a fresh new way to say "Wish you were here."

Honey, I Shrunk the Audience

Beside Journey Into Your Imagination is Epcot's sleeper hit, the 3-D film *Honey, I Shrunk the Audience.* This show is so much fun that several families reported their kids insisted on seeing it more than once. Based on the popular movie series, the presentation begins as Dr. Wayne Szalinski is about to pick up the award for Inventor of the Year. The scene quickly dissolves into mayhem as the audience is accidentally "shrunk," one son's pet snake gets loose, and the other's pet mouse is reproduced 999 times. Although the 3-D images are dazzling, the effects go far beyond the visual—you actually

The Scare Factor
Honey, I Shrunk the Audience was very, very highly rated by the families we surveyed. If your child does happen to be unnerved by the special effects, have him take off the 3-D glasses and either pull up his legs into the seat or sit in your lap. That way he won't see the images clearly and won't feel the tactile sensations.

feel the "mice" running up your legs, and the kid-pleasing, dog-sneezing finale is not to be missed.

Test Track

Test Track is the longest, fastest ride in all of Disney World—and the only Epcot attraction that can honestly be called a thrill ride.

Insider's Secret

Test Track draws the longest lines in Walt Disney World. How do you spell relief? F-A-S-T-P-A-S-S

The idea is that guests are testing automobiles before they are brought to market. You begin the ride inside, checking out how your vehicle responds to conditions of cold, heat, and stress—but it's the stress level of the passengers that soars when you move to the speed test, break through a barrier, and burst outside of the building. Once outside, the cars reach speeds of up to 65 miles per hour, with

Helpful Hint

Be prepared for the fact that this attraction is more apt to be closed than any other ride in all of Disney World.

hills, curves, and hairpin turns. Twenty-eight cars are on the track at the same time, each outfitted with its own in-board computer. In other words, the track isn't pulling the cars, as is the case in most driving rides; the Test Track cars are driving

The Scare Factor

Children must be 40 inches tall to ride, and an adult must accompany children under 7. It's all about speed, with no flips or plunges, and kids we surveyed loved Test Track.

themselves. The track is almost a mile long in total, adding up to a powerfully exciting ride.

Horizons

Horizons is closed as we go to press, with no indication if it will be revamped and reopened or cleared out to make way for a new pavilion.

Wonders of Life

Devoted to celebrating the human body, the Wonders of Life pavilion resembles a brightly colored street fair full of hands-on exhibits. You can check out your health profile via computer, get advice on your tennis or golf swing, and test your endurance on a motorized bike. Like the Land pavilion, the Wonders pavilion houses three major attractions and is crowded by 11 A.M.

- Body Wars. Body Wars uses flight-simulation technology to take riders on a turbulent high-speed chase through the human body. After being miniaturized to the size of a pinhead and injected into a patient, the crew is briefed to expect a routine medical mission for the purpose of re-

The Scare Factor

No expectant mothers or kids under 3 are allowed to board, and Body Wars does indeed have its queasy moments, more because of the accuracy of flight-simulation technology than the bouncing of the spaceship. Those prone to motion sickness should skip the trip, as well as anyone put off by the sheer subject matter. More people reported losing their lunch on Body Wars than on Star Tours, the major motion-simulation ride at MGM.

moving a splinter from the "safe zone just under the skin" But when shapely Dr. Lair is sucked into a capillary, your crew is off on a rescue chase through the heart, lungs, and brain.

@ *The Making of Me.* This 15-minute film provides a fetus-eye view of conception, gestation, and birth. Martin Short travels back in time to show us his own parents as babies and then chronicles how they met and ultimately produced him. (One glaring anachronism: Martin must have been the only kid born in America in the 1950s who was delivered through Lamaze.) Although the film is direct and unflinching, it's appropriate for any age.

Let one parent queue up while the other takes the kids around to some of the interactive exhibits. Coach's Corner—which gives visitors a chance to have their golf, tennis, or baseball swing videotaped, replayed in slo-mo, and then analyzed by Nancy Lopez, Chris Evert, or Gary Carter—is especially fun.

@ Cranium Command. One of the funniest presentations in Epcot, Cranium Command mixes Audio-Animatronics with film. The preshow is vital to understanding what's going on—General Knowledge taps an unfortunate recruit, Fuzzy, to pilot "the most unstable craft in the fleet"—the brain of a 12-year-old boy. If he fails in his mission, Fuzzy will be demoted to flying the brain of a chicken or, worse, a talk-show host.

Fuzzy tries to guide his boy through a typical day of junior high school without overloading his system—which isn't easy, especially when the body parts are played by this cast: Charles Grodin as the right brain, Jon Lovitz as the left brain, Hans and Franz from *Saturday Night Live* pumping it up in the role of the heart, Norm from *Cheers* as the stomach, and, in a particularly convincing performance, Bobcat Goldthwait as adrenaline.

Universe of Energy

This technologically complex presentation can be enjoyed by any age on any level. Ask the attendant at the door how long until show time and don't queue up until the wait is 10 minutes or less; this is an almost 30-minute presentation, and there's no point in wearing out the kids before you begin.

Disney has made the preshow and postshow a lot snappier by bringing in Ellen DeGeneres, Alex Trebek, and Jamie Lee Curtis. The premise is that Ellen dreams she goes on *Jeopardy!* and is thoroughly skunked in the science category by smarty-pants Jamie Lee; Bill Nye the Science Guy convinces her that we all need to know more about energy.

The Disney twist comes when the 97-seat theater begins to break apart in sections that align themselves in sequence and move toward a curtain. Your theater has become your train, and the curtain slowly lifts to reveal an Audio-Animatronics version of the age when coal deposits first began to form. The air reeks of sulfur as it presumably did during the prehistoric era, the light is eerie blue, and all around you are those darn dinosaurs. After your train has once again metamorphosed into a theater, there's a final film segment in which a newly educated Ellen gets her *Jeopardy!* revenge.

Despite its proximity to the front gate, this is not a good choice for the morning; save it for afternoon or early evening, when you'll welcome the chance to sit for a half-hour. The Universe of Energy seats a large number of people at a time, meaning that lines form and dissipate quickly. If the line looks

The Scare Factor
Few families report that their kids were afraid of the dinosaurs; in fact, for most kids the dinosaurs are by far their favorite part of the attraction.

prohibitive, check out nearby pavilions and return in 20 minutes. You may be able to walk right in.

Innoventions

Innoventions is the arcade of the future, where you can try out new Sega Genesis games before they hit the market, fly on a virtual reality magic carpet, and play with beyond-state-of-the-art technology such as video controller chairs and computers that translate voice dictation directly into the printed word.

Innoventions is a showcase for such corporations as Apple, IBM, Motorola, Sega, and AT&T. The products displayed have either just come on the market or are straight from the inventor and not yet available. Choices range from toilets that clean themselves to a stationary bike with a Nintendo attached—the idea is that you'll become so absorbed in the game that you won't notice how hard you're pedaling.

By far the most popular are the virtual reality games; people line up for five minutes on a machine, and many become so hooked that they reenter the line over and over for the chance to be a cue ball in a pool game or a driver in the Indy 500. (Observers can see what the player sees on an overhead screen.) Cast members are quick to point out that these much-maligned games are what pushed the envelope in computer technology, especially in the area of graphics. Preteens and teens will obviously be dazzled, but there are Pico computer games for preschoolers as well.

If you plan to spend much time in Innoventions, pick up a map as you enter. Well-informed cast members are on hand to answer questions or help you get the hang of the games and experiments. Exhibits change frequently, which keeps things fresh.

Helpful Hint
Innoventions becomes crowded in midmorning, as people enter the Epcot gates and make a dash for the first thing they see. Visit in early evening or during IllumiNations.

If the blinking and beeping become too overwhelming, parents can take a break outside at the nearby Expresso and Pastry Cafe. The Fountain of Nations between Innoventions East and West—so named because it contains water from all the countries of the World Showcase—puts on a lovely evening show.

World Showcase

Pretty by day and gorgeous by night, the World Showcase comprises the pavilions of 11 nations—Mexico, Norway, China, Germany, Italy, America, Japan, Morocco, France, the United Kingdom, and Canada—stretching around a large lagoon. Some of the pavilions have full-scale attractions (listings follow); others have only shops and restaurants. Demonstrations, musical presentations, and shows are scheduled throughout the day, and the characters, dressed in culturally appropriate costumes, frequently appear in the afternoons.

Most important from an educational and cultural perspective, each pavilion is staffed by citizens of the country it represents. Disney goes to great pains to recruit, relocate, and, if necessary, teach English to the shopkeepers and waiters you see in these pavilions, bringing them to Orlando for a year and housing them with the representatives from the other World Showcase nations. It's a cultural exchange program on the highest level. (One Norwegian guide told me her room-mates were from China, Mexico, and Canada.)

These young men and women save the World Showcase from being merely touristy, add an air of authenticity to every aspect of the experience, and provide your kids with the chance to rub elbows, however briefly, with other cultures. So even if pavilions such as Morocco and Japan don't have a ride or film, don't rush past them: Stop for a pastry and chat with the person behind the counter.

Helpful Hint

The World Showcase used to be a big yawn for kids under 8. But if you buy them a World Showcase Passport at Port of Entry, they can collect stamps and a handwritten message from each World Show-case nation they visit. Given kids' passion for col-lecting, a desire to fill their Passport will motivate them to move from country to country. It's the Epcot equivalent of collecting character auto-graphs, and it makes a great souvenir.

In addition, *Family Fun* magazine has begun sponsoring Kids' Zones, where children can learn a craft appropriate to the country they're visiting. For example, they can paint the Eiffel Tower in Paris, make an origami bird in Japan, or learn how to write their names in Arabic in Morocco. Although the crafts vary with the seasons, the hands-on interaction with a World Showcase employee is a real kick, and stopping at the Kids' Zones is a great way to break up the afternoon.

World Showcase Attractions

O Canada!

This 20-minute CircleVision 360 film is gorgeous, stirring—and difficult to view with kids under 6. In order to enjoy the effect of the circular screen, guests are required to stand during the presentation, and strollers are not allowed in the theater. This means babies and toddlers must be held, and preschoolers, who can't see anything in a room of standing adults, often clamor to be lifted up as well. So we regretfully suggest that families with young kids pass up this presentation, as well as the equally lovely *Wonders of China.* If you're dining at Epcot during your parents' night out, this would be a good time to take in those World Showcase attractions that just aren't oriented toward kids.

Impressions de France

What a difference a seat makes! Like all the Epcot films, *Impressions de France* is exceedingly well done, with lush music and a 200-degree wide-screen feel. It's fairly easy to get in, even in the afternoon, and no one minds if babies take a little nap.

The American Adventure

This multimedia presentation, combining Audio-Animatronics figures with film, is popular with all age-groups. The tech-

Helpful Hint

The America pavilion becomes quite crowded in the afternoon, but because it's located at the exact midpoint of the World Showcase lagoon, it's impractical to skip it and work your way back later. If you're faced with a half-hour wait, enjoy the excellent Voices of Liberty preshow or have a snack at the Liberty Inn next door.

nological highlight of the show comes when the Ben Franklin robot actually walks upstairs to visit Thomas Jefferson, but the entire 30-minute presentation is packed with elaborate sets that rise from the stage, film montages, moving music, and painless history lessons.

Wonders of China

Another lovely film—when Disney directors and photographers went to China to shoot it, they were the first Westerners ever allowed to film many of these sites. But again, the theater was not really designed with families in mind.

Maelstrom

In this Norwegian boat ride, your Viking ship sails through fjords and storms, over waterfalls, and past a threatening three-headed troll—all within four minutes. Riders disembark in a North Sea coastal village, where a short film is presented. A Viking ship–styled play area is located to the left of the Norway pavilion—a welcome addition for kids.

The Scare Factor

This ride sounds terrifying, but the reality is far tamer than the description. The much-touted "backward plunge over a waterfall" is so subtle that passengers in the front of the boat are not even aware of the impending doom. Some preschoolers are put off by the darkness, the swirling mists, and the troll, but the ride is generally fine for kids 6 and up.

El Rio del Tiempo: The River of Time

There's rarely a wait at this little boat ride, located inside the romantic Mexico pavilion. Reminiscent of It's a Small World in the Magic Kingdom, El Rio is especially appealing to younger riders.

General Information About Epcot Restaurants

Two years ago Disney changed the reservation system it employed for years, replacing it with "priority seating," which basically means that if you show up at a restaurant at the prearranged time, you'll receive the next table available that fits the size of your party. The problems begin when 15 families of four show up all at once with the same priority seating time; our readers report waits of anywhere from 10 minutes to an hour, with about 20 minutes being typical.

Still, it's better than being a walk-in, the lowest life form in the Disney World food chain, so if you'd like to try a certain restaurant, arrange priority seating up to 60 days in advance by calling 407-WDW-DINE (some restaurants will allow up to 120 days). If you're staying on-site, dial 55 from your hotel room phone.

The following are some general tips for the obligatory Epcot dining experience.

@ If you haven't arranged for priority seating, make your plans first thing in the morning at the WorldKey Information Center beside Spaceship Earth. Visitors who have no priority seating times arranged sometimes get seated by simply showing up at the restaurant door, especially if they try a large restaurant like the Biergarten or eat dinner very early.

Money-Saving Tip

If you're trying to save money, remember that lunchtime selections are just as impressive as dinner, and the fare is much cheaper.

ℯ The Epcot dining experience doesn't come cheap. Dinner for a family of four will run about $60 without alcohol. But, as throughout Disney World, portions are very large, even on items from the kiddie menu. Two children can easily share an entree; for that matter, so can two adults.

ℯ Kids are welcome at any Epcot eatery, although some are more entertaining for youngsters than others. (See the following section for details.) High chairs, booster seats, and kiddie menus are universally available.

The World Showcase restaurants offer "Mickey's Child Deals" for about $4. The food is a nod to the country whose cuisine is being represented—for example, skewered chicken in Morocco and fish and chips in the United Kingdom. But the entrees are smaller, less spicy, and look enough like chicken nuggets and fish sticks that the kids will eat them.

Casual attire is acceptable anywhere in the park. It may seem strange to eat oysters with champagne sauce while wearing a Goofy sweatshirt, but you'll get used to it.

ℯ Be bold. Your hometown probably has good Chinese and Italian restaurants, but how often do you get to sample Norwegian or Moroccan food?

Full-Service Restaurants at Epcot

Epcot, especially in the World Showcase area, is known for its restaurants. This is your chance to try an admittedly Americanized version of a whole new cuisine, and to be swept into a full-scale cultural experience, combining food, music, entertainment, and architecture to create the illusion that you've traveled the globe.

Quick Guide to Full-

Restaurant	Description
Akershus (Norway)	Lot of fish, picky eaters may rebel
Biergarten (Germany)	Rousing, noisy atmosphere
Bistro de Paris (France)	Classic French cuisine, very elegant, very adult
Le Cellier (Canada)	A good spot for beef and salmon—as well as buffalo
Chefs de France (France)	The ambience of a Paris sidewalk cafe
The Coral Reef	Great view of the Living Seas tank
The Garden Grill	American food, restaurant rotates
Marrakesh (Morocco)	Exotic surroundings, belly dancers
Nine Dragons (China)	Cuisine representing every region of China
L'Originale Alfredo di Roma (Italy)	Most popular restaurant in the World Showcase
Rose and Crown Dining Room (United Kingdom)	Pub atmosphere and charming service
San Angel Inn Restaurante (Mexico)	Service is swift and friendly
Teppanyaki Dining Room (Japan)	Chefs slice and dice in the best Benihana tradition

For descriptions of ratings, prices, priority seating, and suitability for kids, see pages 316–317.

Service Restaurants at Epcot

Rating	Price	Priority Seating	Suitability	Details on
★★	$$	Recommended	Moderate	Page 326
★	$$	Recommended	High	Page 326
★★★	$$$	Necessary	Low	Page 327
★	$$	Recommended	Low	Page 329
★★★	$$$	Necessary	Moderate	Page 329
★★	$$$	Necessary	High	Page 331
★★	$$	Recommended	High	Page 333
★	$$	Suggested	Moderate	Page 337
★	$$	Suggested	Moderate	Page 338
★★	$$$	Necessary	Moderate	Page 339
★★	$$	Recommended	High	Page 340
★★	$$	Recommended	High	Page 341
★★★	$$$	Necessary	High	Page 342

Money-Saving Tip
If you want to save both time and money, stick to the fast-food places for meals—but arrange priority seating at a sit-down restaurant for a truly off time, say 4 P.M. or 10 P.M., and just have dessert. You can soak up the ambience for an investment of 30 minutes and 20 bucks.

Notable Fast-Food Restaurants at Epcot

"Fast food" is a somewhat relative term at Epcot, where long lines are the norm during peak dining hours. But the choices are far more varied and interesting than those at the Magic Kingdom. And the views are so lovely—especially in the Mexico, Japan, and France pavilions—that Epcot blurs the distinction between fast food and a real meal.

- The skewered chicken and beef at the Yakitori House in the Japan pavilion is tasty, and the little courtyard outside gives the feel of a Japanese tea garden.

Money-Saving Tip
As is the case in many of the World Showcase eateries, a child's combination plate is more than adequate for an adult, especially if you'll be snacking in a couple of hours.

- The Cantina de San Angel in the Mexico pavilion serves tortillas and tostadas at tables clustered around the lagoon.

- You'll find open-faced salmon or ham sandwiches and exceptional pastries at Kringla Bakeri og Kafe in the Norway pavilion. The kids can play on the nearby Viking ship while adults relax.

- If your kids are suffering from hamburger withdrawal, there's always the Liberty Inn at the America pavilion.

- If you find yourself in Future World at lunchtime and your party can't agree on a restaurant, visit Sunshine Season in the Land pavilion. The food court here has plenty of variety, including clam chowder, quiche, barbecue, stuffed potatoes, scooped-out pineapples filled with fruit salad, and killer chocolate chip cookies.

- La Maison du Vin in the France pavilion and the Weinkeller in the Germany pavilion offer wine tastings. The fee is minimal, and you get to keep the souvenir glass. A case of Chardonnay is the last thing you need with you when you're riding Test Track, so if you find something you like, the bottles can be sent to Package Pickup for you to retrieve as you exit the park or, if you're staying on-site, delivered directly to your room.

Epcot Extras

The Magic Kingdom isn't the only place to see the characters, catch a show, watch fireworks, or buy souvenirs. Epcot provides all of that entertainment but with an international spin.

Characters

The afternoon character shows at the World Showcase Lagoon brings as many as 20 characters to a single spot, and the crowds of kids vying for their attention are never as large as those at the Magic Kingdom—especially if you choose the first show of the day. Check the entertainment schedule on your map for times.

In the afternoons the characters appear in their appropriate World Showcase nations. For example, you can meet Aladdin in Morocco and Mary Poppins in Great Britain. Check your entertainment schedule for times.

World Showcase Performers

Singers, dancers, jugglers, and artisans from around the globe perform throughout the World Showcase daily. Most of these presentations (which are detailed in your daily entertainment guide) are not especially oriented toward children—although kids over 7 will catch the humor of the World Showcase Players in the United Kingdom, who put on wacky farces with lots of audience participation. The young gymnasts in the China pavilion appeal to children of all ages.

Older kids will enjoy the Beatles clone group The British Invasion, also in the United Kingdom. Or check out Off-Kilter, who offer "High Energy Progressive Celtic Music" in Canada. This translates

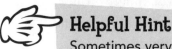

Helpful Hint

Sometimes very special performers, such as pint-sized Chinese acrobats, are showcased in Future World. These acts, especially the ones that feature youngsters, draw high ratings from kids in every age-group.

to rock music with bagpipes, and the show is a must-see. Another crowd pleaser is the Living Statues in France, where remarkably unlifelike actors pose as classical statues and interact with guests. Get the cameras ready for this one.

IllumiNations

This display of laser technology, fireworks, syncopated fountains, and classical music is a real-life Fantasia and an unqualified Disney World classic. Very popular, very crowded, and a perfect way to end an Epcot day, IllumiNations takes place on the World Showcase Lagoon, and the performance coincides with the park closing time. Try to watch from the Mexico or Canada pavilion so you'll be able to beat most of the crowd to the exits afterward. (If you're staying at the Swan, Dolphin, BoardWalk, or Yacht and Beach Clubs and thus leaving via the "backdoor" exit, try the Great Britain or France pavilion.)

Shopping

You'll see things in Epcot that aren't available anywhere else in Disney World: German wines, silk Chinese robes, a collection of piñatas that would put any Mexican marketplace to shame, and a shop devoted to English teas are all within strolling distance of each other. However, you don't want to end up carrying those hand-knit Norwegian sweaters and that Venetian crystal around the park with you, so if you make major purchases, either have them sent to Package Pickup near the front gate or, if you're staying on-site, have them delivered to your hotel.

Afternoon Resting Places at Epcot

- Universe of Energy
- *Circle of Life* or *Food Rocks,* in the Land pavilion

- *Honey, I Shrunk the Audience*
- *The Making of Me,* in the Wonders of Life pavilion
- The American Adventure
- *Impressions de France*

Best Restroom Locations at Epcot

The restrooms within the Future World pavilions are always crowded, and those around Innoventions aren't much better. But there are places where you can take a relatively quick bathroom break:

- At Baby Services, located on the bridge between Future World and the World Showcase

- Behind Kringla Bakeri og Kafe in the Norway pavilion

- Between the Morocco and France pavilions

- Near the Group Sales Booth at the Entrance Plaza (a good place to stop as you exit the park)

- In Future World, the restroom near the Garden Grill Room in the Land pavilion

Tips for Your Last Hour at Epcot

- If you're staying for IllumiNations, you'll need to find a good spot around the World Showcase Lagoon 30 minutes in advance during the off-season, 45 to 60 minutes in advance during the on-season. If the idea of such a long wait dismays you, you can bring desserts and have an evening snack while you wait. Or one parent can hold the turf while the other takes the kids souvenir shopping.

◉ Not staying for IllumiNations? The show pulls a lot of people to the World Showcase Lagoon, so this is an excellent chance to ride any Future World attractions you may have missed earlier, especially Test Track. Or drop by Innoventions on your way out. Just be sure to be at the exit gate before IllumiNations ends and the onslaught of people begins.

Tips for Leaving Epcot

◉ Families staying for IllumiNations should prepare themselves for a crush of people. You may want to turn in rental strollers before the show begins and just carry younger kids to the exits; it can be nearly impossible to push a stroller in the mob. On top of everything else, in order to make the fireworks more effective, the lights are dimmed at the end of IllumiNations, so you are exiting in the dark. Whatever their age, hold on to your children's hands during the exodus; this is the time of the day when you're most apt to be separated from your party.

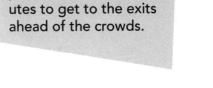

Time-Saving Tip
If you're not staying for IllumiNations, be out of there before it ends. Once you see the fireworks begin in earnest, you have about 5 minutes to get to the exits ahead of the crowds.

◉ Those staying at the Epcot resorts should watch IllumiNations from the Great Britain and France pavilions and exit via the "backdoor." If there's a line for the water taxi, you may be better off walking back to your hotel.

@ If you're not in the first wave of people to hit the exits (which is most likely if you're watching from the areas near the Mexico or Canada pavilions), have a snack, browse the stores, and aim to exit about 20 minutes behind the main crowd.

CHAPTER 7

Disney-MGM Studios Theme Park

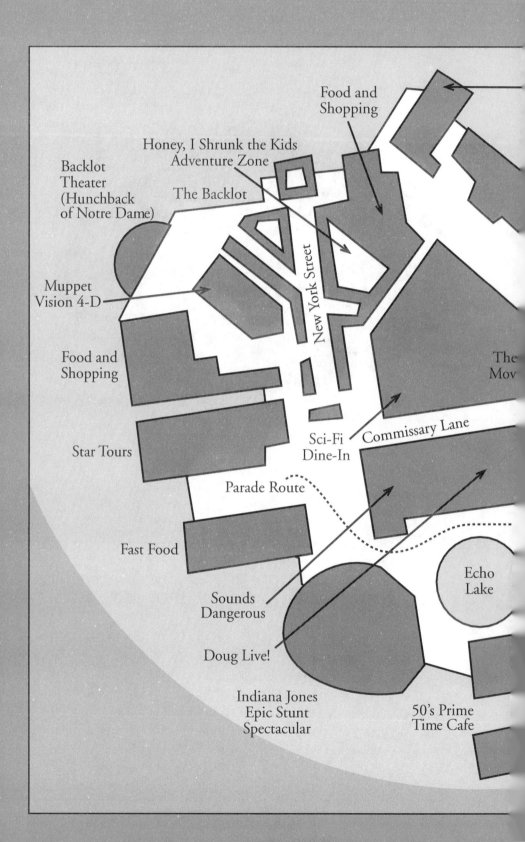

Food and Shopping

Honey, I Shrunk the Kids Adventure Zone

Backlot Theater (Hunchback of Notre Dame)

The Backlot

Muppet Vision 4-D

New York Street

Food and Shopping

The Mov

Star Tours

Sci-Fi Dine-In

Commissary Lane

Parade Route

Fast Food

Echo Lake

Sounds Dangerous

Doug Live!

Indiana Jones Epic Stunt Spectacular

50's Prime Time Cafe

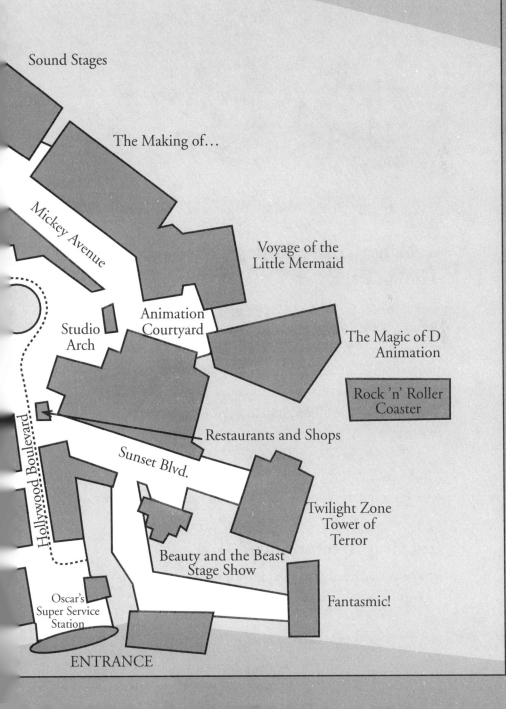

Disney-MGM Studios

Studios Backlot Tour

Sound Stages

The Making of…

Mickey Avenue

Voyage of the Little Mermaid

Animation Courtyard

Studio Arch

The Magic of D Animation

Rock 'n' Roller Coaster

Restaurants and Shops

Sunset Blvd.

Hollywood Boulevard

Twilight Zone Tower of Terror

Beauty and the Beast Stage Show

Oscar's Super Service Station

Fantasmic!

ENTRANCE

DISNEY WORLD SCENE 1 TAKE 17

Getting to the Disney-MGM Studios Theme Park

Compared to the Magic Kingdom, getting to MGM is a snap. Shuttle buses run approximately every 15 minutes from all on-site hotels. Remember that on-site guests who drive to the theme parks don't have to pay for parking.

If you're staying at the Swan, Dolphin, BoardWalk, or Yacht and Beach Clubs, you're a 10-minute water taxi ride from the MGM gate.

If you're staying off-site and have a car, note that the MGM parking lot is small. If you get there at opening time, you can forgo the parking lot tram and walk to the front gate.

Getting Around MGM

MGM is a relatively small park with no in-park transportation such as trains or buses. In other words, you'll walk.

Tips for Your First Hour at MGM

@ On-site resort guests can enter MGM one hour early on Wednesday and Sunday. The blackboard halfway down Hollywood Boulevard lets you know which attractions are operative; the whole park doesn't open early, but at least three major attractions will be ready to ride.

@ One parent can handle stroller rental at Oscar's Super Service Station while the other picks up a map/entertainment schedule at Guest Relations or Crossroads of the World.

@ If your kids are old enough and bold enough for a big-deal ride, go straight to the Rock 'n' Roller Coaster, then move on to the Twilight Zone Tower of Terror on Sunset Boulevard.

Younger kids? If an early show of the Voyage of the Little Mermaid is scheduled, you should head there the minute you enter the gate. Your entertainment schedule will tell you if an 8:30 or 9 A.M. show is planned.

@ If you haven't made dining plans yet, pause at the Hollywood Junction Red Car Station, where Sunset Boulevard meets Hollywood Boulevard, to arrange priority seating for any restaurant you'd like to try. The booth has sample menus.

@ Board the Great Movie Ride.

@ Board Star Tours.

@ If you haven't had breakfast, check out the pastries at Starring Rolls.

MGM Touring Tips

◉ With the exception of Voyage of the Little Mermaid, save theater-style presentations such as Doug Live!, Beauty and the Beast, the Indiana Jones Epic Stunt Spectacular, the Hunchback of Notre Dame Stage Show, and Sounds Dangerous for afternoon or evening. Tour continuous-loading attractions such as the Tower of Terror, the Great Movie Ride, the Rock 'n' Roller Coaster, and Star Tours early in the day.

◉ MGM is the park where the newer Disney films are showcased, so parades and shows are constantly being updated. The Aladdin parade makes way for the Toy Story parade, followed by Hercules, and then Mulan, and Tarzan, and so on.

Therefore, the parades and shows described in this chapter could be scrapped if Disney decides it's time to plug its latest film. Consult your entertainment schedule and maps for the latest offerings because the changes can be quite abrupt.

◉ Save the Backlot and Animation tours for after lunch or early evening.

◉ Remember—what's new is always hot: See recently opened attractions like the Rock 'n' Roller Coaster early.

Insider's Secret
The Disney people post a gigantic blackboard at the end of Hollywood Boulevard, keeping visitors updated on approximate waiting times at various attractions. Consult it whenever you're in doubt about what to do next.

☙ For one of the coolest photo ops in all of WDW, pull the handle on the umbrella outside the Hollywood Art School in the backlot section. You'll be "Singing in the Rain" within seconds!

☙ If any Disney Channel shows are in production on the day of your visit, Guest Relations can tell you how to become a member of the studio audience.

> **Helpful Hint**
> Disney Channel shows being taped require that audience members be at least 12 years old and, for some shows, 17.

☙ MGM is small and easily crisscrossed, so don't feel obligated to tour attractions in any particular geographic sequence. Those 4- and 5-year-olds who would need a stroller at the Magic Kingdom or Epcot can do without one here.

☙ Also, after the dinner hour, popular restaurants such as the SciFi Drive-In sometimes will accept walk-ins, especially if you're just dropping by for dessert. As at the other theme parks, the restaurants are still serving food as the park officially closes, so if you didn't make it into one of the big-deal restaurants earlier in the day, now's your chance.

☙ Fantasmic!, a 25-minute evening spectacular is an absolute must-see. Performances take place on a lake beside the Tower of Terror, and you should be in place 90 minutes before the stated show time to guarantee a good seat in the on-season. Show up an hour early in the off-season.

Quick Guide to

Attraction	Location	Height Requirement
The ABC Sound Studio	Hollywood Blvd.	None
Afternoon Parade	Hollywood Blvd.	None
The Backstage Pass	Mickey Ave.	None
Beauty and the Beast Stage Show	Sunset Blvd.	None
Disney Channel Filming	Mickey Ave.	None
Doug Live!	Hollywood Blvd.	None
Fantasmic!	Sunset Blvd.	None
The Great Movie Ride	Hollywood Blvd.	None
The Honey, I Shrunk the Kids Adventure Zone	New York Street	None
The Hunchback of Notre Dame Stage Show	New York Street	None
The Indiana Jones Epic Stunt Spectacular	Hollywood Blvd.	None
The Magic of Disney Animation Tour	Animation Courtyard	None
The Making of . . .	Mickey Ave.	None
The MGM Backlot Tour	Mickey Ave.	None
MuppetVision 4-D	New York Street	None
Twilight Zone Tower of Terror	Sunset Blvd.	40 inches
Rock 'n' Roller Coaster	Sunset Blvd.	48 inches
Star Tours	Hollywood Blvd.	40 inches
Voyage of the Little Mermaid	Animation Courtyard	None

Scare Factor

0 = Unlikely to scare any child of any age.
! = Has dark or loud elements; might rattle some toddlers.
!! = A couple of gotcha! moments; should be fine for school-age kids.
!!! = You need to be pretty big and pretty brave to handle this ride.

MGM Attractions

Speed of Line	Duration of Ride/Show	Scare Factor	Age Range
Slow	15 min.	!	All
n/a	10 min.	0	All
Fast	25 min.	!	5 and up
Fast	30 min.	0	All
n/a	n/a	0	12 and up
Moderate	17 min.	0	All
Fast	25 min.	!!	5 and up
Fast	2.5 min.	!	5 and up
Slow	n/a	0	2 and up
Fast	30 min.	0	All
Fast	30 min	!	All
Moderate	35 min.	0	All
Fast	25 min.	!	All
Fast	35 min.	!	5 and up
Fast	20 min.	0	2 and up
Fast	10 min.	!!!	6 and up
Moderate	3 min.	!!!	7 and up
Moderate	10 min.	!!	5 and up
Slow	20 min.	!	4 and up

The MGM Don't-Miss List

Rock 'n' Roller Coaster (if your kids are over 7)

Star Tours

The Great Movie Ride

The Indiana Jones Epic Stunt Spectacular

Voyage of the Little Mermaid

The Hunchback of Notre Dame stage show

Beauty and the Beast stage show

Twilight Zone Tower of Terror
(if your kids are over 7)

MuppetVision 4-D

Fantasmic!

The MGM Worth-Your-While List

The Magic of Disney Animation Tour

Honey, I Shrunk the Kids Adventure Zone

The ABC Sound Studio, *Sounds Dangerous*

Doug Live!

The Backstage Studio Tour

The parade

MGM Attractions

Twilight Zone Tower of Terror

The Twilight Zone Tower of Terror combines the spooky ambience of a decaying, cobweb-covered 1930s-style Hollywood hotel with sheer thrills. The clever preshow, for which Disney spliced together clips from the old TV series in order to allow the long-deceased Rod Serling to narrate the story, invites you to enter an episode of *The Twilight Zone.* The story begins on Halloween evening in 1939 when five people boarded the hotel elevator: a movie star and a starlet, a child actress and her nanny, and the bellboy. The hotel was struck by lightning, the elevator dropped, and the five passengers were permanently transported into the Twilight Zone.

After watching the preshow, guests are directed to a cage "freight" elevator that will ascend—you guessed it—13 stories. You're seated with a lap bar, and each elevator holds about 25 people. On the way up, the elevator will stop to reveal a hallway that literally vanishes before your eyes.

But it's the second stop that will really get you. The elevator will move forward past a series of holographic images, the doors eventually opening onto a panoramic view of the park from more than 150 feet in the air. Then you free-fall; it takes only two seconds to hit the bottom, but it's a squealer—and then they haul you up and do it again.

The Scare Factor

In 1999 the Tower of Terror was changed to up the thrill potential. Where once you fell only a couple of times, in the new version there's a real yo-yo effect, with riders being lifted and dropped up to six times.

The Tower can be crowded, but the line moves swiftly for this 10-minute ride. If you miss it in the morning, return in the evening for an even more intense version of the experience.

Originally, I recommended this ride for ages 7 and up, and many kids in the 7 to 11 age range will still love this ride (or perhaps even love it more) in the newer, wilder form. But it's no longer true that the scary part of the ride lasts a mere 3 seconds; now you're in the shaft for long enough to get out a couple of real good screams.

Rock 'n' Roller Coaster

The Rock 'n' Roller Coaster Starring Aerosmith features a soundtrack perfectly synchronized to reflect the movements of the coaster. The story is that guests are visiting a concert by their favorite band in 24-passenger stretch limos.

You're quickly accelerated into your first total flip and the mazelike track, which seems to extend from the neck of an electric guitar, will go on to make a total of three inversions along with innumerable twists and turns. At one point you rip through the "O" in the HOLLYWOOD sign.

The coaster is fun and addictive and even those

Helpful Hint

Lines get long in the afternoon, so once you ride in the morning be sure to get a FAST-PASS so you can easily return later in the day.

The Scare Factor

Loud and wild, especially at takeoff, the coaster is designed for preteens, teens, and young adults. With a 48-inch height requirement, suffice it to say this will be too much for kids 7 and under.

wary of coasters tend to love this smooth, fast ride. One comfort: since the whole ride is inside a building, you never go very high, so it shouldn't overly alarm those with a fear of heights. Rock 'n' Roller is more about speed than plunging.

The Great Movie Ride

Housed in the Chinese Theater at the end of Hollywood Boulevard, the Great Movie Ride debuted as an instant classic. Disney's largest ride-through attraction, it loads steadily and fairly swiftly, but this 25-minute ride draws large crowds and is best toured either early in the morning or in the last hour before the park closes.

Each tram holds approximately 40 riders, and your tour guide provides an amusing spiel as you glide past soundstage sets from *Casablanca, Alien, The Wizard of Oz,* and other great films. The Audio-Animatronics figures of Gene Kelly, Julie Andrews, and Clint Eastwood are among Disney's best.

Things suddenly turn ugly as your car stalls and the movie scenes come to life. Depending on which car you've boarded, you're about to be overrun by

Insider's Secret
Most of the waiting area is inside the Chinese Theater; if you see a line outside, rest assured that there are hundreds more tourists waiting inside, and skip the attraction for the time being.

either a gangster on the lam or a desperado trying to escape John Wayne. Your tour guide may be gunned down or your tram taken hostage, but don't fret too much. In a later scene, drawn from *Indiana Jones and the Temple of Doom,* expect another stunning twist of fortune—just in time to reestablish justice and guarantee a happy ending.

The Scare Factor
On the Great Movie Ride, you'll encounter the
Alien from *Alien,* the Wicked Witch from *The Wizard of Oz,* and any number of no-gooders on your
trip. Some of the scenes are startling and intense,
possibly scary for kids under 7. But the fact that
your tram driver disappears and reappears does
underscore the fact that it's all "just pretend."

Star Tours

Motion-simulation technology and a slightly jostling cabin
combine to produce the real feel of flight in Star Tours. With
the hapless Captain Rex at the helm, your crew is off for what
is promised to be a routine mission to the Moon of Endor.
But if you think this mission is going to be routine, you don't
know diddly about Disney. "Don't worry if this is your first
flight," Rex comforts visitors as they board, "it's my first one,
too." One wrong turn later and you're ripping through the
fabric of space at hyperspeed, headed toward combat with the
dreaded Death Star.

George Lucas served as creative consultant, and the
ride echoes the charming as well as the terrifying elements
of his *Star Wars* series. The chatter of R2-D2, C-3PO, and
assorted droids makes even the queues enjoyable. Star Tours
is the best of both worlds, with visual effects so convincing
you'll clutch your arm rails but actual rumbles so mild that
only the youngest children are eliminated as potential crew
members.

Like the Tower of Terror, this ride takes only 10 minutes
start to finish, so the lines move at an agreeable pace. It's still
better to ride in the morning if you can.

The Scare Factor

Most kids love this attraction, especially if they've seen the *Star Wars* movies. "Like being inside a video game," my own 9-year-old enthuses. Any child over 5 should be fine, and Disney attendants are happy to help families traveling with younger children break up their party so that everyone except the baby gets to ride. One warning: Although not as intense as the similar Body Wars at Epcot, Star Tours can cause motion sickness.

Doug Live!

Doug is the 12-year-old star of one of the most popular shows in ABC's "One Saturday Morning" lineup. Four parents are chosen from the audience to play the rock group, The Beets, and one lucky child gets the meaty role of Quail Kid. This show, with the plot driven by Doug's familiar attempts to win the affections of Patti Mayonnaise, is light-hearted and uplifting, with a combination of music, live action, and cartoon graphics. A must for fans of the TV series, skippable for others; because you sit for the performance in a comfortable, cool theater, this is a good choice for afternoon.

The ABC Sound Studio

Drew Carey's spy spoof, "Sounds Dangerous," is the latest incarnation of the ABC Sound Studio. No longer are audience volunteers chosen to add the sound effects; now the theater has headsets that make the noises—which emanate as Drew upends a jar of killer bees, drives a car, has a haircut, and visits the circus—eerily intimate.

For long periods of the show you sit in total darkness to accentuate the sound effects, and this unnerves some young kids. At nearly every performance at least one toddler is shrieking, which obviously undercuts the enjoyment of everyone in the theater, not to mention the spooked child in question. But for kids with no fear of the dark, the show is an entertaining introduction to the world of old-time radio, where sound told the story.

Helpful Hint
This theater is the smallest at MGM, so check the size of the line before you queue up. Sounds Dangerous is generally a good choice for afternoon.

The SoundWorks exhibits in the postshow area are also a lot of fun. Try the Movie Mimics, where you can dub your own voice into films starring Clark Gable, Snow White, or Roger Rabbit.

The Magic of Disney Animation Tour

Visitors can meet a Disney animation artist who will show you how to draw a character, and you also get a walk-through tour of the Disney Animation building—the East Coast home of Walt Disney Feature Animation. A special presentation at the Disney Classics Theater lets you relive moments from Disney films, from *Snow White and the Seven Dwarfs* to *Mulan.* Because there is a fair amount of sitting, this is a good choice for afternoon. Up to 150 people tour at once, so you can usually get in with a 10- to 15-minute wait.

The Indiana Jones Epic Stunt Spectacular

Note: Indiana Jones will be shut down for rehab for six full months in 2000; if you're going in 2001 it should again be operational.

Next to Star Tours, the Rock 'n' Roller Coaster, and the Tower of Terror, this is the favorite MGM attraction of teens and preteens. You may think the lines are the most spectacular part of the show, but, because the 2,000-seat theater is so huge, people standing as far back as the 50's Prime Time Cafe are usually seated. Line up about 20 minutes before show time, and be aware that afternoon shows are sometimes a mob scene. If that's the case, try it again during one of the last two seatings of the evening.

As in the other theater presentations, audience volunteers are chosen. (Your odds of being tapped improve if you show up early and are near the front of the line.) Professional stunt-people re-create daring scenes from the *Indiana Jones* series, and this 30-minute show is a great chance to learn how those difficult and dangerous stunts end up on film. The finale is spectacular.

The MGM Backlot Tour

The Backlot Tour, which once took nearly two hours, has now been split into segments to make it more palatable to families with young kids. You can take the 35-minute tram segment first, and then stop and play in the Honey, I Shrunk the Kids Adventure Zone or have a snack before queuing up for the second segment of the tour, the Backstage Pass.

The tour begins with a stop at the special effects water tank, where audience volunteers re-create a naval battle scene. Then you stroll through the props department before being loaded onto a tram that scoots you through wardrobe and past huge outdoor sets representing a typical small town and a large city. The highlight of the tram segment is a stop in Catastrophe Canyon, where you'll be caught in a flash flood, an oil explosion, and an earthquake. (If you're sitting on the left side,

The Scare Factor

In Catastrophe Canyon, you'll be shaken and splashed, but the disaster lasts only about 30 seconds, and the tour guide immediately explains how it is all done. Most kids find the Canyon the best part of the Backlot Tour.

prepare to get wet.) Later you'll ride behind the Canyon and see how the disasters were created.

After you disembark from your tram, you'll be near the Honey, I Shrunk the Kids Adventure Zone and the Studio Catering Co. snack bar.

The Honey, I Shrunk the Kids Adventure Zone

The Adventure Zone is based on the popular Disney movie of the same name. "Miniaturized" guests scramble through a world of giant Legos, 9-foot Cheerios, and spider webs three stories high. Kids are generally so entranced by all the tunnels and neat little hiding areas that many a parent has had to go in to retrieve his tots—and then found he didn't want to leave himself!

Children 2 to 5 can enjoy the Junior Adventurers area, with its downsized maze and slide, where they can play in safety away from the rougher antics of the older kids. It is strongly recommended that toddlers stay out of the three-story spider web, which requires you to climb all the way through before exiting—a daunting task for little legs. Families with preschoolers must stay alert inside the Adventure Zone: When a child enters

Helpful Hint

This attraction is very popular with kids 8 and under. The only complaint? It needs to be about four times larger!

a tunnel or climbs to the top of a slide, it's often difficult to judge exactly where she'll emerge. For that reason, the attraction could be called "Honey, I Lost the Kids"!

The Backstage Pass

Disney uses this section of the backlot to hype whatever movie is presently in the theaters. The tour includes some fun segments where audience volunteers are inserted into the movie, and special effects are explained and reproduced. The tour is fairly long and can be boring for young kids who won't get much of what's going on; it's probably skippable, unless you're a big fan of whatever film is featured.

Voyage of the Little Mermaid

Using puppets, animation, and live actors to retell the beloved story of Ariel and Prince Eric, Voyage of the Little Mermaid remains one of the most popular shows at MGM. Come early or prepare for an hour-long wait.

The special effects in this 20-minute show are the best Disney has to offer; during the brilliant storm scene, you'll feel like you're really underwater, and the interplay between the cartoon characters, puppets, and live actors is ingenious. Toddlers may find certain scenes too real for comfort, but everyone else is certain to be dazzled.

MuppetVision 4-D

Look for the hot air balloon with Kermit's picture, and you'll find the *MuppetVision 4-D* movie. The show combines slapstick with sly wit, and everyone from preschoolers to adults will find something to make them laugh. (The preshow is nearly as clever as the main

Helpful Hint
The 3-D effects are more convincing if you sit near the back of the theater.

The Scare Factor

Although *MuppetVision 4-D* tested highly among kids ages 2 to 5, some parents reported that kids under 2 were unnerved by the sheer volume of the finale.

show, so be sure to watch while you wait.) The 3-D glasses in themselves are a kick, and the 20-minute movie is funny, touching—and loud. A good choice for midmorning, when you've ridden several rides and would like a chance to rest.

Beauty and the Beast Stage Show

This 30-minute show re-creates musical scenes from the film of the same name. Be at the theater at least 10 minutes before show time to guarantee a seat, 20 minutes if you expect to be near the stage. It's a good choice for afternoon; the theater is covered and large enough to seat several hundred people at once.

Recognizing the enduring popularity of the production, Disney moved it to a larger theater on Sunset Boulevard and provided enough shade to make the afternoon shows pleasant. The new Theatre of the Stars, modeled on the Hollywood Bowl, is the perfect setting for this Broadway-caliber show.

The Hunchback of Notre Dame Stage Show

Who is best qualified to tell the story of Quasimodo? Obviously, it's the gypsies who dwell in the Court of Miracles deep beneath the streets of Paris.

In the Hunchback of Notre Dame, the imagineers have opted not to make the special effects bigger, newer, and wilder but rather to return to age-old magic tricks and illusions. In order to dazzle or confuse their audience, the gypsies do not rely on a pyrotechnic pow but rather on transforming one thing into something else. Puppets may change into live performers with the twirl of a cape, and Quasimodo's first bell-ringing appearance is especially dramatic—but in creating these effects the gypsies use no technology that would not have been available in the fifteenth century.

The Hunchback of Notre Dame Stage Show is in the relatively small Backlot Theater. In order to ensure a good seat, you'll need to show up at least 20 minutes early. A juggler/comedian keeps you entertained while you're waiting.

Helpful Hint
Some families who were less than dazzled with the movie automatically skip this show; don't—the show is more fun than the movie.

The Making of . . .

This is a film about the making of Disney's latest film. Although you might learn a little about casting and production, the main idea is to promote Disney movies. Unless you have a special interest in the film described, this attraction is skippable.

Fantasmic!

In Fantasmic!—which features lasers, fireworks, lighting effects, and music—Mickey performs in his role as the Sorcerer's Apprentice, fighting off a horde of evil Disney characters with

The Scare Factor
The show is intense—every Disney villain you can think of shows up for the cartoon Armageddon—and also loud enough to frighten many preschoolers. The scariest thing is the crowd. Be sure to either link hands and hold on as you exit or hold your seat and let the bulk of the crowd pass.

a variety of special effects including the projection of film images on a screen of water. Based on the long-popular show at Disneyland, Fantasmic! is the perfect way to top off a day at MGM.

Afternoon Parade

A themed parade featuring one of Disney's current releases runs every afternoon. The time (usually 1 P.M.) and the route are outlined in your map. Stake out curb space 30 minutes in advance during the on-season; because the parade route is short, the crowds can be 8 to 10 people deep, and no place on the parade route is substantially less crowded than another. Although not as elaborate as those in the Magic Kingdom, the parades are popular, full of clever in-jokes, and extremely well done.

Disney Channel Filming

On given days, Disney Channel shows may be in production on MGM backlots. If so, a sign will be posted at the front gates telling which show is taping and when, with instructions to go to Guest Relations if you want to be in the studio audience. Many shows require members of the audience to be at least 12, others 17.

Time-Saving Tip

Watching a taping is time-consuming and involves a lot of sitting, so visitors on a tight touring schedule or those with kids under 12 are advised to skip the taping sessions.

Meeting the Characters at MGM

MGM is a great place to meet the characters. They appear more frequently than at the Magic Kingdom or Epcot, and there are fewer kids per square foot vying for their attention.

Check the tip board or your entertainment schedule for times, get your camera ready, and check out these locations.

- A variety of characters greet visitors as they enter the park, usually around 8:30 or 9 A.M. The same characters return to the entrances around 3 P.M.

- The classic characters can be found on Mickey Avenue; look for their trailers. The beginning of Sunset Boulevard is another good place for star-spotting.

- Breakfast and lunch buffets featuring characters from recent films are offered every day during the on-season and periodically during the off-season. Call 407-WDW-DINE to see who is appearing during your visit.

- If a parade or ceremony is scheduled for the Celebrity of the Day, the characters will be there in full force. Although the theme changes, the 1 P.M. parade is also a sure bet for spotting characters.

- Periodically the *Star Wars* crew can be found outside the Star Tours ride.

- And the Muppets are sometimes "on location" outside *MuppetVision 4-D*.

Full-Service Restaurants at MGM

The food here is fun, with greater variety than you'd find at the Magic Kingdom and more pizzazz to the service. Make reservations by phone if you're staying on-site; otherwise, priority seating can be arranged each morning at a special booth on Sunset Boulevard for the 50's Prime Time Cafe, the SciFi Drive-In, Mama Melrose's Ristorante Italiano, and the Hollywood Brown Derby.

Quick Guide to Restaurants

Restaurant	Description
50's Prime Time Cafe	This restaurant is almost an attraction in itself
The Hollywood and Vine "Cafeteria of the Stars"	Large, attractive art deco cafeteria
The Hollywood Brown Derby	Restaurant is elegant and lovely
Mama Melrose's Ristorante Italiano	Pizza and a wacky New York ambience
The SciFi Drive-In Theater	Kids give this one high marks

For descriptions of ratings, prices, priority seating, and suitability for kids, see pages 316–317.

As at Epcot, the food is expensive and the service slow, especially during peak dining hours. If you just want to see the inside of the SciFi Drive-In or 50's Prime Time Cafe, make your reservation for 3 P.M. or for 10 minutes before the park is slated to close and just have dessert.

Notable Fast-Food Restaurants at MGM

@ Located near Star Tours, the Backlot Express lives up to its name and serves up burgers and chicken within min-

Full-Service at MGM

Rating	Price	Priority Seating	Suitability	Details on
★★	$$	Recommended	High	Page 332
★★	$	Not offered	Moderate	Page 334
★★★	$$$	Recommended	Moderate	Page 335
★★	$$	Suggested	Moderate	Page 337
★★	$$	Recommended	High	Page 341

utes. This large restaurant is a good place to grab a bite during the most crowded hours of the day.

@ Kids can't resist the big green Tyrannosaurus at Dinosaur Gertie's. Gertie's is the place to get ice cream while waiting in line for the Indiana Jones Epic Stunt Spectacular.

@ Starring Rolls is your best bet for a fast breakfast, as well as a great spot to pick up cookies, brownies, and pastries before the afternoon parade.

@ Stop by one of the Echo Lake Produce or Anaheim Produce fruit stands if you're looking for a fast, healthy snack.

Tips for Your Last Hour at MGM

If you're watching Fantasmic! you'll need to enter the stadium at least an hour in advance—90 minutes during the on-season. That's quite a wait, so you may want to eat dinner while you hold your seat. The stadium serves hot dogs and snacks, or you could buy food from somewhere else in the parks and take it in with you.

If you're not watching Fantasmic! the last hour before closing is a great time to hit those attractions that were posting long waits earlier in the day. The park virtually empties out as everyone heads toward the show, so it's a good chance to ride the Rock 'n' Roller Coaster or any other biggie that was swamped earlier.

Tips for Leaving MGM

Although a terrific show that more than justifies the inconvenience, Fantasmic! draws virtually everyone in the park to one spot at closing and thus makes exiting a nightmare.

Those watching from the Mickey section have the best shot at getting out fast and beating the crowds to the shuttle tram or water taxi. If you're located near the water or in one of the sections to the extreme right or left of the stadium, you have little chance of exiting early. Sit tight and wait for the crowd to disperse then eat or shop your way through the park, allowing most of the people to exit ahead of you.

CHAPTER

8. The Animal Kingdom

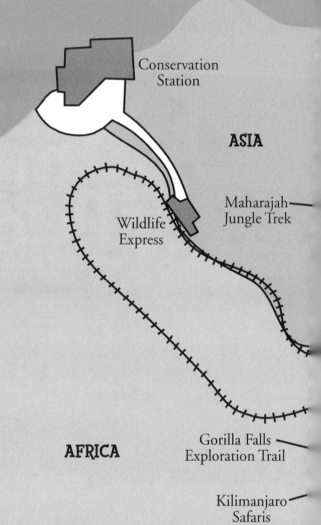

Conservation
Station

ASIA

Maharajah
Jungle Trek

Wildlife
Express

AFRICA

Gorilla Falls
Exploration Trail

Kilimanjaro
Safaris

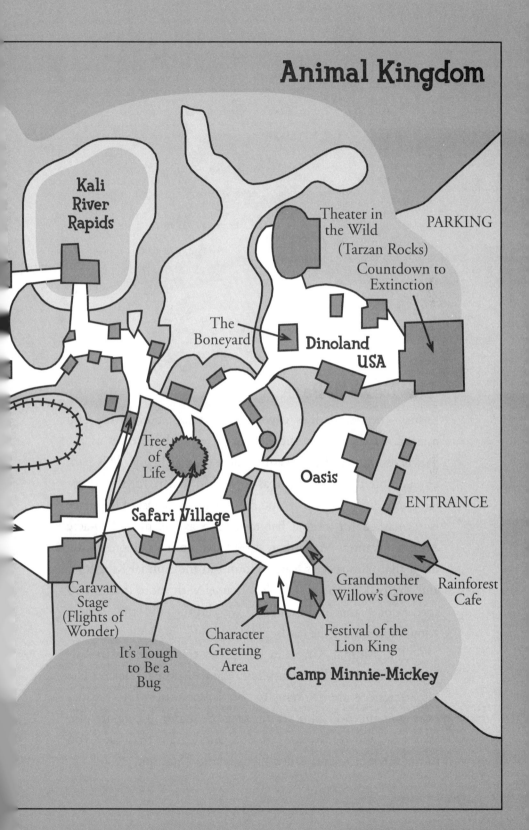

Animal Kingdom

Kali
River
Rapids

PARKING

Theater in
the Wild
(Tarzan Rocks)

Countdown to
Extinction

The
Boneyard

Dinoland
USA

Tree
of
Life

Oasis

Safari Village

ENTRANCE

Caravan
Stage
(Flights of
Wonder)

Grandmother
Willow's Grove

Rainforest
Cafe

It's Tough
to Be a
Bug

Character
Greeting
Area

Festival of the
Lion King

Camp Minnie-Mickey

The Newest Park

Disney's newest park is devoted to animals, both living and mythic. At the center, the 14-story Tree of Life serves as the park icon, much like Spaceship Earth does at Epcot. This park covers more than 500 acres, as compared to 107 for the Magic Kingdom, 157 for MGM, and 300 for Epcot. Most of the space is earmarked for animal habitats, such as the huge 100-acre African savanna. More than 1,000 live animals, representing more than 200 species, can be found in the Animal Kingdom, and the park is also a botanical marvel with more than 3,000 species of plants represented. "We didn't build the Animal Kingdom," one of the landscapers told me. "We grew it."

The Animal Kingdom comprises the Oasis, Safari Village, Africa, Asia, Dinoland, and Camp Minnie-Mickey. The big attractions are Kilimanjaro Safaris, Countdown to Extinction, and the 3-D film *It's Tough to Be a Bug*. There are also four stage shows, a water raft ride, and a train that takes you to the interactive area called Conservation Station.

Getting to the Animal Kingdom

The Animal Kingdom parking lot is extremely small; all on-site hotels run direct shuttles, and many off-site hotels do as well. If possible, arrive by bus. If you're coming by car, be sure to arrive early, before the parking lot is filled to capacity.

Getting Around the Animal Kingdom

The only real means of crossing the park is on foot. The layout is basically circular, with the Tree of Life in the center.

Sounds easy enough, but the area around the main entrance near Safari Village can become so crowded that it is nearly impassable in the middle of the day. So if you're trying to move around the park, a better bet is to cut through the Asia section, essentially going behind the Tree of Life. It looks like you're going out of your way (and you are), but the traffic flow works more in your favor.

Tips for Your First Hour in the Animal Kingdom

- So far, the Animal Kingdom has not been included in the Early Entry cycle but has opened at 7 A.M. every day during the on-season, 8 A.M. during the off-season. If you want to see maximum animal movement and minimal people movement, set your alarm and go early.

- The Oasis is the entry area, much like Main Street in the Magic Kingdom, and it will be open 30 minutes before the stated entry time. (On designated days Safari Village will also be open early. If it is, see *It's Tough to Be a Bug* first.)

@ Head to the Kilimanjaro Safaris. If the wait is less than 30 minutes, ride.

@ Enter the Tree of Life and see the 3-D film *It's Tough to Be a Bug.*

Animal Kingdom Touring Tips

@ Try and hit Kilimanjaro Safaris early. Save shows and interactive exhibits for the afternoon.

Helpful Hint
Come early or expect horrific crowds. The Animal Kingdom has only four or five major attractions, so these are mobbed by afternoon.

@ Don't feel that you have to see all the live shows, which may be too much sitting for young children. Festival of the Lion King is a must-see, but read the descriptions of the others and choose the ones that sound most interesting or age appropriate.

Because of the relatively small number of attractions, the Animal Kingdom can be toured in four to six hours. This means the park will be mobbed between 10 A.M. and 2 P.M. but should begin to clear out somewhat by midafternoon. If you can't be there first thing in the morning, consider arriving about 3 P.M.

If you arrive in the afternoon, see the live shows and ride the trains and boats first, saving the biggies like Countdown to Extinction, *It's Tough to Be a Bug,* and Kilimanjaro Safaris for the last two hours before the park

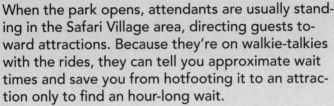

Insider's Secret
When the park opens, attendants are usually standing in the Safari Village area, directing guests toward attractions. Because they're on walkie-talkies with the rides, they can tell you approximate wait times and save you from hotfooting it to an attraction only to find an hour-long wait.

closes. If you don't see everything you'd like to, you can always come back another afternoon.

@ Avoid weekends and summers, when Florida locals swell an already-crowded park to peak capacity.

@ Because of their proximity, and because neither park requires a full day to tour, consider combining a visit to the Animal Kingdom with a stop at Blizzard Beach.

Animal Kingdom Attractions

The attractions may be few in number, but they're powerful experiences. Most of them are designed for the whole family to enjoy together.

Safari Village Attractions

Tree of Life, Featuring **It's Tough to Be a Bug**

The Tree of Life is an absolutely amazing edifice, one of the most gorgeous pieces of architecture Disney has ever produced. You'll have plenty of time while you're in line to pick out the dozens of animal carvings seamlessly twisted into the mammoth trunk of the tree.

The 3-D film inside, called *It's Tough to Be a Bug,* is state-of-the-art and a real highlight for all ages. Like *Honey, I Shrunk*

Quick Guide to

Attraction	Location	Height Requirement
The Boneyard	Dinoland	None
Character Greeting Area	Camp Minnie-Mickey	None
Countdown to Extinction	Dinoland	46 inches
Cretaceous Trail	Dinoland	None
Festival of the Lion King	Camp Minnie-Mickey	None
Flights of Wonder at Caravan Stage	Asia	None
Gorilla Falls Exploration Trail	Africa	None
Grandmother Willow's Grove	Camp Minnie-Mickey	None
Tarzan Rocks at Theater in the Wild	Dinoland	None
Kali River Rapids	Asia	42 inches
Kilimanjaro Safaris	Africa	None
Maharajah Jungle Trek	Asia	None
The Tree of Life, featuring *It's Tough to Be a Bug*	Safari Village	None
Wildlife Express to Conservation Station	Africa	None

Scare Factor

0 = Unlikely to scare any child of any age.
! = Has dark or loud elements; might rattle some toddlers.
!! = A couple of gotcha! moments; should be fine for school-age kids.
!!! = You need to be pretty big and pretty brave to handle this ride.

Animal Kingdom Attractions

Speed of Line	Duration of Ride/Show	Scare Factor	Age Range
n/a	n/a	0	All
Moderate	n/a	0	All
Moderate	10 min.	!!!	7 and up
Fast	5 min.	0	All
Moderate	25 min.	0	All
Fast	25 min.	0	All
Moderate	10 min.	0	All
Fast	12 min.	0	All
Fast	30 min.	0	All
Moderate	7 min.	!	4 and up
Moderate	20 min.	!	6 and up
Fast	10 min.	0	All
Slow	8 min.	0	All
Fast	10 min.	0	All

The Animal Kingdom Don't-Miss List

It's Tough to Be a Bug

Kilimanjaro Safaris

Countdown to Extinction (if your kids are 7 or older)

Festival of the Lion King

The Animal Kingdom Worth-Your-While List

Kali River Rapids

Flights of Wonder

Pocahontas Show (for kids 7 and under)

Tarzan Rocks

The exploration trails, including Gorilla Falls and Maharajah Jungle Trek

the Audience, the show combines visual and tactile effects, and the cast of buggy characters, including the Termitinator and an accurately named Stinkbug, are so funny that almost everyone leaves this attraction laughing. The best special effect of all is at the very end; it's a real "gotcha".

Helpful Hint

The Tree of Life is so visually impressive that many visitors entering the park will head there first. If you can't see it early in the morning, save it for late afternoon.

Africa Attractions

Kilimanjaro Safaris

This is the Animal Kingdom's premier attraction, a ride that simulates an African photo safari. Guests board open-top lorries for a 2-mile ride through the African savanna. Water and plant barriers are so cunningly incorporated that the animals appear to be running free. Your guide helps you tell the impalas from the gazelles, and at times the lorry comes startlingly close to the wildlife. The story line is that you're helping the reserve's game warden look for elephant poachers who have abducted a baby elephant, Little Red.

Disney has gone to great pains to give the animals as much freedom as possible and ample space to roam, which means that some safari trips yield more sightings than do others. On our last we had great views of the rhino herd and came unbelievably close to one bold giraffe, while the lions were posed so gracefully on their rocks that they might have been a poster for a Disney film. Others have reported seeing more—or less—but one rule of thumb is that the animals are more active when it's cooler. In other words, go in the morning if you can. This ride is the Dumbo of the Animal Kingdom, posting waits two or three times those at any other attraction.

Be aware, however, that although Little Red is ultimately rescued in the end and the ride ends on a happy note, the poachers have shot the mother of a baby elephant—shades of

The Scare Factor
Your Kilimanjaro Safaris vehicle will bump and bounce quite convincingly and, by the final segment, when you're chasing the elephant poachers, the ride gets pretty wild.

Bambi—and this may be upsetting to younger children. The imagineers have created this ride not only to be fun and exciting but also to underscore some points about the dangers facing animals in the wild.

Gorilla Falls Exploration Trail

Located just as you leave Kilimanjaro Safaris, this is a self-guided walking trail. The landscaping is gorgeous, you can linger as long as you like, and at one point you pass through the area where Gino the silverback gorilla lives. (The dominant male in a gorilla troop is called the silverback because he is ordinarily older than the other animals and often has gray hairs mixed in with the black.) Gino and his harem are on one side of the trail, and the bachelor gorillas are on the other side.

At different points along the trail, you'll pass everything from mole rats to hippos, but kids seem to especially like the meerkats and warthogs in the Pumbaa and Timon exhibit.

Wildlife Express to Conservation Station

This 10-minute train ride gives you a glimpse of the animal care that goes on behind the scenes, even showing you where the animals sleep at night. The ride offers a little rest after a morning of touring, and the trains themselves are positively nifty looking.

You disembark at Conservation Station, an utterly out-of-the-way exhibit in the farthest-flung section of the park. In the Affection Section, kids can touch and cuddle small animals; or you can tour the veterinary labs, meet wildlife experts, or enjoy an audio show called "Song of the Rainforest." Low-key with several interactive exhibits, this is a good choice for the afternoon but skippable if you're on a tight touring schedule.

Dinoland Attractions

Countdown to Extinction

Guests are strapped into "high-speed" motion-simulation vehicles and sent back in time to the Cretaceous period to save the iguanodon (a gentle, plant-eating dinosaur) from extinction.

It's a truly noble mission, but it ain't easy. On the way, Disney throws everything it has at you: asteroids, meteors, and, oh yeah, a few people-eating dinosaurs. A combination track ride and motion-simulation ride, Countdown to Extinction can be rough and wild—but it is also lots of fun.

The Scare Factor
The 48-inch height requirement, which surpasses even Space Mountain's, should clue you in that this is a pretty intense experience. The attraction does incorporate atmospheric scariness with a wild-moving ride. Fine for 7 and up, iffy for preschoolers.

Theater in the Wild, Featuring Tarzan Rocks

This large amphitheater is home to some of Disney's most ambitious stage shows. Check your entertainment schedule for show times and be there about 20 minutes early to ensure a good seat, 30 minutes on a busy day. If the kids are restless, one parent can hold the bench while the other takes the kids to the nearby Boneyard. *Tarzan Rocks,* the current offering, features an excellent live band, aerial ballet, dazzling roller-skating stunts, and favorite characters from the film. There's something for any age, preschoolers to teens. (Note: *Tarzan Rocks* is playing as we go to press, but as at all Disney theaters, the show is subject to change.)

The Boneyard

A great attraction for preschoolers, the Boneyard is a playground designed to simulate an archaeological dig site. Kids can dig for fossils, excavate bones, and play on mazes, bridges, and slides. The park is visually witty—where else can you find slides made from prehistoric skeletons?—and has funny surprises, such as a footprint that roars when you jump on it.

Visit the Boneyard after you've toured the biggies and the kids are ready to romp for a while. The sand can become hot in the Florida afternoons, however, so remember the sunscreen and water bottles and don't stay too long.

Cretaceous Trail

The Cretaceous Trail allows you to stroll down a shady path among plants that have survived from the Cretaceous period, around 30 million years ago, when dinosaurs roamed the earth. Plants range from simple spore bearers to magnolias, the first flowering trees. It's the adult equivalent of the Boneyard—a quiet place to decompress after you've fought the beasts at Countdown to Extinction.

Camp Minnie-Mickey Attractions

Character Greeting Area

Camp Minnie-Mickey is the Animal Kingdom equivalent of Toontown—you'll find three separate greeting areas where you can line up to meet the characters, all adorably decked out in safari gear. The greeting areas are especially mobbed just before and after the *Festival of the Lion King* show, so plan to get your photos and autographs at a different time.

Festival of the Lion King

Every Disney park seems to have a sleeper hit—an attraction that ends up being far more popular than the imagineers anticipated—and this is it for the Animal Kingdom.

The 25-minute show features what you might expect—singers, dancers, the characters from the popular movie—but it is also chock-full of surprises in the forms of acrobatic "monkeys," flame swallowers, and "birds" that dramatically take flight. The costuming is incredible, the performers are exceedingly talented, and the finale is guaranteed to give you goosebumps.

The show is currently staged eight times a day, and in order to ensure you'll be seated at all, you need to line up 30 to 40 minutes in advance. The show is a good choice for early afternoon, just after lunch, when you're fairly well rested.

Grandmother Willow's Grove

This smaller show, nice for younger kids, features Pocahontas, Grandmother Willow, and live animals. A strong message about conservation and wildlife protection is woven into the story. Show times are indicated on your entertainment schedule. Another good choice for afternoon.

Asia Attractions

Caravan Stage, Featuring Flights of Wonder

A lovely display of birds in free flight. You'll see falcons, vultures, hawks, and toucans that demonstrate their unusual talents. The birds fly very low over the heads of the audience, and the background story of the show is quite funny.

You should be able to be seated if you show up 10 to 20 minutes early. Again, show times are noted on your entertainment schedule, and stage shows are generally a good choice for afternoon.

Kali River Rapids

Guests will board eight-passenger rafts for a descent down a raging river through rapids and waterfalls. Expect to get very, very wet, quite possibly soaked, depending on where you are sitting

The Scare Factor

A very mild ride, with one sizable descent on the way. Fine for anyone—unless they're afraid of getting splashed! The height requirement is 42 inches.

in the raft. Bring your trusty $5 poncho, if you have one, stow cameras in the lockers before you board, and be sure to keep your feet up on the center bar. A wet fanny is an inconvenience; drenched socks and shoes can lead to blisters and ruin your whole trip.

This water ride also illustrates the dangers of clear-cutting jungles; you'll pass through a variety of landscapes during your wet journey, from lush to barren, illustrating how irresponsible harvesting leaves the land vulnerable to erosion.

Quick Guide to Full-in the Animal

Restaurant	Description
Rainforest Cafe	Great fun!

For descriptions of ratings, prices, priority seating, and suitability for kids, see pages 316–317.

Maharajah Jungle Trek

Another lovely walking path, this one re-creates the habitats of Asia. You'll encounter Bengal tigers, Komodo dragons, gibbons, and other animals on your trek. You can spend anywhere from 10 minutes to an hour on the path. Note: The tigers are more active in the morning.

River Cruise with Radio Disney

You board a boat in the Asia section, then travel along the river that circles the Tree of Life. Geared toward kids, expect lively music mixed with animal information—and long waits for what is essentially a pretty simple ride. Available in the on-season only.

Service Restaurants Kingdom

Rating	Price	Priority Seating	Suitability	Details on
★★	$$	Not accepted	High	Page 340

Food Choices in the Animal Kingdom

The park has only one full-service restaurant, Rainforest Cafe. Kids love the Rainforest Cafe, as evidenced by the popularity of the branch at Downtown Disney, but the restaurant neither accepts reservations nor arranges priority seating. To dine there, drop by the booth about an hour before you'd like to eat. They'll take your name and give you an estimated seating time. Then continue to explore Safari Village—shopping, touring the Tree of Life, or seeing the 3-D film—while you wait.

Fast-food spots are scattered throughout the park, including Restaurantosaurus, which serves McDonald's food; the Pizzafari; and Flame Tree Barbecue. Tusker House Restaurant offers the tastiest food in the park, in my opinion, and the selections usually include salad or vegetables. But the Animal Kingdom has relatively few food venues for so many people. Lines will undoubtedly be long, so your best option may be to avoid eating in the park altogether. Eat a big breakfast before you go, snack while at the park, and have another meal after you exit.

A morning character breakfast is currently being held at Restaurantosaurus. Call 407-WDW-DINE for exact times and prices.

Tips for Your Last Hour at the Animal Kingdom

There is currently no big closing show at the Animal Kingdom, so leaving isn't really a problem. Because the park is small, many people have finished their touring and are leaving the park by midafternoon, just as the afternoon wave of guests is coming in.

Tips for Leaving the Animal Kingdom

The parking lot is small, and bottlenecks occur regularly. For this reason, on-site visitors should come and go by bus if they can. If you have a car, a shuttle tram will deliver you to it.

Blizzard Beach is located near the Animal Kingdom, and they often share shuttles. You may want to bring your suits along and spend the morning at the Animal Kingdom and the afternoon in the water park.

CHAPTER 9

The Disney World Water Parks

1. Coronado Springs Resort
2. Wide World of Sports
3. Swan Resort
4. Dolphin Resort
5. Yacht & Beach Club Resorts
6. Disney's BoardWalk
7. Magic Kingdom Main Entrance
8. Car Care Center
9. Transportation & Ticket Center Parking
10. Transportation & Ticket Center
11. Polynesian Resort
12. The Grand Floridian
13. Contemporary Resort
14. Wilderness Lodge
15. Fort Wilderness Campground
16. Dixie Landings Resort
17. Port Orleans Resort
18. Old Key West Resort
19. Lake Buena Vista Golf Course
20. Disney Institute
21. Disney Institute Villas
22. Disney's West Side
23. Pleasure Island
24. Caribbean Beach Resort

25. Animal Kingdom Lodge
26. Disney Village Hotels
27. All-Star Resorts

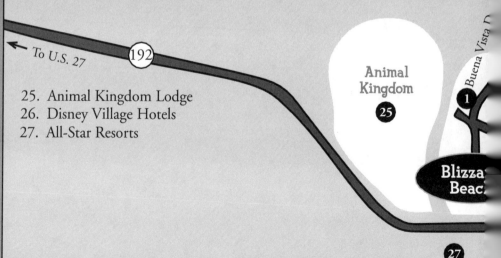

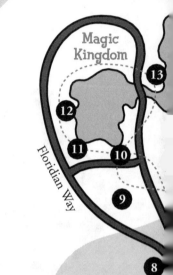

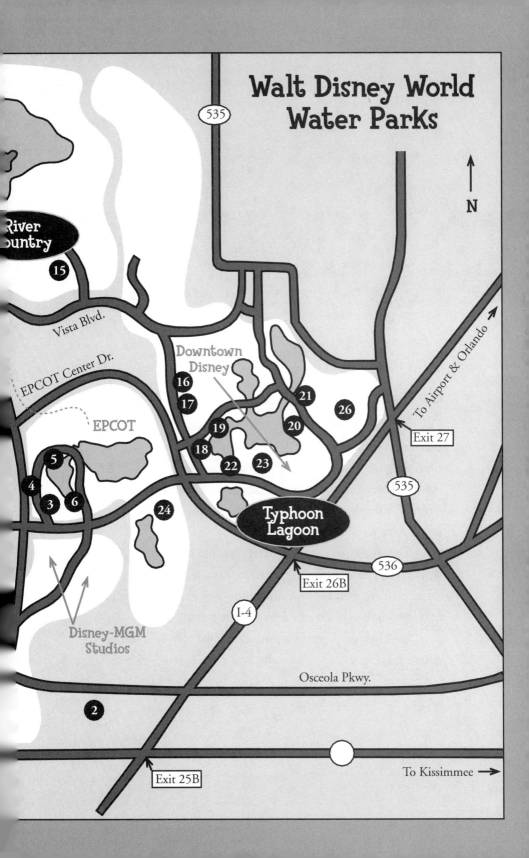

Walt Disney World Water Parks

535

N

River Country

15

Vista Blvd.

EPCOT Center Dr.

Downtown Disney

EPCOT

16

17

19

18

22

23

21

20

26

To Airport & Orlando

Exit 27

535

5

4

3

6

24

Typhoon Lagoon

536

Exit 26B

Disney-MGM Studios

I-4

Osceola Pkwy.

2

Exit 25B

To Kissimmee →

Getting to the Water Parks

On-site visitors should take the bus to Typhoon Lagoon or Blizzard Beach. Getting to Typhoon Lagoon may involve sitting through stops at all three bus pickup points at Downtown Disney; and Blizzard Beach often shares a bus with the Animal Kingdom, so expect a slightly longer commute than you'd have to the major parks.

Off-site guests driving to Typhoon Lagoon and Blizzard Beach should definitely be there before the stated opening time. During midday and afternoon hours in the summer, the parking lots are often filled to capacity.

Headed to River Country? Either drive directly, or if you're staying on-site, take the bus or monorail to the Magic Kingdom. The River Country launch will carry you across the lake to the park entrance.

Quiz: Which Water Park Is Right for You?

The most important thing in a water park is
A. The slides
B. The waves
C. The pools

The ages of our kids are
A. Preteens and teens
B. A mix—they're 11, 8, and 4
C. Preschoolers and toddlers

Long lines are
A. To be expected. This is Disney World, after all.
B. Tolerable at the big-deal rides,
but I like to get away from the crowd sometimes.
C. The last thing I want when I'm trying to relax.

When we go to a water park, we
A. Go early and stay all day.
B. Show up in the evening and use the time to unwind.
C. Just drop in for a couple of hours to cool off.

I'd most like to lie by the pool with
A. Who has time to lie by the pool?
B. The latest Tom Clancy book and a piña colada.
C. A big old shade tree and a slice of watermelon.

As a family, we're looking for
A. Excitement.
B. Variety.
C. Relaxation.

Mostly A's? Hit the slopes of Blizzard Beach.

Mostly B's? There's a wave with your name on it at
Typhoon Lagoon.

Mostly C's? Wade into River Country.

River Country

Billed as an "ol' swimming hole perfect for splashin' and slidin'," River Country was completely overshadowed by the openings of Typhoon Lagoon and Blizzard Beach.

This small 5-acre park never gets as crowded as Typhoon Lagoon and Blizzard Beach, which are 10 times larger. River Country draws far fewer preteens and teens, and the water level in the center of Bay Cove is only about chest deep on an 8-year-old.

Helpful Hint

River Country remains a good choice for families with young kids or anyone who doesn't swim very well.

Bay Cove, the largest section of River Country, features swing ropes, two waterslides, and White Water Rapids, an exhilaratingly bumpy inner-tube ride down a winding 230-foot-long creek. The nearby swimming pool offers two small but steep slides that shoot riders into midair; kids smack the water eight feet below with such force that they can barely stagger out of the pool and make it up the stony steps to try it again . . . and again.

Younger kids will prefer the Ol' Wading Pool, a roped-off sandy-bottomed section of Bay Cove with four small slides cut into a wall of boulders, designed specifically for preschoolers. Because older kids are kept out of this section and the slides empty into a mere 18 inches of water, parents can relax on the many lounge chairs scattered along the Ol' Wading Pool beach.

Again, the Park Hopper Plus pass lets you in gratis, but individual tickets are available at $15.95 for adults, $12.50 for kids. River Country is a fine place to picnic, and there are a couple of fast-food stands on-site.

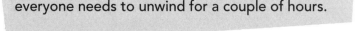

If you're coming by car or taking a shuttle, be aware that the River Country parking lot is quite far from the park. You'll catch a shuttle from the parking lot, drive through Fort Wilderness Campground, and be let out near the gates. Those coming from Fort Wilderness or those who have taken the launch from the Magic Kingdom to Fort Wilderness have only a short walk to the River Country entrance.

Helpful Hint
Although Typhoon Lagoon and Blizzard Beach can take up a whole day, a swift-moving 10-year-old can try out every attraction at River Country in two hours flat. For this reason, it's a good water park to drop into when the theme parks are sweltering and everyone needs to unwind for a couple of hours.

River Country Touring Tips

- Although the oversized swimming pool is heated, making fall and spring swimming a delight, it's obviously impossible to heat the bay. River Country is usually closed during December, January, and February and can be chilly during the spring and fall. Call 407-824-4321 for information about hours of operation.

- Families not returning to their hotels in midafternoon can use River Country to break up a day in the Magic Kingdom. Stow your bathing suits in one of the lockers beneath the Main Street Railroad Station in the morning. When the park heats up and fills up in the afternoon, exit the Magic Kingdom and take the launch marked "Campground and Discovery Island." (The 15-minute boat ride is so pleasant that it almost constitutes an afternoon getaway in itself.) If you're staying off-site, this option is less time-consuming than returning to your hotel pool. After a few hours in the cool waters of River Country, you can hop back on the launch and be in the Magic Kingdom within minutes.

@ Horseback riding is located near the River Country parking lot; if you're planning to try the trail rides during your Disney stay, it makes sense to combine the horseback riding with an afternoon at River Country. Great for younger kids, the pony rides and Fort Wilderness petting farm are located right at the River Country main entrance. The ponies are available from 10 A.M. to 5 P.M., cost $2 to ride, and are incredibly gentle.

Insider's Secret
If you enter River Country early in the morning, head for White Water Rapids first. This is the first attraction to draw lines.

Helpful Hint
Remember that you're swimming in a lake, not a pool. The netting does a good job on critter control, but this is not the day to wear your new $90 white swimsuit.

Typhoon Lagoon and Blizzard Beach Touring Tips

- The water parks draw a rowdy teenage crowd, which means young kids and unsteady swimmers may get dunked and splashed more than they like. If your children are very young, you might be better off at River Country—or staying in the children's sections (Ketchakiddee Creek in Typhoon Lagoon or Tike's Peak in Blizzard Beach), which are off limits to older kids.

- Always crowded, the water parks are extra packed on weekends since they're popular with locals as well as tourists.

- Many visitors arrive with their swimsuits on under their shorts and shirts, which saves time. It's also a good idea to bring your own towels because towel rental is $1 per towel and the towels are small. There are plenty of lockers, which rent for $5 with a refundable deposit. The locker keys come on rubberized bands that slip over your wrist or ankle so that you can easily keep them with you while in the water.

- You can "rent" life vests for free, although they do require a driver's license or credit card for deposit. Snorkeling equipment can be picked up for no charge at Hammerhead Fred's near the Shark Reef at Typhoon Lagoon. An instructor runs you through the basics before letting you loose in the saltwater pool.

- Because you're constantly climbing uphill all day, half the time dragging a tube or mat behind you, the water parks are extremely exhausting. If you spend the day at a water park, plan to spend the evening touring passive attractions, such as films or shows—or make this your parents' night out and leave the kids with a sitter.

@ The water parks are a good place to picnic, although there are also several places to get fast food.

@ The Lost Kids Station at Typhoon Lagoon is across a bridge and so far from the main water areas that lost children are very unlikely to find their way there on their own. At Blizzard Beach it's at Shoeless Joe's rentals, far from the swimming action. Instruct your children, should they look up and find themselves separated from you, to tell one of the Disney employees. (They all wear distinctive nametags.) The Disney people will escort the children to the Lost Kids Station, and you can meet them there. Because both of these parks are full of meandering paths, with many sets of steps and slides, it's easy to get separated from your party. Set standard meeting places and times for older kids.

Helpful Hint
If your kids have rubberized beach shoes with nonskid bottoms, be sure to throw them in your beach bag. The sidewalks can be slippery and the pavement can be hot.

@ If you have the Park Hopper Plus pass and it's summer, consider visiting more than one water park—they're very different experiences. Typhoon Lagoon gets the nod for its pool area: The pool there is huge and has those incredible surfing waves. Blizzard Beach has a superior whitewater ride and more big-deal slides. Typhoon Lagoon is more relaxing and visually attractive; Blizzard Beach is the pow park, focusing on high-speed thrills.

@ Typhoon Lagoon and Blizzard Beach are often closed for refurbishing during January and February. If you're planning a winter trip, call 407-824-4321 to make sure at least one of the parks will be open during the week you plan to visit.

Insider's Secret

Whichever you choose, be sure to visit a water park early in your Disney World visit. Several families reported that they saved this experience until late in their trip and then found it was the highlight of the whole vacation for their kids. "If we'd known how great it was, we'd have come every day." lamented one father. "As it turns out we only went to Blizzard Beach once—on the morning of the day we were due to fly out."

Typhoon Lagoon

Disney has dubbed its 56-acre Typhoon Lagoon as the "world's ultimate water park," and the hyperbole is justified. Where else can you slide through caves, picnic with parrots, float through rain forests, and swim (sort of) with sharks? Typhoon Lagoon opened in 1989 as the largest water park in the world and was instantly so popular that it was hard to get in. The opening of the even-bigger Blizzard Beach in 1995 has taken off a bit of the pressure, but it is still difficult to get into Typhoon Lagoon during peak touring times.

Helpful Hint
If you're visiting during a holiday or midsummer, plan to arrive at the water parks at opening time—or wait until evening.

Typhoon Lagoon occasionally becomes so swamped with swimmers that it closes its gates. On a regular basis during the holiday weeks, the park becomes so crowded that no one is admitted after 10 A.M., to the great dismay of families who have put on their bathing suits, swabbed themselves with sunscreen, and prepared for a day in the pools.

For anyone with a Park Hopper Plus pass, entrance to Typhoon Lagoon is included. Otherwise admission is $27.95 for adults and $22.50 for children 3 to 9.

Typhoon Lagoon Attractions

Humunga Kowabunga

This ride consists of two waterslides that propel riders down a mountain at 30 miles per hour. No kids shorter than 48 inches are allowed.

Helpful Hint
For women and girls, a one-piece suit is your best bet. A young Disney employee informed me that the most desired duty in all of Typhoon Lagoon is to stand at the bottom of Humunga Kowabunga, helping riders out of the chute—apparently at least one woman per hour loses her swimsuit top during the descent.

Storm Slides

Three curving slides deposit riders in the pool below. Kids of any age can ride, but it's suggested that they be good swimmers because although the pool isn't deep, you do enter the water with enough force to temporarily disorient a nervous swimmer. Most kids 7 to 11 (and some who are younger) love these zesty little slides, but if you're unsure if yours are up to it, wait at the edge of the pool where the slide empties so you can help them out.

Each of the three slides—the Rudder Buster, Jib Jammer, and Stern Burner—offers a slightly different route, although none is necessarily wilder than the others.

Mayday Falls

A Disney employee helps you load into the giant rubber tubes and gives you a gentle shove. What follows is a fast, giggly journey that more than once makes you feel as if you're about to lose your tube. No kids shorter than 48 inches are allowed.

Keelhaul Falls

This corkscrew tube ride is full of thrills. Kids shorter than 48 inches are provided with their own smaller tube, and lots of kids as young as 4 reported that they loved this ride.

Gangplank Falls

Weather whitewater rapids in four-passenger rafts. Slower and milder but much bumpier than Mayday or Keelhaul, Gangplank is a good choice for families with kids too young for the other whitewater rides. Gangplank Falls loads slowly, however, and the ride is short, so hit it early in the morning, especially if you think your kids will want to go down more than once.

If the kids are small, sometimes more than four people are allowed into a raft.

Surfing Lagoon

Ride machine-made waves up to 6 feet high in a 2.5-acre lagoon. The waves come at 90-second intervals and are perfectly designed for tubing and bodysurfing. Every other hour the pool is emptied of tubes and the wave machine is cranked up to allow for body-surfing. A foghorn blast alerts you to when a big 'un is on its way. Although the Surfing Lagoon lets anyone in, don't take small children too deep during the hours designated for bodysurfing—every 90 seconds 400 shrieking teenagers will bear down on your head. A special bonus: Surfing lessons are available in the morning before the park opens. Call 407-824-SURF for details.

Whitecap Cove and Blustery Bay

The Surfing Lagoon has two small, roped-off coves, where smaller waves lap upon toddlers and babies.

Castaway Creek

This is a meandering 2,000-foot stream full of inner tubes. Guests simply wade out, find an empty tube, and climb aboard. It takes about 30 minutes to circle the rainforest, and there is a bit of excitement at one point when riders drift under a waterfall. But there are numerous exits along the creek, so anyone who doesn't want to get splashed can hop out before the falls. In general a very fun, relaxing ride, appropriate for any age or swimming level.

Shark Reef

This is a saltwater pool where snorkelers swim "among" exotic marine life, including sharks. The sharks are behind Plexiglas, of course, and are not too numerous, so anyone expecting the casting call for *Jaws* will be disappointed.

Take the kids down to the viewing area first and let them observe the marine life and other snorkelers and then make up their own minds.

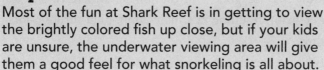
Helpful Hint

Most of the fun at Shark Reef is in getting to view the brightly colored fish up close, but if your kids are unsure, the underwater viewing area will give them a good feel for what snorkeling is all about.

Ketchakiddee Creek

This is a water playground sized for preschoolers, with geysers and bubblers in the shape of crocodiles and whales, as well as slides and a small whitewater raft ride. No one taller than 48 inches is allowed to ride, which is a pleasant change from most of the park rules, although parents are encouraged to enter the area and help their kids. Lifeguards are everywhere, and lots of chairs are set out nearby for adults.

Mt. Mayday Scenic Trail

This footpath leads almost to the top of Mt. Mayday, where the shipwrecked Miss Tilly is impaled, and offers views of the slides and rides below.

Blizzard Beach

When word got out in the travel industry that Disney was opening another water park, there was great speculation as to the theme. Having already designed the ultimate country swimming hole and the ultimate tropical lagoon, what could the imagineers come up with this time?

A melting ski lodge, of course. Blizzard Beach is built on the tongue-in-cheek premise that a freak snowstorm hit Orlando and a group of enterprising businesspeople built Florida's first ski resort. The sun returned in due time, and for a while it looked like all was lost—until someone spied an alligator slipping and sliding down one of the slushy slopes. Blizzard Beach was born. The snow may be gone, but the jumps, sled runs, and slalom courses remain, resulting in a high-camp, high-thrill ski lodge in the palms.

Blizzard Beach centers on "snowcapped" Mt. Gushmore. You can get to the top via ski lift or a series of stairs, but how you get down is up to you. The bold can descend on the Summit Plummet or Slush Gusher, but there are medium-intensity flumes, inner-tube runs, and whitewater rafts as well. The motif extends into every element of the park: There is a chalet-style restaurant, Plexiglas snowmen, and innumerable sight gags like ski marks running off the side of the mountain. The original skiing alligator has returned as the resort mascot, Ice Gator.

Blizzard Beach was built in response to Typhoon Lagoon's popularity and draws huge crowds. Come early in the morning or prepare for monster waits. A Park Hopper Plus pass gets you in free; otherwise, admission is $27.95 for adults, $22.50 for children 3 to 9.

Blizzard Beach Attractions

Summit Plummet

The icon of the park, this slide is 120 feet tall, making it twice as long as Humunga Kowabunga at Typhoon Lagoon. A clever optical illusion makes it seem that riders are shooting out the side of the mountain into midair; the real ride is very nearly as intense, with a 60-degree drop that feels more like 90. Top speeds on Summit Plummet reach 55 miles per hour, a full 10 miles per hour more than on Space Mountain—and you don't even have a seat belt. The height requirement is 48 inches. In short, this flume is not for the faint of heart.

Slush Gusher

This is another big slide, but this time with a couple of bumps to slow you down. Still a big-deal thrill, akin in intensity to Humunga Kowabunga at Typhoon Lagoon.

Runoff Rapids

You take a separate set of stairs up the back of Mt. Gushmore to reach these three inner-tube rides. You'll have a choice of tubes that seat one, two, or three people. (Remember, the heavier the tube, the faster the descent.) The Rapids are great fun, and each path provides a slightly different thrill, so many people try it over and over. But you'll have to carry your own raft up the seven zillion stairs (157, to be exact!); visit early in the morning before your stamina fails.

Snow Stormers

This is a mock slalom run that you descend on your belly while clutching a foam rubber "sled." The three slides are full of twists and runs that splash water back into your face, and if you'd like, you can race the sledders in the other two tubes to the bottom. Snow Stormers is so much fun that, like Runoff Rapids, hardly anyone does it only once.

Toboggan Racers

Eight riders on rubber mats are pitted against one another on a straight descent down the mountain. The heavier the rider, the faster the descent, so the attendant at the top of the slide will give kids a head start over adults. Not quite as wild as Snow Stormers, this ride is a good choice for getting kids used to the feeling of sliding downhill on a rubber sled.

Teamboat Springs

The whole family can join forces here to tackle the whitewater as a group. The round boats, which an attendant will help you board at the top, carry up to six people, and the ride downhill is zippy and fun, with lots of splashes and sharp curves. This is one of the best-loved rides in the park, drawing an enthusiastic thumbs-up from preschoolers to grandparents. Because parents and kids can share a raft, this is another good first ride to test young children's response before moving on to Snow Stormers or Runoff Rapids. It's much longer, wilder, and more fun than Gangplank Falls, the comparable whitewater ride at Typhoon Lagoon.

Downhill Double Dipper

On this individual tube ride, you go through a water curtain and tunnel, emerge into a free fall, and then exit through a long steep tube. At one point in the ride, your tube is completely airborne. The Double Dipper is fun and addictive, but if your kids are young, test them on nearby Runoff Rapids first.

Ski Patrol Training Camp

This special section is designed for kids 5 to 9, and they can walk across icebergs, swing from T-bars, and test their mountaineering skills. There are medium-intensity slides as well. It's a welcome addition for families who have children too old for Tike's Peak but not quite up to the major slides. Interested in rock climbing? The small climbing wall is a good place to give it a try.

Tike's Peak

This is the preschool and toddler section, with yet smaller slides and flumes, igloo-style forts, and a wading pool that looks like a broken ice-skating rink. A separate section for toddlers ensures that they won't be trampled by overenthusiastic 5-year-olds. There are chairs and picnic areas nearby for parents.

Chair Lift

The chair lift offers transportation to Summit Plummet, Slush Gusher, and Teamboat Springs and is also a fun ride in itself.

Melt Away Bay

Unlike the huge Surfing Lagoon at Typhoon Lagoon, this swimming area is relatively small and offers mild swells instead of big waves. Fed by "melting snow" waterfalls, the pool area is attractive and surrounded by chairs and shady huts for relaxing.

Cross Country Creek

This lazy creek circles the park. All you have to do is wade in, find an empty tube, and climb aboard. Expect major blasts of cold water as you float through the "ice cave." (There are exits before the cave if this is just a bit too authentic for you.) It takes about 25 minutes to make a full lap, and it's a pleasant experience for any age.

Helpful Hint

Don't bother bringing your own snorkels, rafts, masks, or water wings. Only official Disney equipment is allowed in the pools.

CHAPTER

10

The Rest of
the World

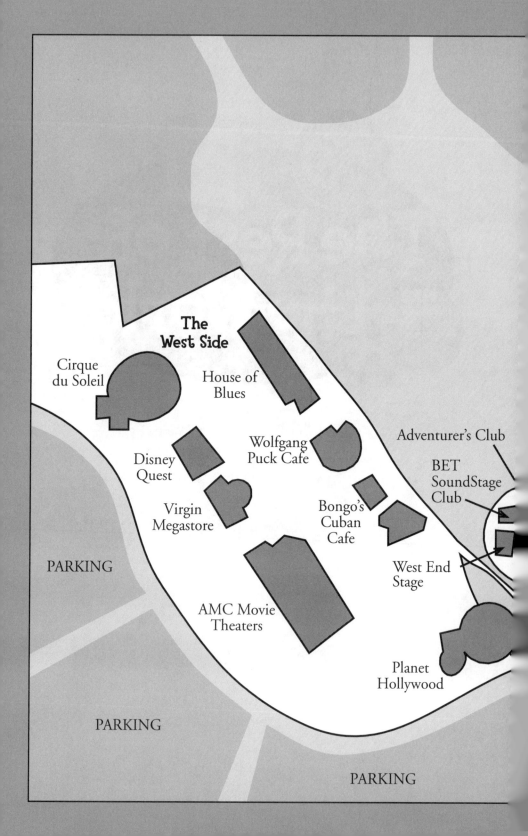

The West Side

Cirque
du Soleil

House of
Blues

Disney
Quest

Wolfgang
Puck Cafe

Virgin
Megastore

Bongo's
Cuban
Cafe

Adventurer's Club

BET
SoundStage
Club

AMC Movie
Theaters

West End
Stage

Planet
Hollywood

PARKING

PARKING

PARKING

Downtown Disney and Pleasure Island

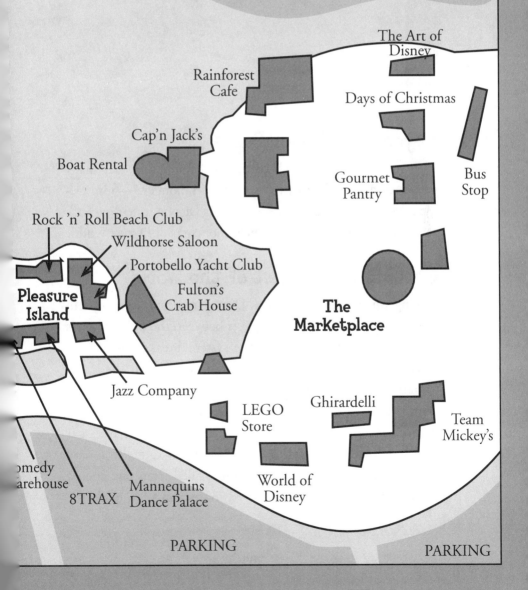

Disney Institute

The Art of Disney

Rainforest Cafe

Days of Christmas

Cap'n Jack's

Boat Rental

Gourmet Pantry

Bus Stop

Rock 'n' Roll Beach Club

Wildhorse Saloon

Portobello Yacht Club

Fulton's Crab House

Pleasure Island

The Marketplace

Jazz Company

LEGO Store

Ghirardelli

Team Mickey's

Comedy Warehouse

8TRAX

Mannequins Dance Palace

World of Disney

PARKING

PARKING

Beyond the Major Parks

The major parks get much of the media attention, but many guests report that their best Disney World moments—from racing a Mouse Boat around the Seven Seas Lagoon to settling back at a comedy club—happen in the minor parks of Disney World.

Getting to the Rest of the World

Staying on-site? Although the Disney transportation system does a good job of shuttling guests between the on-site hotels and the major theme parks, the system breaks down a bit when it comes to the minor parks. Always consult the transportation guide you're given at check-in for the best route from your particular resort to anywhere on Disney property. If it involves more than two transfers, and you don't have a car with you, consider taking a cab. They're easy to get from any on-site resort, and the cost of being hauled from one end of Disney property to another is never more than a few bucks.

Staying off-site? If you have your own car, use it. Off-site hotels rarely offer shuttle service to anything other than the major parks. If you don't have a car, call a cab.

Getting to Downtown Disney

Buses run from all on-site hotels to Downtown Disney and make three stops—at the Marketplace, Pleasure Island, and West Side. Those staying at Dixie Landings, Port Orleans, or Disney's Old Key West have boat service directly to the Marketplace, by far the most pleasant way to get there. In addition, on-site and off-site guests can drive directly to Downtown Disney. There is no charge for parking, but the parking lot sometimes fills at night; if so, valet parking ($6) is your best option.

Getting to the Disney Institute

You can take a bus to any major park or Downtown Disney and transfer there. If you have your own car, definitely drive.

Getting to the Wide World of Sports

Buses are an option, but few run to this out-of-the-way location, and those that do require transfers. Check your transportation guide for the best route from your resort. Some guests report horrific commute times, so if you have your own car, definitely drive. If not, consider a cab.

Getting from One Resort to Another

Your simplest option is to use the theme park that is nearest your home resort as a transfer station. For example, if you're staying at the Yacht Club and have dinner reservations at the Maya Grill in Coronado Springs, take the water taxi over to MGM and catch a Coronado Springs bus from there.

The Don't-Miss List for the Rest of the World

Downtown Disney, for shopping and dining

Cirque du Soleil (expensive but unique)

DisneyQuest (if you have kids over 10)

Pleasure Island (for an adult night out)

Character Breakfasts (if you have kids under 7)

The Worth-Your-While List for the Rest of the World

Mouse Boats

Miniature Golfing at Winter Summerland or Fantasia Gardens

A day at the Disney Institute

BoardWalk, for dining and club-hopping

Downtown Disney

The enormous entertainment, dining, and shopping complex known as Downtown Disney has three major sections: the Marketplace, Pleasure Island, and West Side. The three sections are linked by walking paths, shuttle buses, and ferry service; not surprisingly, Downtown Disney is packed at night, when the restaurants and clubs are going full force.

Families who would like to try out some of the food, shopping, and entertainment of Downtown Disney without fighting the crowd would be well advised to go in the afternoon. Explore DisneyQuest and the shops, and then eat your main meal at a truly off time, like 4 P.M. Downtown Disney is a fun way to take a break from theme park touring in the middle of your vacation.

Time-Saving Tip

Warning: Buses stop at all three sections of Downtown Disney, meaning even a direct shuttle to your resort can be a 30-minute ride, so plan accordingly. Dixie Landings, Port Orleans, and Old Key West run water taxis to Downtown Disney. It's not only a faster commute than the buses but a much more pleasant one as well.

Downtown Disney Marketplace

World of Disney, the largest Disney store on earth, is a great place to start. You'll find a bit of everything here, so if you've been mentally making a list during your trip ("I want the ESPN shirt for Sean, the Dumbo teapot for Aunt Sara, and a stuffed Pooh for Tracy"), World of Disney is the perfect place for one-stop shopping.

The Days of Christmas shop is another must-see, as is Team Mickey, which features sporting equipment and clothes. A padded softball "autographed" by all the characters makes a special gift for a very young athlete. The LEGO Store is just amazing, with a play area out front where kids can relax and build for a while as well as stunningly complex LEGO models scattered around the lagoon. And if money is no object, stop off at the Art of Disney, where you'll find Disney animation cels and other collectibles.

The Rainforest Cafe is great fun because birds and fish (real) and rhinos and giraffes (fake) surround your table while you eat. Check out the incredible barstools with their parrot and zebra legs. Long waits are standard at the Rainforest Cafe, but you can always put your name in and then shop for a while until you're called.

The marketplace has a small playground and sand area, as well as neat splash fountains to keep younger kids entertained. Or venture down to the dock at the Buena Vista Lagoon to rent one of the zippy Mouse boats. The cost is $17 per half-hour; kids under 12 must ride with an adult. Although the boats appear to be flying, they really don't go very fast, and they're a fun, safe diversion for all ages.

Pleasure Island

At the Pleasure Island Nightclub Theme Park, the motto is "It's New Year's Eve every night!" The island comes alive at 7 each evening when its three dance clubs, two comedy clubs, jazz club, and 1970s-style disco open their doors. A different

Money-Saving Tip
The $18.86 admission gives you unlimited access to all the clubs. If you have a Park Hopper pass, you're entitled to free admission to Pleasure Island. (Even if you don't have the Park Hopper pass, you still shouldn't have to pay full price—there are numerous discount coupons to be found in the freebie magazines at your hotel. These are the only Disney tickets that are regularly discounted.) And if you just want to see the shops and restaurants of Pleasure Island, there is no admission charge until 7 P.M., when the clubs open.

featured band puts on a show each evening, winding down just before midnight, when a street party culminates in the New Year's Eve countdown, complete with champagne, fireworks, and confetti.

Children under 18 are welcome if accompanied by a parent or guardian (except for Mannequins and the BET Sound Stage). Although Pleasure Island is clearly geared toward adults, some families do bring their kids. This is a wholesome, Disneyesque nightclub environment—that is, there's no raunchy material at the comedy club, drunks are discreetly handled, and security is tight. So if for some reason you are reluctant to leave your children with a sitter at the hotel, Pleasure Island is fine.

Pleasure Island Touring Tips

- @ If you choose Pleasure Island for parents' night out, get an in-room sitter for the kids. Most hotel services close down at midnight, and if you stay for the fireworks and street party, you won't be back until after that. With an in-room sitter, the kids can go to bed at their usual hour.

- @ You won't be pressured to drink in the clubs, but if you do, you'll soon learn that the alcohol is expensive.

- @ Even if you don't dance, Pleasure Island is worthwhile. Nearby barstools let you watch the dancers, and the comedy club and live bands are very entertaining.

Pleasure Island Touring Plan

- @ Arrive about 7 P.M. Take in the Comedy Warehouse first. (The dance clubs don't gear up until later.) This 30-minute show, a combination of improvisation and Disney spoofs, is proof positive that comedians don't have to be profane to be funny. And because so much of the material is truly improvised, some guests return to the Comedy Warehouse several times in the course of the evening to see an essentially different routine each time.

@ For something completely different, try the Adventurer's Club, a lavish, eccentric hideaway based on British hunting clubs of the 1930s. You won't be in the bar for long before you realize some of your fellow patrons are actors—and the barstools are sinking and the masks on the walls are moving. Every 30 minutes or so, a seemingly spontaneous comedy routine erupts among the actors; the séance routines are especially memorable. The biggest hoot is the twice-nightly New Members Induction Ceremony, during which hapless bar inductees are encouraged to learn the club salute, club creed, and all-purpose theme song.

Insider's Secret

Unfortunately, many people just walk in, peruse the bizarre decor of the Adventurer's Club, and leave before they have a chance to really get into this particular brand of comedy. Give it time! The Adventurer's Club is definitely worth an hour of your evening. There's nothing like this back home—unless you're from the Congo—and the club is a favorite among Orlando locals.

@ Next, stop by the new Jazz Company, which features live music and draws an interesting crowd. The Jazz Company has a wide selection of wines, many offered by the glass, and a light menu, so if you plan to spend a lot of time here, you may not need to eat supper first. The tables are small, the music is relatively subdued, the clientele is more mellow—making this the most romantic of the Pleasure Island clubs.

@ At 8Trax, polyester and disco are still king. It's fun to watch the thirty-somethings sitting in their beanbag chairs, valiantly pretending they don't remember the words to old Bee Gees hits. At other times the club spins back even further in time to late 1960s psychedelia. Sometimes special guests—such as former cast members from *The Brady Bunch*—appear, adding even more camp to the atmosphere.

@ Divide your remaining hours between the four dance clubs. The Rock 'n' Roll Beach Club offers a live band and an informal, pool-shooting, beer-drinking, resort-style ambience; Mannequins is darker and wilder and features canned music, strobe lighting, and a revolving dance floor. Want to learn how to two-step? Try the country-western club, Wildhorse Saloon. Developed by Black Entertainment Television, the BET club features jazz, soul, R&B, and hip-hop music. BET also has concerts, featuring headliners as well as local talent.

> **Helpful Hint**
> Be sure to be back outside for the street party and countdown to New Year's.

@ Flat-out bizarre entertainment can be found all up and down the street. On a recent evening, there were female bodybuilders posing in bikinis, a Velcro wall begging to be leapt against, and a Russian mime troupe.

Downtown Disney West Side

The West Side expansion of restaurants means that people staying on-site without a rental car are no longer tied to restaurants of the theme parks. Far more varied dining, with a casual atmosphere suitable for families, is a bus ride away.

Bongo's Cuban Cafe, created by Gloria Estefan, offers an Americanized version of Cuban dishes, a wildly tropical decor, and loud Latin music. Reservations are taken only for parties of 10 or more, so be prepared to put in your name and spend a while exploring the West Side. Dan Aykroyd's House of Blues serves up Cajun and Creole cooking along with some jazz, country, rock 'n' roll, and, yes, blues music. The Gospel Brunch, which offers plenty of food and an absolutely uplifting atmosphere, runs from 10:30 A.M. to 1 P.M. on Sundays and is an especially good choice for families. The price is $28.00 for adults, $15.00 for kids 4 to 12; tickets can be purchased by calling 407-934-2583 or 407-934-BLUE.

The more sophisticated Wolfgang Puck Cafe serves terrific pizzas at the downstairs Express. Request the upstairs dining room for tonier adult dining. Priority seating is suggested there, so set up a time on the evening you've gotten a sitter for the kids and are heading over to Pleasure Island.

Although not new, Planet Hollywood is always fun. The giant blue globe parked right beside Pleasure Island holds props from a variety of movies, the bus from the movie *Speed* hovers overhead, and even the menus—printed with high school graduation pictures of stars—are entertaining.

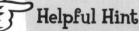

Helpful Hint

The West Side is also home to a 24-screen AMC theater and a Virgin Megastore, which sometimes has concerts out front.

Film clips run constantly on giant screens, and the whole atmosphere is heady, loud, and cheerful. No reservations are taken, and the place can get packed at mealtime; 90-minute waits are not uncommon at 6 P.M. Try to visit in midafternoon, or because the desserts are among the best in town, stop off for a late-night sweet spree as you're leaving Pleasure Island. (The Ghirardelli brownie is beyond compare.)

At the West Side, you'll also find two of Disney World's hottest new attractions, DisneyQuest and Cirque du Soleil.

DisneyQuest

Most people call DisneyQuest an arcade simply because there isn't a name for this totally new type of play environment. Within DisneyQuest you'll find five levels of traditional arcade games as well as high-tech interactive experiences that basically allow you to enter into a video game. For example, in Virtual Jungle Cruise, you board rafts and literally pick up a paddle to help yourself steer through the rapids, and there are also games where you land your spacecraft on an alien planet in an effort to rescue settlers, engage in a virtual sword fight with comic book bad guys, and become the puck in a hockey-style pinball game.

The centerpiece attraction, the one everyone talks about, is CyberSpace Mountain. Bill Nye the Science Guy helps you design your own virtual roller coaster. You build in as many flips, spirals, and hills as you'd like; program in the speed of the car; and even get to name the sucker. When you've finished, your coaster is given a scariness rating from 1 to 5, meaning you can either design a gentle, rolling, grade-1 coaster suitable for kids or a flip-you-over, slam-you-down, rip-roaring grade-5 coaster. (If you end up with a coaster too wild or too tame for your taste, you can redesign it.) Then you enter a booth, are strapped into a car, and you ride a virtual re-creation of the route you just designed, complete with flips.

Needless to say, preteens and teens can get hooked on this stuff very fast, and DisneyQuest is primarily designed for them. (Some parents park older kids at the arcade while they eat at one of the West Side restaurants.) But there are games for the younger kids as well, and any age can enjoy the Create Zone, where the Animation Academy lets you learn how to draw a character or Sid's Make a Toy helps you design a virtual toy (and—guess what—you can purchase its duplicate in the DisneyQuest gift shop!).

DisneyQuest usually opens about 10:30 A.M., and day-times are the best time to come because it can become very crowded at night. Disney has tried several ticketing options for DisneyQuest, but the present plan is a single entry price (adults $27.00, kids 3–9 $21.00), which lets you play as many games as you'd like for as long as you like—an alarming thought for the parents of an 11-year-old boy.

Cirque Du Soleil

After a week at Disney World, probably the last thing you're itching to do is pay $62.00 for adults, $38.00 for kids, to watch a 90-minute acrobatic show. But Cirque du Soleil positively wowed the families we surveyed.

More than 60 performers stage the show, which runs twice daily, five days a week. (Usually 5:30

> **Helpful Hint**
> Cirque du Soleil, staged in the dramatic white tent-top building near DisneyQuest, is a show unlike any you'll see anywhere else.

and 8:30 P.M. Wednesday through Saturday and 2:30 and 5:30 P.M. on Sunday, but call 407-939-7600 to confirm times and prices.) Although the flexibility and athleticism of the troupe will amaze you, it's their ability to use props, sets, costumes, and their bodies to set a mood and tell a story that make the Cirque du Soleil experience so unique. Don't expect any elephants or people being shot out of cannons; these performances are more like theater than traditional circuses.

Helpful Hint
Kids need to be 8 or older to get into the unique ambience of Cirque du Soleil.

The show being staged at press time is *La Nouba,* but the shows are changed on a regular basis. For more information online, check out www.cirquedusoleil.com.

BoardWalk and the ESPN Center

Not up for the sprawl of Downtown Disney? At night, the shops, restaurants, and nightclubs in front of the BoardWalk Inn take on a whole new glitter. A variety of services and entertainment—magic acts, comics, face painting, hair braiding, and midway games—take place along the waterfront. Eat dinner at Spoodles, the Flying Fish Cafe, or one of the BoardWalk's other fun restaurants (arrange priority seating by calling 407-WDW-DINE), and then rent a surrey bike ($10.75 for 30 minutes) for a wild lap around the lagoon.

The ESPN Center is a good stop for sports enthusiasts. The center contains a broadcast and production facility (meaning athlete celebs are sometimes on hand) and the ultimate sports bar featuring—and I'm quoting—"the best ballpark cuisine from around the country." This bold claim translates into sandwiches, salads, and burgers, all sized for hearty appetites; try the Bloody Mary chili.

Two clubs are open strictly to adults 21 and older: The elegant Atlantic Dance nightclub features everything from swing music to disco, but it's all designed to get you moving. Live bands appear on occasion. (Expect a $5 cover charge.) Jellyrolls offers dueling pianos and a sing-along bar. (There is usually a $3 cover charge on weekends.) Either is a good alternative to Pleasure Island if you'd like some live entertainment but just don't have the stamina for club hopping.

Helpful Hint

So you won't miss a single play, at the ESPN Center 70 TVs showing games blare constantly—even in the bathroom!

The fact that the BoardWalk is not as vast and crowded as Downtown Disney appeals to many visitors; you can have a good meal and some entertainment here without getting back into the mouse race. And at night, with the glowing Yacht and Beach Clubs visible just across the water and the fireworks of Epcot in the distance, the BoardWalk ranks as one of the most beautiful and romantic spots in all of Disney World. Pull up a rocker and let the world go by.

On-site guests can take monorails or buses to any theme park and then transfer to the BoardWalk bus. If you're staying at the Yacht and Beach Clubs, the Swan, or the Dolphin, just walk. If you have a car, you can either park in the BoardWalk lot or pay for the $6 valet parking (it's free if you're staying at a Disney resort), which is emphatically worth it on weekend evenings, when the resort parking lot tends to fill up.

Disney Extras

The Disney Institute

Educational may not be the first word that comes to mind when you think of Disney World, but the Disney Institute is aiming to change that. The Institute was created specifically to give guests the chance to sample programs in animation, cooking, gardening, photography, tennis, and other subjects. Guests can stay in a secluded, campuslike enclave and spend their days taking classes, enjoying the world-renowned performers who appear each evening, and working out at the spectacular Sports and Fitness Center. Or you can drop in for a one-day class and sample a bit of what the Institute has to offer.

The Disney Institute opened in 1996 in what was once the Disney Village Resort, located near Downtown Disney and Pleasure Island. The accommodations are either townhouses with full kitchens and sitting rooms or bungalows with mini-kitchens. The villas are clustered around a huge lake and the Institute's village green. Guests can rent bikes or golf carts or simply walk to classes.

Although the laid-back, small-town atmosphere provides much of the Institute's charm, the real draw is the programs. The classes are part of the package—you take as many or as few as you like, with no additional charge. Some classes are designed specifically for kids, but some are created for parents and children to enjoy together. See "Camp Disney at the Disney Institute" in Chapter 1 for details on programs for kids 7 to 10 and 11 to 15.

The instructors are the best in their fields, some of them Disney imagineers trained to lead guests through creativity exercises, storytelling, or computer animation "the Disney way."

There is an instructor for every 15 students, and many classes are even smaller, ensuring lots of individual attention. The Institute reservations system averages 45-minute phone calls because the counselors are prepared to talk guests through all the available options. Most guests request a catalog and select their courses ahead of time, but if a program looks unexpectedly interesting once you arrive, the Institute is quite flexible.

Helpful Hint
People often arrive in Orlando and get fired up to try something they'd never do at home—such as acting or rock climbing.

Counselors are on hand in the lobby to help guests drop or add programs.

The 38,000-square-foot Sports and Fitness Center is the cornerstone of the campus; you can take classes or create your own fitness program using the dozens of beyond-state-of-the-art machines. There's also a full-service spa, a basketball court, and adjacent golf and tennis.

A variety of packages is available, some of which include dining in the Institute restaurant, Seasons, and admission into the theme parks. You don't have to be staying at the Institute to check it out. Half-day and full-day packages, ranging in price from $69 to $99, are also available and give you a chance to try one or two classes. In fact, a day at the Disney Institute offers a nice midweek break from touring. For information or reservations, call 800-4WONDER (496-6337). For a free video, call 800-654-8666.

The Parades, Fireworks, Dinner Shows, Character Breakfasts, and Holiday Special Events

Parades

If you love a parade, you've come to the right place. Included in the festivities are the following:

- Afternoon parade at the Magic Kingdom, usually at 3 P.M.

- The electrical nighttime parade that runs at both 9 and 11 P.M. during the busy season at the Magic Kingdom and on selected dates during the off-season.

- Electric Water Pageant, visible from the beaches of the Seven Seas Lagoon from 9 to 10:20 P.M. nightly.

- March of the Animals is presented daily at the Animal Kingdom. Show times vary, so check your map.

- The MGM parade, which features the new movie Disney is currently hyping. Usually starts at 1 P.M., but times vary, so check the entertainment schedule.

- Mind-blowing holiday parades at Easter, Fourth of July, and Christmas.

Fireworks

A 5- to 10-minute display explodes in the sky above Cinderella Castle at 10 P.M. nightly during the on-season. Just before the fireworks begin, you'll see one of the Magic Kingdom's niftiest—but least advertised—little extras: Tinkerbell's Flight. A young gymnast, dressed in tights and zestily hacking the air with a magic wand, slides down a wire suspended from the top of Cinderella Castle to a rooftop in Tomorrowland.

IllumiNations

Don't miss this laser, fountain, light, and music extravaganza at closing time each evening at Epcot. See "IllumiNations" in Chapter 6 for more information.

Fantasmic!

One of Disney's best special events, Fantasmic! is staged nightly at the Disney-MGM Studios. The multimedia show combines music, lasers, fireworks, and a classic good-versus-evil story line.

Quick Guide to Full-in the Rest

Restaurant	Description	Location
Bongo's Cuban Cafe	An Americanized version of Cuban dishes	West Side
Fulton's Crab House	Offers a variety of elegant seafood dishes	Pleasure Island
House of Blues	Cajun and Creole cooking along with blues music	West Side
Official All-Star Cafe	Loud and raucous	Disney's Wide World of Sports
Planet Hollywood	Always fun, film clips run constantly	West Side
Portobello Yacht Club	Northern Italian cuisine	Pleasure Island
Rainforest Cafe	Great fun, but long waits	Marketplace
Wolfgang Puck Cafe	Terrific pizzas and sushi	West Side

For descriptions of ratings, prices, priority seating, and suitability for kids, see pages 316–317.

Service Restaurants of the World

Rating	Price	Priority Seating	Suitability	Details on
★	$$	Not accepted	Moderate	Page 328
★★	$$$	Recommended	Low	Page 333
★★	$$	Not accepted	High	Page 335
★★	$$	Not accepted	Moderate	Page 338
★★	$$	Not accepted	High	Page 339
★★	$$$	Recommended	Moderate	Page 340
★★	$$	Not accepted	High	Page 340
★★	$$$	Only upstairs	Low	Page 343

Dinner Shows

Book all the dinner shows you would like to attend before you leave home by calling 407-WDW-DINE. Reservations are accepted up to two years in advance and are especially crucial for the Hoop-de-Doo Musical Revue, which requires a lot of hoop-de-doo just to get tickets. The on-site dinner shows include the following:

- Hoop-de-Doo Musical Revue. The Revue plays three times nightly (5, 7:15, and 9:30 P.M.) at Pioneer Hall in Fort Wilderness. You'll dine on ribs and fried chicken while watching a hilariously hokey show that encourages lots of audience participation; $38.00 (includes gratuity) for adults and kids over 12, $19.50 for kids 3 to 11, and American Express cardholders get an additional 10 percent off.

- Polynesian Luau. You'll enjoy authentic island dancing and not-particularly-authentic island food at this outdoor show at the Polynesian Village Resort. The two seatings are at 6:45 and 9:30 P.M. Prices are $38.00 for adults and kids over 12, $19.50 for kids 3 to 11.

If you're staying off-site and don't want to return to the Disney World grounds in the evening, or if you've waited too late to book a Disney show, be advised that Orlando is chock-full of engaging family-style dinner shows that can often be booked on the same afternoon. See "Off-Site Dinner Shows for the Whole Family" in Chapter 16 for details.

Character Breakfasts

The character breakfasts take at least a couple of hours and probably should be skipped if you're on a very tight touring schedule—or if you're watching your pocketbook carefully. But families that stay at Disney World for four or five days give the breakfasts very high marks, especially if they schedule them near the end of their stay, when the kids have had plenty of time to warm up to the characters.

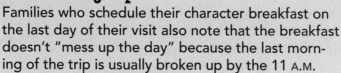

Time-Saving Tip
Families who schedule their character breakfast on the last day of their visit also note that the breakfast doesn't "mess up the day" because the last morning of the trip is usually broken up by the 11 A.M. checkout time at most Orlando hotels.

The food is pedestrian at the character breakfasts, but who cares? Because it takes a while to meet all the characters (usually between five and seven circulate among the diners) and eat, either come early or, if you're able to make a reservation, try to book the first seating of the day. Prices generally run about $15 for adults, $8 for children. The more elaborate Sunday brunches are also more expensive: about $20 for adults, $10 for kids. Priority seating can be arranged up to 60 days in advance for the Magic Kingdom, Animal Kingdom, and MGM seating, 120 days for Epcot and resort seating; call 407-WDW-DINE before you leave home.

There are buffet character breakfasts at the Grand Floridian (featuring the Mary Poppins and Alice in Wonderland characters), the Beach Club, the Wilderness Lodge, and the Polynesian (all featuring the classic characters). Old Key West features a menu-style character breakfast with the Winnie the Pooh gang. During especially crowded seasons of the year, additional breakfasts may be added.

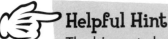

Helpful Hint
The biggest character breakfast of all is at Chef Mickey's in the Contemporary Resort. It features Mickey, Minnie, Donald, Daisy—you get the idea.

Character breakfasts within the theme parks have become increasingly popular during the past three years. In the Magic Kingdom, you can meet Cinderella and her friends at the "Once upon a Time" breakfast at Cinderella's Royal Table or the Winnie the Pooh characters at the Crystal Palace. In MGM, characters from recent Disney films circulate among the diners at the Hollywood and Vine Cafeteria.

If your family isn't much for breakfast, you can also see the characters in the evening. 1900 Park Fare in the Grand Floridian offers an evening character buffet, and the Liberty Tree Tavern in the Magic Kingdom offers a patriotic dinner with the characters dressed in Revolutionary-era outfits. Or try the Garden Grill Room in the Land pavilion at Epcot. Arrange priority seating in advance by calling 407-WDW-DINE.

Jolly Holiday Packages Featuring Mickey's Very Merry Christmas Party

Disney World is at its most magical during the holidays. Hours are extended, special parades and shows debut, and a meet-the-characters show and party runs on selected evenings. If you fantasize about seeing it snow on Main Street, this is your chance. (We're talking real snow here, not confetti. It's generated from the rooftops of Main Street and blown down upon the crowd below.) Tickets for Mickey's Very Merry Christmas Party should be purchased in advance but are also included in a Jolly Holidays Package, a special all-inclusive holiday deal. Call 407-W-DISNEY for details.

It is quite possible to celebrate Christmas at Disney without getting caught in the crush. The decorations go up just after Thanksgiving, and the special shows, packages, and holiday parties begin soon thereafter. A family visiting in early December can see all the special stuff—except, of course, for the Christmas Day parade—without having to face the harrowing holiday crowds.

One recent Christmas, when my family visited, we were agog at the hotel decorations. Aladdin's hometown of Agrabah was reconstructed out of gingerbread at Port Orleans; the Yacht and Beach Clubs offered the gingerbread villages of the Little Mermaid and Belle. The on-site hotels hosted fun little parties for their guests, with visits from Santa, stockings for the children, eggnog and cookies, and Victorian carolers giving a homey feel to a hotel holiday.

Helpful Hint

If school schedules rule out an early December trip, note that the week before Christmas is slightly less hectic than the week between Christmas and New Year's Eve.

Each hotel has its own themed tree as well—a nautical tree for the Yacht Club, starfish and seashells at the Beach Club, Native American tepees and animal skulls for the Wilderness Lodge, and the sweeping pink poinsettia tree at the Grand Floridian. The themed decorations are so drop-dead fabulous that Disney offers Christmas tours of the resorts, which are popular with Orlando locals.

So if you're visiting Disney World between Thanksgiving and New Year's Eve, be sure to save some time just to check out the lobbies of the on-site hotels.

That Sportin' Life: On Water

Most on-site hotels have lovely marinas with a variety of watercraft to meet every age-group's needs. The two major recreational lagoons in Disney World are the Seven Seas Lagoon, which is in front of the Magic Kingdom and serves Fort Wilderness and the Magic Kingdom resorts, and the Buena Vista Lagoon at the Disney Village Marketplace. In addition, the Yacht and Beach Clubs share a lagoon with the Swan and the Dolphin Resorts; the Caribbean Beach Resort, Coronado Springs, Port Orleans, and Dixie Landings all have their own canals and lagoons with watercraft for rent.

Because rates at Disney World are "adjusted" frequently, it's not a bad idea to confirm rental prices in advance. In the on-season, reservations are a good idea. To make them from your hotel room or for general information on Disney World sporting options, call 407-824-2621.

You do not have to be a guest of an on-site resort to rent the boats, although the marina will ask for either a resort ID or a Disney World ticket, along with a current driver's license for the larger boats. If you're staying off-site and don't want to bother commuting to an on-site hotel, try the Downtown Disney Marketplace.

Water options include the following:

Boat rental. The Disney fleet includes Mouse boats ($17 for 30 minutes), canopy boats ($20 for 30 minutes), sailboats ($8 for 30 minutes), pontoons ($22 an hour), pedal boats ($6 for 30 minutes), and canoes ($6 an hour). The most popular are the Mouse boats, those zippy little two passenger speedboats you see darting around the Buena Vista and Seven Seas Lagoons. Drivers must be 12 years old (14 at Downtown Disney), although kids of any age will enjoy riding alongside Mom and Dad.

Waterskiing. A boat, a driver, and full equipment can be rented at Fort Wilderness, the Polynesian, the Grand Floridian, and the Contemporary marinas. The cost is $100 an hour for up to five people, and reservations can be made 14 days in advance by calling 407-824-2621.

Fishing. Angling is permitted in the canals around Fort Wilderness. Rent rods and reels at the Bike Barn. You can fish from shore or take a canoe or pontoon boat deeper into the canals. Resort guests can also drop a line at Dixie Landings.

Helpful Hint

If your kids just want to play around with the idea of fishing, you can drop a line for catfish at Ol' Man Island in Dixie Landings. Dixie Landings and Port Orleans guests also have their own fishing excursions that can be arranged through Guest Relations.

Want a bit more action? Guided two-hour expeditions leave daily from Dixie Landings, and up to five people can be accommodated for $160.00, which includes the boat, the guide, the equipment, and snacks. Trips also depart daily from the Downtown Disney marina. Make reservations up to 14 days in advance by calling 407-824-2621.

Swimming. All the Disney World hotels have private pools, but the pools at the Swan and the Dolphin are best for serious swimmers because they have special lanes reserved for laps. The newer hotels—the Yacht and Beach Clubs, Wilderness Lodge, Coronado Springs, the BoardWalk, Port Orleans, and Dixie Landings—boast elaborately themed pool areas, some of which almost qualify as miniature water parks.

Surfing. Surfing lessons are sometimes offered at Typhoon Lagoon before the park opens: Call 407-WDW-SURF for details.

That Sportin' Life: On Land

Tennis. Several on-site hotels (the Contemporary, the Grand Floridian, the Yacht and Beach Clubs, the Village Resort Villas, the Swan, and the Dolphin) have courts that can be reserved 24 hours in advance. Call 407-824-3578 for details. The tennis courts at Fort Wilderness and Disney's Old Key West operate on a first-come, first-served basis.

There is considerable variation in fees. A court costs $15 at the Grand Floridian, the Contemporary, the Swan, and the Dolphin; tennis is $3 at Disney's Old Key West and the Yacht and Beach Clubs.

If you'd like private lessons or to participate in a clinic, consider staying at the Contemporary, which has lessons for $60 an hour. You can also get a package that allows the entire family court time for the duration of your stay. The Contemporary also runs clinics, which include videotaped analysis of your play by the club pro. Call 407-824-3578 for details. The Disney Institute also provides an extensive tennis clinic.

Golf. There are now five courses on the Disney World grounds, with greens fees running about $100 for Disney World hotel guests, about $115 for those staying off-site. With such pricey fees, anyone planning to golf a lot should consider the World Adventure or some other package. (Magic Kingdom Club members also get price breaks.) Or you can play in the early evening, when twilight fees drop to as low as $50.

The five courses are the Palm and Magnolia, two fairly demanding courses located near the Magic Kingdom; the Lake Buena Vista Course, which is near the Disney Institute Villas; and Osprey Ridge and Eagle Pines, which share the Bonnet Lakes Golf Club. Beginners and kids are better off at the nine-hole Oak Trail near the Magnolia, which is a walking course with fees of $24 for adults, $12 for kids under 17. (Two adults can get a reduced rate of $32, and two kids can play for $16.)

To reserve a tee time or arrange for participation in a golf clinic, call 407-WDW-GOLF. Disney World guests can make tee-off and lesson reservations up to 30 days in advance; those staying off-site can (and should) make reservations 7 days in advance.

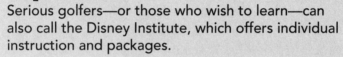

Helpful Hint
Serious golfers—or those who wish to learn—can also call the Disney Institute, which offers individual instruction and packages.

Miniature golf. Fantasia Gardens, an 18-hole miniature golf course across the street from the Disney-MGM Studios is real eye-candy because of the whimsical statues of characters featured in the classic movie *Fantasia*. The course itself is fairly challenging, with caves, tunnels, and moving obstacles. A second course, Fantasia Fairways, is a miniature version of a real golf course, with sand traps, water hazards, and roughs. The holes are up to 100 feet long, but you play them with a putter. It's difficult enough to drive a veteran golfer to curses and probably not a good choice for kids.

The courses can be crowded but are different enough from your miniature golf course back home to justify the time and money invested. Prices are $9.25 for adults, $7.50 for kids. For more information, call 407-560-8760.

"Would you like to play in snow or sand?" That's the first question you're asked at Disney's Winter Summerland, the new miniature golf course located near Blizzard Beach. Your first clue that there's strange weather ahead: Santa, his sleigh pulled by flamingos, has crash-landed on the roof and skidded through a combination snowbank-sandbank into the wackiest campground on earth.

If you opt to play the icy white "greens" of the winter course, you'll find a snow castle, slalom ski runs, a hockey rink where the sticks are obstacles, and a snowman who squirts you when you successfully sink a putt. Holiday music fills the air, but next door on the summer course the Beach Boys serenade you amid sand castles, pools, and barbecues—and an occasional snoring Santa taking a break on the beach. (Those in the know say summer is the more challenging season—must be all those sandtraps.)

There are plenty of surprises on the course, and at least three hidden Mickeys. Rates are $9.25 for adults, $7.50 for kids 3 to 9. Just pay the guy in the Winterbago.

Running. Jogging trails cut through the grounds of nearly every Disney World hotel. Consult Guest Services for a map of your particular resort. Fort Wilderness has a 2.3-mile exercise trail complete with posted period stops for chin-ups, sit-ups, and a host of other tortures. The sprawling Caribbean Beach Resort and the Wilderness Lodge, with its invitingly shady trails, are also good choices for runners.

Horseback riding. Guided trail rides leave the Fort Wilderness grounds five times a day. Disappointingly, children under 9 are forbidden, even though the horses are gentle and the pace is slow. The cost is $21.00, and reservations can be made up to 14 days in advance. Call 407-824-2621 before you leave home for reservations and information.

Health clubs and spas. The Contemporary, Grand Floridian, Swan, Dolphin, Yacht and Beach Clubs, BoardWalk,

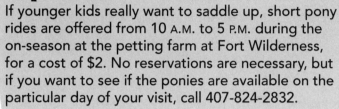

Helpful Hint

If younger kids really want to saddle up, short pony rides are offered from 10 A.M. to 5 P.M. during the on-season at the petting farm at Fort Wilderness, for a cost of $2. No reservations are necessary, but if you want to see if the ponies are available on the particular day of your visit, call 407-824-2832.

Coronado Springs, and Disney's Old Key West all have health clubs, and the cost is anywhere from $6 to $12 per visit with reduced length-of-stay rates—well worth it when you consider that most of the health clubs have whirlpools and saunas, a nice wrap-up to a day spent walking around the theme parks. Most of the health clubs are for the exclusive use of that particular hotel's guests, but the facilities at the Contemporary, Swan, and Dolphin are open to all on-site guests.

Helpful Hint

There are full spa facilities at the Grand Floridian and Disney Institute. An aromatherapy massage can be a lifesaver on day four of a seven-day trip.

If working out is really important to you, stay at the Disney Institute. The health club there is one of the most complete in Florida, with an amazing variety of machines; full tennis, golf, and basketball facilities; and classes in everything from boxing to yoga. Staying somewhere else? Limited use of the fitness center facilities is currently available on a daily basis, although this is subject to change when the Institute is full. Call 407-827-1100 for details.

Cycling. Bikes ($5 an hour or $12 a day) or tandems ($7 an hour) can be rented at the Bike Barn in Fort Wilderness, at the Villas of the Disney Institute, or at Dixie Landings, Port Orleans, Coronado Springs, Disney's Old Key West, the Wilderness Lodge, and the Caribbean Beach Resort.

Still have questions? You can get general sports information by calling 407-824-2621.

Disney's Wide World of Sports

This new multimillion-dollar complex houses competitions, tournaments, and vacation-fitness activities with facilities to accommodate 25 different sports. It's the spring training home of the Atlanta Braves, and the training site for the Harlem Globetrotters. The facility allows Disney to play host to a wide variety of tournaments and sports festivals, and tickets to premium events can be arranged through TicketMaster (407-839-3900).

Ever dreamed of firing off a pass like John Elway? Running through defenders for a 40-yard gain? Or how about saving the game with a field goal in the final seconds? Your football fantasies can all come true at the NFL Experience at Disney's Wide World of Sports. An interactive football playground designed to resemble a training camp, the NFL Experience gives fans the chance to test their passing in Quarterback Challenge, brush up their receiving skills in Down and Out, and push sleds against the time clock in The Big Move.

Two of the most popular elements are the timed obstacle course, and Sudden Death, where participants attempt to kick a field goal against a simulated defensive line composed of life-sized tackling dummies on a moving track. And if both your offense and your defense fail, you can at least Look Like a Pro by stepping behind body cast replicas of famous players for a fun photo op.

Entrance to the entire Wide World of Sports Complex is $9 for adults, $7 for kids 3 to 9; the hours for the NFL Experience are 10–5. Call 407-363-6000 for details. While the NFL Experience is a huge hit with kids 8 to 14, younger kids can test their mettle in The Kid's Zone. The whole family can have the thrill of playing in the pros—and none of the bruises.

Afterwards have lunch at the All-Star Café which has big screens running constant sporting events and a slew of athletic memorabilia.

Dining at Disney

Full-Service Restaurants at Disney

You've come to ride, but you also need to eat. The good news is that the variety and quality of the on-site restaurants has vastly improved in the ten years I've been doing this guide. The bad news is that as the size of the parks and the crowds has increased, so has the hassle factor in getting seated at your favorite restaurant. Read on for tips on how to choose the best spot for your family—and get in with minimal fuss.

Arrange priority seating in advance by dialing 407-WDW-DINE. Once in Orlando, those staying at on-site hotels can call from their rooms or make plans via Guest Services. Those staying at off-site hotels can make reservations once they enter the theme parks.

Definition of Restaurant Ratings

★ Okay in a pinch
★★ Decent food
★★★ A big-deal meal

Price

$ Inexpensive; adult dinner is about $10

$$ Moderate; adult dinner is about $15

$$$ Expensive; adult dinner is about $20 and up

Priority Seating

Not Offered: This restaurant does not accept priority seating, unless you have a party of 10 or more. Your best bet is to show up at an off-time, get a buzzer, and shop or explore nearby areas while you wait for your table.

Suggested: This restaurant is rarely crowded, which may mean that the type of food is unfamiliar to most Disney World guests, the restaurant isn't very good, or it's a perfectly fine place that happens to be in an out-of-the-way location. Unless you're dining during peak hours or touring during a crowded time of the year, you'll probably be able to be seated as a walk-in.

Recommended: This restaurant draws average crowds. Unless you're touring in the off-season or dining at off hours, you'll need to arrange priority seating either from the theme parks or, if you're staying at an on-site hotel, from your room.

Necessary: This is a popular restaurant; arrange priority seating before you leave home.

Suitability for Kids

High: Not only is the place informal, with at least a few food choices designed to appeal to kids, but there's also either some sort of entertainment going on or the locale itself is funky and interesting.

Moderate: This restaurant is reasonably casual and family-oriented.

Low: This is one of Disney World's more adult restaurants, with a romantic ambience, sophisticated menu choices, and leisurely service.

Quick Guide to Full-

Restaurant	Description	Location
Akershus (Norway)	Lots of fish, picky eaters may rebel	Epcot
Artist Point	Excellent food in a rustic setting	Wilderness Lodge
Biergarten	Rousing, noisy atmosphere	Epcot
Big River Grille & Brewing Works	Casual restaurant located on the BoardWalk	BoardWalk
Bistro de Paris (France)	Classic French cuisine, very elegant, very adult	Epcot
Boatwright's Dining Hall	Specializes in tame Cajun cooking	Dixie Landings
Bonfamille's Cafe	Toned-down Creole food	Port Orleans
Bongo's Cuban Cafe	Offers an Americanized version of Cuban dishes	West Side
California Grill	One of WDW's absolute best	Contemporary
Cape May Cafe	Breakfast buffet is very popular	Beach Club Resort
Captain's Tavern	Provides a variety of seafood, chicken, and steaks	Caribbean Beach
Le Cellier (Canada)	A good spot for beef and salmon—as well as buffalo	Epcot
Chefs de France (France)	The ambience of a Paris sidewalk cafe	Epcot
Chef Mickey's	At character breakfast, Mickey and crew wander among diners	Contemporary
Cinderella's Royal Table	A chance to meet the princess and her pals	Magic Kingdom
Citricos	Outstanding wine selection	Grand Floridian
Concourse Steakhouse	Open, airy, and a bit loud	Contemporary

Service Restaurants

Rating	Price	Priority Seating	Suitability	Details on
★★	$$	Recommended	Moderate	Page 326
★★★	$$	Recommended	Moderate	Page 326
★	$$	Recommended	High	Page 326
★	$$	Not accepted	Moderate	Page 326
★★★	$$$	Necessary	Low	Page 327
★	$$	Suggested	Moderate	Page 327
★★	$$	Suggested	Moderate	Page 327
★	$$	Not accepted	Moderate	Page 328
★★★	$$$	Necessary	Low	Page 328
★★	$$	Recommended	High	Page 328
★	$	Suggested	Moderate	Page 328
★	$$	Recommended	Low	Page 329
★★★	$$$	Necessary	Moderate	Page 329
★★	$$	Recommended	High	Page 329
★★	$$$	Necessary	High	Page 329
★★★	$$$	Necessary	Low	Page 330
★★	$$$	Recommended	Low	Page 330

(continued)

Quick Guide to Full-

Restaurant	Description	Location
Coral Cafe	Sophisticated food, but a loud lobby location	Dolphin
The Coral Reef	Great view of the Living Seas tank	Epcot
Crystal Palace	Winnie the Pooh visits guests as they dine	Magic Kingdom
ESPN Club	Selections are pure ballpark chow	BoardWalk
50's Prime Time Cafe	Want to be in a '50s sitcom?	MGM
Flying Fish Cafe	One of WDW's absolute best	BoardWalk
Fulton's Crab House	Offers a variety of elegant seafood dishes	Pleasure Island
The Garden Grill	American dishes and the Disney characters	Epcot
Grand Floridian Cafe	Great variety, pleasant ambience	Grand Floridian
Gulliver's Grill at Garden Grove	Kids will be entertained, but food is basic	Swan
Harry's Safari Bar and Grill	Atmosphere is fun and funky	Dolphin
The Hollywood and Vine "Cafeteria of the Stars"	Large, attractive art deco cafeteria	MGM
The Hollywood Brown Derby	Elegant and lovely	MGM
House of Blues	Cajun and Creole cooking along with blues music	West Side
Juan and Only's Bar and Jail	Food is plentiful and tasty	Dolphin

Service Restaurants

Rating	Price	Priority Seating	Suitability	Details on
★	$$	For large parties	Moderate	Page 330
★★	$$$	Necessary	High	Page 331
★★	$$	Recommended	High	Page 331
★	$	Not accepted	Moderate	Page 331
★★	$$	Recommended	High	Page 332
★★★	$$$	Necessary	Low	Page 333
★★	$$$	Recommended	Low	Page 333
★★	$$	Recommended	High	Page 333
★★	$$	Suggested	Moderate	Page 333
★	$$$	Suggested	Moderate	Page 334
★★	$$$	Recommended	Moderate	Page 334
★★	$	Not offered	Moderate	Page 334
★★★	$$$	Recommended	Moderate	Page 335
★★	$$	Not accepted	High	Page 335
★★	$$	Recommended	Moderate	Page 335

(continued)

Quick Guide to Full-

Restaurant	Description	Location
Kimonos	The mood is hushed, unrushed, and not for kids	Swan
Kona Cafe	Pacific Rim food with a tropical emphasis	Polynesian
Liberty Tree Tavern	Sunday dinner cuisine and the characters in Revolutionary garb	Magic Kingdom
Mama Melrose's Ristorante Italiano	Pizza with a wacky New York ambience	MGM
Marrakesh (Morocco)	Exotic surroundings and belly dancers	Epcot
Maya Grill	Desserts alone worth the trip	Coronado
Narcoossee's	Some of the best fresh seafood in Disney World	Grand Floridian
Nine Dragons (China)	Cuisine representing every region in China	Epcot
Official All-Star Cafe	Loud and fun	Disney's Wide World of Sports
'Ohana	Family-friendly place	Polynesian
L'Originale Alfredo di Roma	Most popular restaurant in the World Showcase	Epcot
Palio	Swank and colorful, but pricey	Swan
Planet Hollywood	Always fun, film clips run constantly	West Side
The Plaza Restaurant	Try the sundaes	Magic Kingdom
Portobello Yacht Club	Northern Italian cuisine	Pleasure Island
Rainforest Cafe	Great fun, but long waits	Animal Kingdom/ Disney Marketplace
Rose and Crown Dining Room (UK)	Pub atmosphere and live entertainment	Epcot

Service Restaurants

Rating	Price	Priority Seating	Suitability	Details on
★★	$$	For large parties	Low	Page 336
★★	$$	Suggested	Moderate	Page 336
★★	$$	Recommended	High	Page 336
★★	$$	Suggested	Moderate	Page 337
★	$$	Suggested	Moderate	Page 337
★★	$$	Recommended	Low	Page 337
★★★	$$$	Recommended	Low	Page 338
★	$$	Suggested	Moderate	Page 338
★★	$$	Not accepted	Moderate	Page 338
★★	$$	Recommended	High	Page 338
★★	$$$	Necessary	Moderate	Page 339
★★	$$$	Recommended	Low	Page 339
★★	$$	Not accepted	High	Page 339
★★	$$	Recommended	High	Page 340
★★	$$$	Recommended	Moderate	Page 340
★★	$$	Not accepted	High	Page 340
★	$$	Recommended	Moderate	Page 340

(continued)

Quick Guide to Full-

Restaurant	Description	Location
San Angel Inn Restaurante (Mexico)	Gorgeous and romantic	Epcot
The SciFi Drive-In	Way campy—you'll eat in cars	MGM
Seasons Dining Room	Menu changes with the seasons	Disney Institute
Spoodles	Mediterranean cuisine, great risotto	BoardWalk
Teppanyaki Dining Room (Japan)	Chefs slice and dice in the best Benihana tradition	Epcot
Tony's Town Square Cafe	Lady and the Tramp theme and generous servings	Magic Kingdom
Victoria and Albert's	The most elegant of all Walt Disney World restaurants	Grand Floridian
Whispering Canyon Cafe	Comfort food, family-style service	Wilderness Lodge
Wolfgang Puck Cafe	Terrific pizzas and sushi	West Side
Yacht Gallery	A fine choice for breakfast	Yacht Club Resort
Yachtsman Steakhouse	One of the premier steak houses in Disney World	Yacht Club Resort

Service Restaurants

Rating	Price	Priority Seating	Suitability	Details on
★★	$$	Recommended	High	Page 341
★★	$$	Recommended	High	Page 341
★★	$$	Recommended	Moderate	Page 341
★★	$$	Recommended	Moderate	Page 342
★★★	$$$	Necessary	High	Page 342
★★	$$	Recommended	High	Page 342
★★★	$$$	Necessary	Low	Page 343
★★	$$	Suggested	High	Page 343
★★	$$$	Only upstairs	Low	Page 343
★★	$$	Suggested	Moderate	Page 344
★★★	$$$	Necessary	Low	Page 344

Restaurant Descriptions

Akershus (Norway)	Epcot	★★ $$
		Moderate

There's a buffet, so you get your food fast and have the chance to see things before you make a selection. But most of the food is apt to be unfamiliar to the kids, and there's a lot of fish, so picky eaters may rebel. A fine spot for hearty eaters because you can load up at the hot and cold buffet tables. Also a good chance to sample a variety of unusual dishes.

Artist Point	Wilderness Lodge	★★★ $$
		Moderate

The most upscale of the Wilderness Lodge eateries, Artist Point offers excellent food in a casual—almost rustic—setting. Best known for the maple-glazed salmon, Artist Point features the cuisine, wines, and artwork of the Pacific Northwest.

Biergarten (Germany)	Epcot	★ $$
		High

There's plenty of room to move about; a rousing, noisy atmosphere; and entertainment in the form of yodelers and an oompah-pah band.

Big River Grille & Brewing Works	BoardWalk	★ $$
		Moderate

This casual restaurant is Disney World's only on-site brew pub. It's a good place to sample four new beers and a couple of spe-

cialty ales, but the food—a variety of chicken, ribs, and salads—is nothing special. Outdoor dining allows you to take in the action of the BoardWalk while you eat.

Bistro de Paris	Epcot	★★★ $$$ Low

Recently reopened, the Bistro is quieter, calmer, and more elegant than its sister, Chefs de France, which is located below it, down on the street. It is also a tad too civilized for kids under 10. Expect classic French cuisine, a wonderful wine selection, and elegantly unrushed service. An added bonus: Request a table by the window at 9 P.M. and you'll see the fireworks of IllumiNations.

Boatwright's Dining Hall	Dixie Landings	★ $$ Moderate

The sit-down restaurant at Dixie Landings specializes in very tame Cajun cooking. The catfish, crawfish, and bouillabaisse are designed to suit mainstream American palates, and the unwalled rooms mean that this place is always noisy. The morning breakfast buffet is a good place to chow down big time before hitting the parks.

Bonfamille's Cafe	Port Orleans Resort	★★ $$ Moderate

Port Orleans also offers a sit-down restaurant, this one far more off the beaten path and sedate. Expect toned-down Creole food such as jambalaya, shrimp Creole, and andouille sausage. Another good choice for a big breakfast.

Bongo's Cuban Cafe	West Side	★	$$
		Moderate	

Created by Gloria Estefan, Bongo's offers an Americanized version of Cuban dishes, a wildly tropical decor, and loud Latin music. Reservations are taken only for parties of 10 or more, so be prepared to put in your name and spend a while exploring the West Side.

California Grill	Contemporary Resort	★★★	$$$
		Moderate	

This Contemporary Resort restaurant is very popular. One clue to the quality: Disney executives lunch here. Not only does the California Grill offer a marvelous variety of cuisine, with stylish preparation, but the views from the top of the Contemporary are also unparalleled, especially during the Magic Kingdom fireworks. Excellent wine selection.

Cape May Cafe	Beach Club Resort	★★	$$
		High	

A bright and airy eatery in the heart of the Beach Club, Cape May Cafe has an excellent seafood buffet at dinner, featuring shrimp, scallops, clams, fish, and a couple of landlubber choices like ribs. The breakfast buffet, during which the characters circulate among the diners dressed in adorable old-fashioned bathing attire, is very popular.

Captain's Tavern	Caribbean Beach Resort	★★	$
		Moderate	

The only full-service dining room in the Caribbean Beach Resort, the Tavern provides a variety of seafood, chicken, and

steaks. Nothing too noteworthy, either in terms of the menu or setting—which is so dark that I once literally walked into a wall.

Le Cellier (Canada)	Epcot	★★ $$ Low

Nothing much going on here in terms of entertainment or setting, but the steaks and salmon are tasty. Exotic choices like buffalo or venison are also on the menu, and the desserts are as big as the prairies of Alberta.

Chefs de France (France)	Epcot	★★★ $$$ Moderate

Older kids might be wowed by the atmosphere and the chance to order a croquette de boeuf en brioche—surely the classiest hamburger they'll ever wolf down. A great view of all the World Showcase action.

Chef Mickey's	Contemporary Resort	★★ $$ High

The Contemporary Resort is a fun setting for a character breakfast as Mickey and crew wander among the diners and the monorail whisks by overhead. The evening buffet features pasta, shrimp, prime rib, and a variety of salads and vegetables.

Cinderella's Royal Table	Magic Kingdom	★★ $$$ High

Located in Cinderella Castle in Fantasyland and nestled high amid the spires of the castle, this restaurant is the most glamorous in the Magic Kingdom. Prime rib is one of the specialties and the food, even at lunch, is whimsically presented.

Cinderella appears downstairs throughout the day to greet diners and pose for pictures. (Ask what times she is scheduled before you make your reservation.)

The "Once Upon a Time" character breakfast, featuring the Cinderella gang (and sometimes other "princess" characters such as Snow White or Belle), is $15 for adults, $8 for kids 3 to 11. Priority seating is necessary.

Citricos	**Grand Floridian Resort**	★★★ $$$ Low

Set to become—along with the California Grill and Flying Fish Cafe—the third star in Disney's crown of fine dining, Citricos offers southern French cuisine in the Grand Floridian. Citricos is known for its outstanding wine list—up to 20 selections are available by the glass, and manager John Blazon recommends a specific wine to be paired with each appetizer and entrée on the menu. A real treat for a parents' night out!

Concourse Steakhouse	**Contemporary Resort**	★★ $$$ Low

Located in the cavernous lobby of the Contemporary Resort, the Steakhouse offers all the beef you'd expect, as well as chicken, shrimp, salmon, and pasta. An okay spot if the kids are along because the place is already a bit noisy but hardly your most romantic choice for a parents' night out.

Coral Cafe	**Dolphin Resort**	★ $$ Moderate

This place has always mystified me: It offers sophisticated-bordering-on-frou-frou food, but it's located smack in the middle

of the Dolphin Resort lobby with everything from convention-attending businessmen to families in dripping bathing suits parading by your table. If you want a special meal for an adult evening, there are far better choices nearby at the Board-Walk or Epcot's World Showcase.

The Coral Reef	**Epcot**	★★	$$$
		High	

One whole wall is glass, giving diners an unparalleled view of the Living Seas tank. Ask for a lower level for the best view. The Dover sole is outstanding.

Crystal Palace	**Magic Kingdom**	★★	$$
		High	

Located between Main Street and Adventureland, the Crystal Palace buffets offer a wide variety of food—even that most elusive of all Magic Kingdom foods: vegetables. The characters from Winnie the Pooh visit guests as they dine.

The Crystal Palace is especially crowded from noon to 2 P.M., so you should aim to go in midafternoon. Priority seating is suggested but not always necessary if you're eating at a really off time, like 4 P.M.

ESPN Club	**BoardWalk**	★	$
		Moderate	

Anchoring one end of the BoardWalk, the ESPN Club is better known for its TVs, which simultaneously broadcast every sporting event you can imagine, than for its food. The Bloody Mary chili is my personal favorite, but the selections include buffalo wings, burgers, nachos, and beer. There's an arcade

next door to entertain the kids. It can get packed on weekends when the big games are broadcast.

50's Prime Time Cafe	MGM	★★
		High	**$$**

With its kitsch decor and ditsy waitresses dressed like June Cleaver, this restaurant is almost an attraction in itself. Meat-loaf, macaroni, milkshakes, and other comfort foods are served in a 1950s-style kitchen while dozens of TVs blare clips from classic sitcoms in the background.

"Hi, kids," says your waitress, pulling up a chair to the Formica-topped table. "You didn't leave your bikes in the driveway, did you? Let me see those hands." Assuming that you pass her clean-fingernails inspection, "Mom" will go on to advise you on your food choices. "I'll bring peas with that. Vegetables are good for you."

The camp is lost on young kids, who nonetheless love the no-frills food and the fact that "Mom" brings around crayons and coloring books and then hangs their artwork on the front of a refrigerator with magnets. But it's baby-boomer parents, who were raised on the sitcoms the restaurant spoofs, who really adore the place. The tacky Tune-In Lounge next door is decorated in exact replicas of the furniture my parents had in their den 40 years ago. Much of MGM is dedicated to nostalgia, but this is nostalgia on a small and extremely enjoyable scale. You can fill up at lunch or dinner for about $10 per person, and the s'mores—so huge that they cover the pink Fiestaware plate—can be split by the whole family for dessert. (The dessert menu is on a Viewmaster!) Priority seating is advised.

Flying Fish Cafe	BoardWalk	★★★ $$$ Low

This is my favorite restaurant on Disney property. The zany, art-deco decor is by Martin Dorf, who also designed the California Grill and Citricos, and the menu changes weekly. The risottos are wonderful, and all the fish dishes excellent, especially the potato-wrapped snapper served with leeks and a cabernet sauvignon reduction. The steaks, charred in herbs on the outside, juicy and tender on the inside, are phenomenal too. And don't even get me going on the chocolate lava cake.

Fulton's Crab House	Pleasure Island	★★ $$$ Low

Located on the moored Empress Lilly Riverboat, Fulton's offers a variety of elegant seafood dishes.

The Garden Grill	Epcot	★★ $$ High

Easily recognizable American dishes, served family style, with some of the food grown in the greenhouses downstairs. The booths are large, which lets you stretch out, and the restaurant rotates, allowing diners to observe scenes from the Living with the Land pavilion's boat ride below. Best of all, the characters, dressed in gingham and dungarees, circulate among the diners.

Grand Floridian Cafe	Grand Floridian	★★ $$ High

The focus of the menu is southern, from the fried chicken and mashed potatoes to the fried catfish. If you'd like a good solid

meal of traditional favorites, simply served, with a pretty view of the Grand Floridian grounds, the cafe is for you. Another good choice for a hearty breakfast.

| *Gulliver's Grill at Garden Grove* | Swan Resort | ★ | $$$ |
| | | **Moderate** | |

Kids will be entertained by the colorful junglelike decor at this restaurant located in the Swan Resort, but the food, alas, is anything but exotic. The menu features your basic steaks and fish, while lunch is mostly sandwiches and salads. If you like this sort of atmosphere, you'll find more critters and better prices at the Rainforest Cafe.

| *Harry's Safari Bar and Grill* | Dolphin Resort | ★★ | $$$ |
| | | **Moderate** | |

Okay, more wildlife, this time at the Dolphin. The atmosphere is fun and funky, with stuffed animals and fake foliage galore. Expensive even for a Disney World restaurant—they must figure all the conventioneers are on expense accounts—Harry's offers the standard fish and beef entrées as well as some unusual dishes such as alligator, boar, and kangaroo. For kids just coming from the parks, the thought of chowing down on Pumbaa and Kanga may be a bit too much.

| *The Hollywood and Vine "Cafeteria of the Stars"* | MGM | ★★ | $ |
| | | **Moderate** | |

This large, attractive art deco cafeteria offers a wide variety of salads and desserts as well as an outstanding rotisserie chicken. The line moves fast, and it's nice to see what you're getting.

Character breakfasts are currently being held in the cafeteria, and you will need priority seating for those.

The Hollywood Brown Derby	MGM	★★★ $$$ Moderate

Signature Cobb salad as well as veal, pasta, and fresh seafood are served at the Derby, where, not surprisingly, caricatures of movie stars line the walls. What may surprise you is the quality of the food, as the Derby has recently taken on a new chef, who has made some creative additions. The restaurant itself is elegant and lovely—like stepping back to Hollywood in its heyday, complete with Cole Porter music being played on a grand piano. Lunch for an adult will run about $12, dinner $18. Priority seating is advised.

House of Blues	West Side	★★ $$ High

Dan Aykroyd's House of Blues serves up Cajun and Creole cooking along with some jazz, country, rock 'n' roll, and, yes, blues music. The Gospel Brunch, which offers plenty of food and an absolutely uplifting atmosphere, runs from 10:30 A.M. to 1 P.M. on Sundays and is an especially good choice for families. The price is $29.68 for adults, $15.90 for kids 4 to 12; tickets can be purchased by calling 407-934-2583 or 407-934-BLUE.

Juan and Only's Bar and Jail	Dolphin Resort	★★ $$ Moderate

Another Dolphin Resort restaurant, another funky decor—this one designed to invoke a Mexican jail. (Somehow I suspect

they're not really this clean or friendly.) Although the Tex-Mex is predictably tame, the food is plentiful and tasty, and the sampler platter is a good way to try a bit of everything.

Kimonos	Swan Resort	★★ $$ Low

If you love sushi and sashimi, you'll adore the austerely elegant Kimono's in the Swan Resort. The servings are fresh, delicious, and beautifully presented. The mood is hushed, unrushed, and not for kids.

Kona Cafe	Polynesian Resort	★★ $$ Moderate

Newly opened in the Polynesian Resort, the Kona Cafe offers Pacific Rim food with a tropical emphasis. The fish dishes are especially good, and the desserts are a feast for the eyes and the palate. The banana-stuffed French toast served at breakfast makes parental eyes glaze over with sheer sugary sweetness, but kids love it, and indeed it's one of the most famous breakfasts in all of Disney World.

Liberty Tree Tavern	Magic Kingdom	★★ $$ High

Located in Liberty Square and decorated in a style reminiscent of Colonial Williamsburg, the Tavern serves salads, sandwiches, and clam chowder at lunch. The evening menu offers classic American cuisine—a sort of "dinner at Grandma's" with turkey and dressing, pot roast, and mashed potatoes. An evening character dinner, featuring the characters in Revolu-

tionary War-era garb, is $20 for adults, $11 for kids 3 to 10. Priority seating is suggested.

Mama Melrose's Ristorante Italiano	MGM	★★ $$ Moderate

This restaurant is tucked away near the MuppetVision 4-D plaza and serves "gourmet" brick-oven pizza and a wide variety of tasty pasta dishes. Expect a rather wacky New York ambience—sometimes Mama herself turns up to inspect the premises—and fairly quick service. The pizzas are a reasonably cheap alternative for lunch; if everyone wants pasta, expect to pay about $10 a head. Occasional specials allow kids to eat free. Priority seating is advised.

Marrakesh (Morocco)	Epcot	★ $$ Moderate

This restaurant offers exotic surroundings, and kids enjoy the belly dancers. The unfamiliarity of the food may pose a problem, but the children's portions are not as spicy as those served to the adults, so if the kids can be persuaded to give it a try, they'll find that roasted chicken tastes pretty much the same the world over.

Maya Grill	Coronado	★★ $$ Low

It's worth a trip to the Coronado Springs Resort just to try the desserts. The entrées are "New World"-influenced, a fusion of Caribbean, Mexican, and Central American cuisines with an emphasis on grilled meats. But the dessert presentation, in

which full-size samples of every offering are brought to your table, will win you over no matter how full you are.

Narcoossee's	**Grand Floridian**	**★★★ $$$** **Low**

Situated in the white octagonal building on the water at the Grand Floridian, Narcoossee's offers some of the best fresh seafood at Disney World as well as one of the prettiest views. Try it at night and you can watch the Magic Kingdom fireworks as you dine.

Nine Dragons ***(China)***	**Epcot**	**★ $$** **Moderate**

There isn't much entertainment going on, but the staff is quite happy to accommodate special requests such as "Can you hold the sweet and sour sauce on the sweet and sour chicken?" You'll find food from every region of China.

Official All-Star ***Cafe***	**Disney's Wide** **World of Sports**	**★★ $$** **Moderate**

This sports bar is the only full-service restaurant at Disney's Wide World of Sports complex. There's lots of sports memorabilia on the walls, as well as TVs blaring sporting events. The mood is loud and raucous, like that of a Planet Hollywood or Hard Rock Cafe, but the food isn't quite up to snuff. Expect pizza, sandwiches, pasta, and burgers.

'Ohana	**Polynesian Resort**	**★★ $$** **High**

A fun family-friendly place in the Polynesian, 'Ohana specializes in skewered meats, tropical fruits and vegetables, and

teriyaki and citrus-based sauces. The food is prepared before your eyes in a large open pit, and there is always some sort of activity, such as hula dancing lessons or limbo contests, to keep kids entertained.

L'Originale Alfredo di Roma	Epcot	★★ $$$ Moderate

The Alfredo in question is the gentleman who created fettuccine Alfredo. This is the most popular restaurant in the World Showcase, usually the first to book up despite the fact that it seats 250 people. Most children like Italian food, but the restaurant is very crowded and service is slow.

Palio	Swan Resort	★★ $$$ Low

The Swan Resort is home to this swank and colorful Italian trattoria. The veal dishes are outstanding, but some families surveyed thought the place was a bit pricey.

Planet Hollywood	West Side	★★ $$ High

Although not new, Planet Hollywood is always fun. The giant blue globe parked right beside Pleasure Island holds props from a variety of movies, the bus from the movie *Speed* hovers overhead, and even the menus—printed with high school graduation pictures of stars—are entertaining. Film clips run constantly on giant screens, and the whole atmosphere is heady, loud, and cheerful. No reservations are taken, and the place can get packed at mealtime; 90-minute waits are not uncommon at 6 P.M.

The Plaza Restaurant	Magic Kingdom	★★ High	$$

The Plaza's sandwiches, burgers, and salads are very filling. Try the milkshakes or the staggeringly large sundaes, which are trotted over from the Sealtest Ice Cream Parlor next door. The Plaza is moderately priced and open for lunch and dinner. Priority seating is advised.

Portobello Yacht Club	Pleasure Island	★★ Moderate	$$$

Northern Italian cuisine, including veal, pasta, grilled chicken, and wonderful appetizers. The patio is especially nice in the spring.

Rainforest Cafe	Animal Kingdom/ Disney Marketplace	★★ High	$$

The Rainforest Cafe is great fun because birds and fish (real) and rhinos and giraffes (fake) surround your table while you eat. Check out the incredible barstools with their parrot and zebra legs. Long waits are standard at the Rainforest Cafe, but you can always put your name in and then shop for a while until you're called.

Rose and Crown Dining Room (UK)	Epcot	★ Moderate	$$

This restaurant has a pub atmosphere with live entertainment, charming service, and mediocre food. If you eat outside, you can watch the FriendShips go by on the lagoon.

San Angel Inn Restaurante (Mexico)	Epcot	★★ High	$$

A beautiful location inside the Mayan pyramid of the Mexico pavilion with the Rio del Tiempo murmuring in the background. The service is swift and friendly, and kids can browse among the market stalls of the Mexican pavilion or ride El Rio del Tiempo while waiting for the food. One of the best bets in Epcot.

The SciFi Drive-In	MGM	★★ High	$$

At least as campy as the 50's Prime Time Cafe, the SciFi seats diners in vintage cars while incredibly hokey movie clips run on a giant screen and carhops whiz by on roller skates. Standard drive-in fare such as milkshakes and popcorn is on the menu, but more elaborate dinners such as seafood salads and mesquite chicken are also offered. Kids adore the setting and give the SciFi high marks.

Dark and relatively quiet, even at high noon, the SciFi is a good place to refresh and regroup after a morning of vigorous touring. Adults should expect to pay about $10 for lunch or $15 for dinner, and, once again, portions are enormous. Priority seating is advised.

Seasons Dining Room	Disney Institute	★★ Moderate	$$

Seasons, in the Disney Institute, features innovative cuisine with an emphasis on fresh Florida ingredients. The menu completely changes four times a year to reflect the best that

area farmers and fishermen have to offer, and the vegetable dishes are especially inspired. The restaurant is in four sections, each decorated to honor one of the four seasons.

Spoodles	**BoardWalk**	★★	$$
		Moderate	

The cuisine at this lively and bustling BoardWalk restaurant is Mediterranean, featuring everything from pasta to tapas to couscous. It's fun to try the sampler platters, which give you a chance to have just a taste of an unfamiliar dish, and Spoodles encourages diners to split entrées, so you often end up dining more or less family style. I like the risotto. Excellent variety, upbeat service, and a favorite of many of our readers.

Teppanyaki Dining Room (Japan)	**Epcot**	★★★	$$$
		High	

Located in the Japanese pavilion of Epcot's World Showcase, Teppanyaki offers teppan dining at large tables where the chefs slice and dice in the best Benihana tradition. Kids enjoy the presentation, which the chefs often jazz up a bit in their honor, and sometimes ladies circulate among the diners demonstrating origami folding as well.

Tony's Town Square Restaurant	**Magic Kingdom**	★★	$$
		High	

Located in the Main Street Hub, this thoroughly enjoyable restaurant is dedicated to Lady and the Tramp, with scenes from the popular film dotting the walls and a statue of the canine romantics in the center. The cuisine, like that of the cafe where the Tramp wooed Lady, is classic Italian, and the por-

tions are generous. Tony's is a good choice for breakfast because, along with the other Main Street eateries, it begins serving before the park officially opens.

The kiddie menus, which feature pictures of Lady and the Tramp to color, are handed out with crayons, and the wait at Tony's is rarely long, making it a good choice for families with toddlers in tow. Tony's is moderately priced (although still expensive for Italian food) and open for breakfast, lunch, and dinner. Priority seating is advised.

Victoria and Albert's	Grand Floridian	★★★ $$$ Low

Extraordinarily elegant cuisine and presentation—with special attention to details such as personalized menus and roses for the ladies. The ultimate spot for a parents' night out.

Whispering Canyon Cafe	Wilderness Lodge	★★ $$ High

Prepare to saddle up and ride stick ponies to your table at this family-style eatery in the Wilderness Lodge. Buckets of chicken, ribs, beef, and veggies are brought straight to your table, with more of an emphasis on quantity than quality. But if you'd like home cooking in a casual atmosphere where the kids can run wild, this is a good bet.

Wolfgang Puck Cafe	West Side	★★ $$$ Low

The Wolfgang Puck Cafe serves terrific pizzas and sushi downstairs. Request the upstairs dining room for tonier adult dining. Priority seating is suggested there, so set up a time on the

evening you've gotten a sitter for the kids and are heading over to Pleasure Island.

Yacht Gallery	Yacht Club Resort	★★ $$ Moderate

Located right off the main drag in the Yacht Club Resort, the Yacht Gallery serves up fish, chicken, and beef in a cheerful nautical-themed room. A fine choice for breakfast, where the buffet offers hearty eaters the chance to load up for a day of touring.

Yachtsman Steakhouse	Yacht Club Resort	★★★ $$$ Low

I'm not sure how a yachtsman got his hands on so much good beef, but this is one of the premier steak houses in Disney World. Offering a full selection of hand-cut steaks and chops, with your choice of sauces, the Yachtsman is expensive and low key, and has the feel of a comfortable private dining room.

Finding Healthful Food

Restaurants that serve meals meeting the low-fat standards set by the American Heart Association are indicated on your map with a red heart. Chefs at most sit-down restaurants are quite willing to adapt recipes, serving sauces on the side and leaving out forbidden ingredients.

Fruit stands can be found on Main Street and in Liberty Square at the Magic Kingdom, near Echo Lake and on Sunset Boulevard in MGM, and between the China and Germany pavilions at Epcot. They make it easier for families on the

move to select grapes or watermelon instead of chips or ice cream and also provide juice instead of the omnipresent theme park soft drink.

Vegetables are harder to find in Disney World than Bugs Bunny T-shirts. Try the Crystal Palace in the Magic Kingdom, the Garden Grill Restaurant at Epcot, and the Hollywood and Vine "Cafeteria of the Stars" at MGM. The 50's Prime Time Cafe is also a good choice for home cooking—and as an added bonus your server will literally force the kids to finish their green beans.

The Disney Cruise Line

The Disney Cruise Line Vacation Package

The number of cruise passengers who are bringing the kids along has risen more than 10 percent in the past two years. A coincidence? Probably not. In the summer of 1998, the Disney Cruise Line's first ship, *Disney Magic,* began sailing from Port Canaveral; a second ship, *Disney Wonder,* joined the fleet in 1999. The full seven-day vacation package combines a stay at Disney World with a three- or four-day cruise. (The longer cruise means a shorter stay in Orlando—your call.) Or, very recently, Disney announced it will begin offering seven-day cruises. See Insider's Secret.

Ports of call include Nassau and Disney's own private island, Castaway Cay. (The only itinerary difference between three- and four-day cruises is that the longer cruise has a full day at sea.) In Nassau, the shopping is great, but Castaway Cay is the real jewel. You can enjoy a whole day of beach activities—youth counselors lead the kids on a "whale excava-

Insider's Secret

Starting in late 2000, Disney will be offering a seven-day Caribbean cruise option. You'll depart Port Canaveral on a Saturday, have Sunday and Monday at sea and then visit St. Maarten, St. Thomas, and St. John. Thursday, you're back at sea and you spend the final full day, Friday, on Disney's private island, Castaway Cay. A great option for families with older kids who can take advantage of the breathtaking snorkeling, especially on St. John—or for those who complained that the shorter cruises didn't give them time to relax and enjoy the ship.

tion," while older kids join their counselors for a special party on the far side of the island and adults recuperate on a white sand beach.

The goal is to make the vacation "seamless" by eliminating all the check-ins, long waits, and innumerable hassles associated with many cruise vacations. You're met at the Orlando airport and transported directly to your resort, where you will find waiting all documentation you need for the entire week. The key to your hotel room will be the key to your stateroom on board ship, and you can use it as a charge card both at Disney World and on the ship.

Disney cruises are perfect for the family who needs a bit of everything in the course of a one-week vacation: time for the adults to relax alone, get a massage, and have a meal without the kids as well as time together as a family. Families whose kids vary in ages are especially sold on the cruises because there are so many kids on board and the age categories in the youth program are very tight, making it equally likely

Helpful Hint

After you've enjoyed three or four days in Disney World, you simply leave your bags in your room and board a comfortable motorcoach for the 90-minute drive to Port Canaveral. When you get to the terminal, no further check-in is needed; simply go directly to your stateroom, and your luggage is delivered within a few hours. The vacation package is designed so that the more relaxing cruise segment follows the rather exhausting theme park segment of the week.

that your 3-year-old and 13-year-old will have each found a friend by the end of the first day. Let's face it—nothing is more relaxing than a vacation where everyone is happy.

To order a brochure and video, call 800-511-1333, or contact your travel agent.

Approximate Costs

So, are you willing to pay for this bliss? Calculating the exact cost of your cruise depends on a few key factors—the time of year, the size of your family, and the level of cabin or stateroom you choose. It's probably a little too late to do anything about the size of your family, but the other two factors are within your control. Guests booking a suite on board ship will lodge at the Grand Floridian during the Orlando part of their vacation; families in an ocean-view stateroom with veranda will stay at a deluxe resort like the Polynesian or Beach Club; and if you choose an inside stateroom on the ship, you'll stay at one of the midpriced resorts like Dixie Landings or Port Orleans while in Orlando.

Money-Saving Tip

As for time of year, off-season savings are not as great as you might imagine; late August to mid-December is value season, when rates are about 10 percent cheaper. Spring and summer are the regular season; the holiday weeks around Christmas and Easter are slightly more expensive.

All the staterooms on board are new and nice, designed for families and therefore 25 percent larger than standard cruise ship cabins—so it's really just a matter of how much space you're willing to pay for and how posh a resort you want in Orlando.

A family of four taking the full seven-day vacation during the summer and staying in a deluxe ocean-view stateroom during their cruise and the BoardWalk during the land segment of the vacation should expect to pay about $6,000. If that same family going that same week is willing to book a regular-sized stateroom and stay at Port Orleans, the price drops to the $5,000 range. Or they could take the three-day cruise for about $3,500.

The price includes round-trip airfare to Orlando, your lodging on board ship, your lodging in Orlando, theme park tick-

Insider's Secret

Disney tries to sell the whole package, so only a few cabins are set aside for the cruise-only option. Call early, or you may be told that only the land-sea package is available.

ets, meals and entertainment on board ship, and transportation between the Orlando airport, your Disney World hotel, and Port Canaveral. In short, most things are included except for your meals during the Orlando segment of the trip and any extras, such as a massage or snorkeling instruction, that you elect to add.

Money-Saving Tip

Early-booking discounts can lower the total cost up to $700 per vacation, but they are available only during periods when booking is slow, and so far there haven't been many weeks like that. Still, it never hurts to try to get an early-booking discount or at least an upgrade to a better stateroom or resort.

Lodging

This is all about location and size. Your cruise brochure contains sketches of all the different cabins, ranging from a standard inside stateroom—which is designed for three people but can sleep four in a pinch—to a two-bedroom suite, which can easily sleep seven people. The majority of the staterooms are in the deluxe ocean-view category, many of them with verandas, and most are about 200 to 250 square feet. (In fact, almost 75 percent of the cabins are outside staterooms, so if you're planning to save a few bucks by booking an inside stateroom, call early.)

Because you're in your cabin so rarely, cruise veterans recommend focusing more on the resort you'll be staying at in Orlando. Once your travel agent has told you which resorts are available in the price category you've selected, turn to Chapter 2 of this book and decide which one is best for you. Then choose the corresponding stateroom on board ship.

Dining

Disney makes this so very special. For starters, you don't dine in the same restaurant every night. "We figured that a family on vacation wouldn't ordinarily eat at the same restaurant three nights in a row," says Amy Foley of the Disney Cruise Line. "So why would a family on a cruise ship want to eat in the same dining room every night?"

Instead, you experience "rotation dining," trying a different onboard restaurant each evening of your cruise. (Your server and tablemates rotate right along with you.) On *Disney Magic* there's Lumiere's, which is decidedly French and the most elegant of the eateries, based on Beauty and the Beast. On the *Wonder* you'll find upscale seafood at Tritons.

On both ships there's Parrot Cay, where the mood and the food are Bahaman and casual, but Animator's Palate is the real show-stopper, an interactive dining experience in which the restaurant transforms into a brilliant palette of color as you dine. As the meal begins, the room is black and white, right down to the framed cartoon sketches on the wall and the servers' somber attire. With each course, color is added—to the artwork, the table settings, and the servers' costumes.

On both the *Magic* and the *Wonder,* adults have a fourth dining option, Palo, an Italian restaurant perched high atop the ship, offering a sweeping view of the ocean. It offers by far the best food on the ship. The excellent wine-tasting classes are held there as well.

Ports of Call

Nassau is your chance to shop, sightsee, or even visit one of the casinos. Older kids might enjoy one of the shore excursions that show you a bit of the island's history and culture or a shore excursion to a Paradise Island beach; kids of any age would love a horse-drawn carriage ride. But in general, frankly, the Nassau stop is to placate the adults on board who miss having a casino.

Helpful Hint

If you don't relish the thought of pushing a stroller through the straw market in search of bargains, relax. The children's programs are still going on back at the ship, so parents have no trouble slipping away a few hours for shopping or a show.

The second port of call is Castaway Cay, a private island where you disembark at the pier (cutting out the time-consuming tendering process often required when a large ship stops at a small island) and stroll onto a pristine beach. Once there, you can rent sailboats or sea kayaks, snorkel, bike, play volleyball, or simply sun yourself. Lunch is cooked right on the island, a party band plays all day, and, in case you left your sunscreen back in the cabin, you can even shop. Castaway Cay is primitive in the same sense that Gilligan's Island was—in other words, not very.

The children's program leads youngsters on scavenger hunts, whale excavations, and sand-castle-building contests; older kids are allowed to explore the whole island under the watchful care of the counselors. Adults can go to the mile-long quiet beach, sip a piña colada, or have an open-air massage in a private cabana. The setup is perfect for families, allowing a mix of time together and time apart.

Kids' Programs

Disney's Oceaneer Club for kids 3 to 8 covers almost an entire deck of the ship, a welcome change from the cramped and depressing quarters many cruise lines designate for youth programs. The Disney characters are often on hand, and the well-trained, unbelievably upbeat counselors lead the youngsters in games, crafts, parties, and costumed plays.

Kids 9 to 12 hang out in Disney's Oceaneer Lab, which has computers, electronic games played on giant video walls, and plenty of games and contests to get the preteen crowd interacting with one another. Teens have their own space, called Common Grounds, designed to resemble a coffee bar.

Helpful Hint
In-room sitting can be arranged if parents of younger kids want to have a late night out without worrying.

Activities run all day long and into the evening, so you can pretty much drop off and pick up the kids whenever you want.

When families first board the ship, counselors meet with parents to explain the program and help kids ease in. Parents are given a pager so that they can be reached at any time.

There are three pools on board: one, shaped like Mickey, with a pint-sized tube slide for little kids; a second "sports pool" for games and the rowdier activities of older children; and a third "quiet pool" for adults.

OnBoard Entertainment

The cornerstone of onboard entertainment is the 975-seat Walt Disney Theater, one of the most technologically advanced

Helpful Hint
Children, already overwhelmed by the size and newness of the ship, sometimes suffer a bit of separation anxiety at the first drop-off. Try to persuade them to join in the first evening, when everyone is new and fast friendships are made. The counselors are trained to look for the shy or nervous children and help them make a smooth transition into the group activities.

theaters in the world and certainly the most remarkable facility of its kind on any cruise ship. Here Disney showcases three distinct Broadway-style shows, some of them new and some based on Disney classics. These are must-see productions, especially Disney Dreams, which is shown on the final evening.

Studio Sea, a family lounge, provides dance music, family-oriented cabaret acts, and participatory game shows starring the audience. The Mickey Mania trivia game is a real blast. At the top of the ship, check out the ESPN skybox, where sports fans are surrounded by multiple screens broadcasting sports events from around the world. The Buena Vista Theater shows a variety of Disney movies daily.

Adults can congregate in the entertainment districts, dubbed Beat Street on the *Magic* and Route 66 on the *Wonder*. Expect a comedy club with an improv troupe, a dance club that alternates between rock and country & western music, and a sophisticated piano bar.

To learn more about the Disney Cruise Line, check out prices, or book a vacation, visit www.disneycruise.com on the Web, or call 407-566-7000.

CHAPTER

13

Disney
After Dark

Disney World After Dark with the Kids

Is there life in Disney World after 8 P.M.? Sure there is. The crowds thin, the temperature drops, and many attractions are especially dazzling in the dark. Orlando is a town that naps but never sleeps, where miniature golf courses and McDonald's stay open all night. During peak seasons the major theme parks even stay open until midnight, so it's easy to have fun at night. But, needless to say, the particular kind of fun you'll have depends on whether the kids are with you.

Evening Activities for the Whole Family

The Evening Parade in the Magic Kingdom

The Main Street Electrical Parade is the current incarnation of Disney's ever-popular evening parade, and it blends lasers, lights, and fireworks for a dazzling display. The parade runs only on selected evenings during the off-season but every night during the on-season. In the busiest weeks there are two showings: the 11 P.M. parade is rarely as crowded as the 9 P.M. one.

Insider's Secret

The evening light parade is a don't-miss. If you're visiting during the off-season, plan your schedule to ensure you'll be in the Magic Kingdom on one of the evenings it's slated to run.

Fantasmic!

Likewise, this evening show at MGM is a must-see.

IllumiNations at Epcot

IllumiNations can be viewed from anywhere around the World Showcase Lagoon at Epcot closing time. With fireworks, laser lights, stirring music, and choreographed fountains spurting in three-quarter time, IllumiNations is a definite must-see.

The Electrical Water Pageant

If you're staying on-site, the Electrical Water Pageant may actually float by your hotel window because it is staged on the Seven Seas Lagoon, which connects the Polynesian, Contemporary, Grand Floridian, and Wilderness Lodge resorts. Times do vary with the season, but generally the Pageant is visible at 9 P.M. at the Polynesian, 9:20 from the Grand Floridian, 9:45 from Wilderness Lodge, and 10:05 from the Contemporary. (Call Guest Relations at your hotel for exact show times.)

If you're not staying on-site, simply ride the monorail to the resort of your choice. The Electrical Water Pageant plays every night, even during off-season. Although it's much shorter and less elaborate show than SpectroMagic or Fantasmic!, nothing can beat the effect of multicolored lights twinkling on darkened water.

Movies

If you're staying on-site, check out the offerings in the theater of the Contemporary Resort. Two different Disney classics show each night at 7 and 9 P.M. Movies are also shown at the evening campfire at Fort Wilderness (with Chip 'n' Dale in attendance), and in many Orlando hotels the Disney Channel is available 24 hours a day. For first-run movies, head to the 24-screen theater at Downtown Disney West Side.

Helpful Hint
The 24-screen theater adjacent to Downtown Disney West Side is a good place to park older kids and teens while parents try out the clubs.

Arcades

It's no secret that kids flip for arcades and all on-site hotels and most off-site ones have them. The most state-of-the-art games are at DisneyQuest in Downtown Disney.

Downtown Disney

The Marketplace and Pleasure Island stores stay open past the park closing times. Some families wait to shop until late at night, and the restaurants here serve food past 10 P.M. as well.

Fireworks

A rousing fireworks display can be seen from anywhere in the Magic Kingdom at about 10 P.M. in the on-season. The show is short but exciting, and at holiday times a more extensive fireworks extravaganza is presented. (Be there a few minutes earlier to witness Tinkerbell's Flight.)

The Rides at Night

At Epcot it is almost always easy to tour Journey into Your Imagination and see *Honey, I Shrunk the Audience* during the dinner hour, when everyone heads out to dine in the World Showcase. Even Test Track lines are a bit better.

In the Magic Kingdom, the Big Thunder Mountain Railroad is much more fun in the dark; Splash Mountain feels like a totally different ride, and Cinderella's Golden Carrousel is especially magical at night.

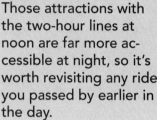

Helpful Hint
Those attractions with the two-hour lines at noon are far more accessible at night, so it's worth revisiting any ride you passed by earlier in the day.

Likewise, at MGM, you can slip onto the Twilight Zone Tower of Terror or the Rock 'n' Roller Coaster while people troop toward Fantasmic!

Night Swimming

Blizzard Beach, Typhoon Lagoon, and River Country all run extended hours in the summer, and the crowds are far thinner after 5 P.M. It stays hot in Orlando well into a summer evening, and, because you don't have to worry about heat exhaustion or sunburn, many families with young kids actually prefer evening swimming. Hotel pools stay open very late as well, some until after midnight.

Miniature Golf

Nighttime is the best time to check out Fantasia Gardens or Winter Summerland.

BoardWalk

Lively and gorgeous at night, the BoardWalk is a hub of family-style activity. After dinner you can rent a surrey bike, try the midway games, or have your face painted or your hair wrapped.

Disney World After Dark
Without the Kids: Finding a Sitter

Why would any decent parent seek a sitter while on a family vacation? Consider this scenario: Meaghan's sucking the inside of her mouth. Loud. Mom keeps making everyone stop while she readjusts the strap of her shoe to accommodate the blister she picked up halfway around the World Showcase Lagoon. You spent $168 to get through the Magic Kingdom gates—and Devin spends the entire afternoon feeding quarters into the same arcade game that's in the local mall back home. Dad has been singing the first line—and only the first line—of "Zip-A-Dee-Doo-Dah" since Thursday. You've asked to see the kiddie menus from nine different restaurants in nine different Epcot countries, and you end up at the American pavilion fast-food joint because Kristy won't eat anything but a hot dog. It's 108 degrees, this trip is costing $108 an hour, and that infernal sucking sound is getting on your last nerve. In short, you have third-day-itis—and it's only the second day of your trip.

Some of the hotels in Orlando have responded with programs designed to get the kids involved with other kids so that parents can have some peace and privacy. Kristy can eat her

Helpful Hint
Although it may seem un-American or even sacrilegious to suggest building time apart into the middle of a family vacation, the truth is that everyone will have more fun if you occasionally break up the group for a while. Even the most devoted of families aren't accustomed to being together 24 hours a day—for every meal, every ride, every potty stop. Every minute.

hot dog, Meaghan can give herself hickeys, and Devin can play Cosmic Invaders 77 straight times without parental glares. The adults can dare to order a meal that will take three hours to enjoy and linger over their coffee. Everyone returns refreshed and recharged, with some happy stories to tell, and you can start the next day actually glad to be together again.

If you decide to schedule a parents' night out during your trip, you'll soon learn that Orlando offers an array of child-care options. Several of the on-site hotels have full-fledged kids' clubs, and where else on earth can your child be bedded down by a real-life Mary Poppins? Among the off-site hotels, there is a large range in cost and quality among the child-care programs; many of the off-site programs are free to hotel guests (at least during certain hours), which can mean big savings for parents.

In-Room Sitters

You'll need to arrange for an in-room sitter if any of the following conditions apply:

> **Insider's Secret**
> The key point is to make your plans before you leave home, either by selecting a hotel that has a kids' club or by arranging for an in-room sitter. If you suddenly get an urge for fine dining at 4 P.M. on a Saturday in July, it will be hard to find a sitter. But if you've checked out your options in advance, it's a breeze.

e You have a child under the age of 4. Very few of the organized kids' clubs will accept children younger than 4, and most require that all children be potty-trained. Under Florida law, children must be 3 and potty-trained to participate in a group-care situation without their parents.

◉ You plan to be out after midnight. Most kids' clubs close down at midnight, some as early as 10 P.M. Parents headed for Pleasure Island or Church Street Station, where the action doesn't begin to heat up until 10 P.M., need in-room sitting.

◉ Your kids are exhausted. If you know in advance you plan to employ an all-out touring schedule, or your children fall apart after 8 P.M., hire an in-room sitter who can put them to bed at their usual time. Most of the kids' clubs at least try to put preschoolers down in sleeping bags by 9 P.M., but this can involve moving them, and possibly waking them, when parents return.

◉ You have a big family. Even with the add-on per-child rate, you'll come out cheaper with an in-room sitter than you would trying to book five kids into a program.

If you decide you'll need in-room sitting, begin by contacting your hotel. Many hotels are happy to arrange the sitting for you through a licensed and bonded agency, and this saves a bit of hassle. The person at the Guest Relations desk is also apt to give you a good recommendation on which service to try; if guests aren't pleased with a sitter or a service, the hotel is undoubtedly the first to hear about it.

Want to make your own plans? For those staying on-site, KinderCare provides trained sitters for all the Disney hotels; call 407-827-5444 at least eight hours in advance. The rate is $12 an hour, $13 an hour for two kids, and there's a four-hour minimum.

At least six independent agencies dispatch sitters to the off-site hotels, but the following two agencies have received especially high marks from our readers:

ABC Mothers   407-857-7447
Super Sitters   407-382-2558

These services stay busy during the summer months, so it's not a bad idea to book them before you leave home. Rates are typically about $9 an hour with a four-hour minimum and an extra-child charge of $1 an hour per child. A $7 transportation fee is also common, meaning that in-room sitting for two kids for four hours would run close to $50—not a cheap option, but for many parents it's well worth the cost.

The independent services can be quite inclusive, with service available 24 hours a day, seven days a week. For families willing to pay the extra bucks, sitters will take the kids out to a fast-food place for supper or even to area attractions. One resourceful divorced father took his two daughters along on a business trip to Orlando and, while he sat in meetings, a Super Sitter trotted the girls around the theme parks.

On-Site Kids' Clubs

The following on-site hotels have kids' clubs (all are area code 407):

BoardWalk	939-5100	Polynesian	824-2000
Contemporary	824-1000	Wilderness Lodge	824-3200
Dolphin	934-4000	Yacht and Beach Clubs	934-8000
Grand Floridian	824-3000		

The clubs generally run in the evening for kids 4 to 12, and the clubhouses are well stocked with Disney-themed toys—as well as computers, video and arcade games, and large-screen TVs. The cost is $4 an hour, and reservations are required. (Not much advance notice is needed, but you can make reservations by contacting Guest Services at the appropriate hotel; on-site guests get first crack at the available slots, but if the clubs don't fill up, space is available to off-site visitors.) The clubhouses are open from 4:30 P.M. until midnight, and cookies and milk are served at bedtime. Kids must be toilet-trained—even Mary Poppins has her limits.

The Polynesian offers the most elaborate kids' program, Kanaka Kids (in the Neverland Club), with buffet food and entertainment for the youngsters. Cost is $8 per hour; call 939-3463 to make reservations. This program is so popular with kids that some families have listed the Neverland Club as one of their children's favorite Disney World attractions.

Helpful Hint
Prices, policy, and planned entertainment change quickly at the kids' clubs, so confirm everything when you make your reservations.

Off-Site Kids' Clubs

Several off-site hotels have their own versions of kids' clubs, with wide-screen TVs, Nintendo games, and wading pools to entertain the children while parents do the town. Most of the programs run only at night. Generally, it is not required that you be registered at the hotel to take advantage of the program, although this policy can change during busy seasons, when the programs are filled. The typical cost is $6–8 an hour with a $3 add-on for each additional kid.

An evening of purely adult dining provides a nice break from the typical vacation restaurant experience, where you frantically color pictures of Pluto and juggle sugar packets in an effort to keep the kids entertained until the food arrives. All of the hotels mentioned are equipped to either escort the kids to the resort coffee shop for a simple meal or order room service so the kids can eat while the parents dine out.

Call the following numbers for more information about off-site resorts with kids' clubs:

Delta Orlando	407-351-3340
Embassy Suites	407-239-1144
Hilton at Disney Village	407-827-4000
Holiday Inn Sunspree	407-239-4500
Hyatt Regency Grand Cypress	407-239-1234

Dining Without the Kids

Certain on-site restaurants are more enjoyable without children, so once you've found a sitter, reserve a table for two at one of these establishments.

At Epcot

Bistro De Paris	Romance Factor ♥♥	$$$

Located upstairs from Chefs de France and accessible by a back staircase entrance, the Bistro is a lovely secluded spot with excellent French fare. The wine list is one of the best in Epcot, and you find few kids at the Bistro de Paris, making it the perfect getaway when you need a break and some adult time.

Marrakesh	Romance Factor ♥	$$

Ready to take a walk on the semi-wild side? The music, architecture, and menu in the Moroccan restaurant are truly distinctive, proving beyond a doubt that you aren't in Kansas anymore. You'll be served lamb, couscous, and honeyed chicken by waiters in floor-length robes while belly dancers weave among the tile tables. (The effect of these dancers on husbands is somewhat akin to the effect meeting Mickey has on toddlers: They're

stunned while it's happening but later remember the experience fondly.) The tables are very close together, lots of families bring the kids, and the place can become quite loud.

| *San Angel Inn Restaurante* | Romance Factor ♥ | $$ |

The menu here goes far past the tacos and enchiladas that most Americans consider Mexican food, and the atmosphere is unparalleled. The restaurant overlooks El Rio del Tiempo, the boat ride that encircles a Mayan pyramid beneath a starry sky. The darkness of the Mexico pavilion, which simulates midnight even at high noon, and the murmur of the Rio are hypnotic. Throw in a couple of margaritas and you may never leave.

| *L'Originale Alfredo di Roma Ristorante* | Romance Factor ♥ | $$$ |

The Alfredo in question is the gentleman who created fettuccine Alfredo. The restaurant in itself is entertaining; you can watch the cooks crank out pasta through a large window, the walls are adorned with clever trompe l'oeil murals, and the waiters and waitresses provide impromptu concerts, ranging from mildly bawdy Italian folk songs to Verdi. Most diners have kids along, making the place a little too loud and crowded for romance.

| *The Coral Reef* | Romance Factor ♥ | $$$ |

Tucked away under the Living Seas pavilion, this Future World restaurant is also expensive, about $100 for dinner for two. Unfortunately, the Coral Reef is less romantic than the World Showcase restaurants. The room is simply too large to

feel cozy, and, as at Alfredo's, most families bring their kids, figuring—and rightly so—that little Nathaniel and Erica can stay busy watching the skin divers while Mom and Dad crack a lobster.

Outside Epcot

Victoria and Albert's	Romance Factor ♥♥♥	$$$

For a very special evening, there is one place in Disney World so elegant and so removed from the classic Disney image that you'll never feel sticky fingers creeping over the top of the booth behind you. Kids are never seen at Victoria and Albert's in the Grand Floridian, where harp music plays, candles flicker, and ties and jackets are required for men.

Where Disney has built a reputation on providing pleasure to the masses, this 50-seat restaurant proves there is also room in Disney World for highly individualized service. When Henry Flagler built the railroad that opened Florida to the oil magnates of the late 1800s, Queen Victoria and Prince Albert sat on the British throne. Now, in one of those "only Disney would go to such trouble" details, all hosts and hostesses in the restaurant call themselves Victoria or Albert.

Your menu will have your own name handwritten on the top; waiters describe the selections for the evening, and the chef often circulates among the tables. At the end of a six-course meal, ladies are presented with long-stemmed roses and their menus. This is the most expensive restaurant in Disney World, hands down—the prix fixe dinner is currently $80 per person, $120 with wine—but it's so special that you'll be talking about it for years afterward. On the evening we visited, the salad was a floral arrangement in a crouton vase—until Victoria tapped the

side of the crouton, releasing the greens into a fan-shaped pattern on the plate; and the coffee service was more elaborate than a Japanese tea ceremony.

The California Grill Romance Factor ♥♥ $$$

Not only does the California Grill offer a marvelous variety of cuisine, with stylish preparation, but, in addition, the views from the top of the Contemporary are unparalleled, especially during the Magic Kingdom fireworks.

Citricos Romance Factor ♥♥ $$$

Located in the Grand Floridian, Citricos is one of Disney's fine restaurants, featuring southern French cuisine and an unparalleled wine selection, many available by the glass. The appetizers are outstanding and the sampler platter gives you the chance to try more than one.

Flying Fish Café Romance Factor ♥♥ $$$

Located on the BoardWalk, the Flying Fish is widely considered to be one of the best restaurants in the entire Disney World complex. Signature dishes include snapper wrapped in a potato crust and yellowfin tuna, but the steaks are outstanding too. Decorated in the same style as its sister restaurant, the California Grill, the Flying Fish is bustling and crowded, with the tables quite close together. Priority seating is a must, but eating at the bar is also a good option since you can watch the chefs as they work.

Maya Grill Romance Factor ♥♥ $$

Serving "New World cuisine" in the Coronado Springs Resort, the Maya Grill is noteworthy for its dessert presentation. Instead of bringing you a dessert tray, servers bring full-sized portions of the evening's desserts—all unspeakably elaborate and beautifully presented—and arrange them in a semicircle around you while they describe each. Anyone who can stoically deny themselves a bit of chocolate and raspberries after this show is a stronger person than I am.

Wolfgang Puck's Cafe Romance Factor ♥♥ $$$

This Downtown Disney establishment is three restaurants in one; the upstairs restaurant is by far the most intimate, with innovative cuisine and a strong wine list.

CHAPTER

14

Universal
Orlando

SandLake Road

To Tampa

Islands of Adventure

Adventure Way

Interstate 4

Hollywood Way

Waterw

CityWalk

Universal Boulevard

To Daytona Beach

Universal Orlando

Turkey Lake Road

Universal Studios
Florida

Vineland Road

Hard Rock Hotel

Waterway

Major Boulevard

RKING GARAGES

Portofino Bay Hotel

Kirkman Road

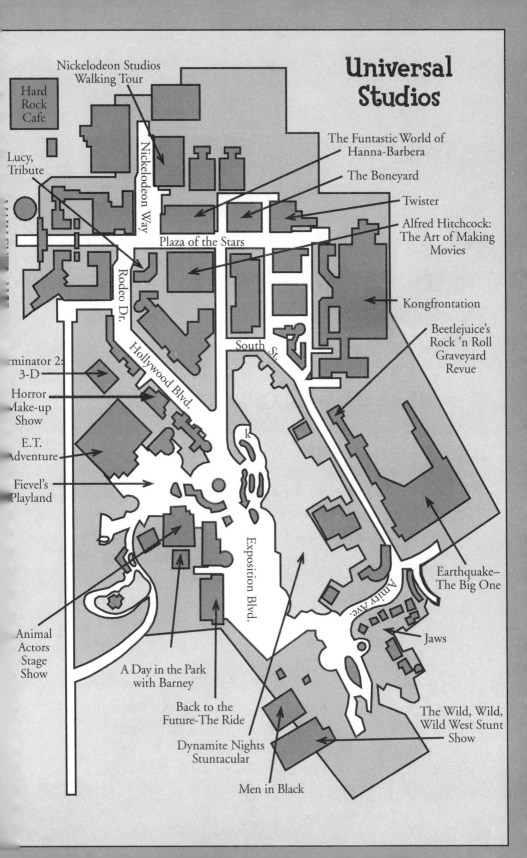

Universal Studios

Hard Rock Cafe

Nickelodeon Studios Walking Tour

Lucy, Tribute

Nickelodeon Way

Plaza of the Stars

The Funtastic World of Hanna-Barbera

The Boneyard

Twister

Alfred Hitchcock: The Art of Making Movies

Kongfrontation

Rodeo Dr.

Hollywood Blvd.

South St.

...minator 2: 3-D

Horror Make-up Show

E.T. Adventure

Fievel's Playland

Beetlejuice's Rock 'n Roll Graveyard Revue

Exposition Blvd.

Amity Ave.

Earthquake– The Big One

Animal Actors Stage Show

A Day in the Park with Barney

Back to the Future-The Ride

Dynamite Nights Stuntacular

Men in Black

Jaws

The Wild, Wild, Wild West Stunt Show

What's Universal Orlando?

Over the past few years Universal Studios in Florida has expanded at an unbelievable rate, buying so much land that the street running through the property has been renamed Universal Boulevard. In 1999 Universal opened Islands of Adventure, a totally new theme park; CityWalk, a dining and entertainment district; and Loews Portofino Bay, a luxury resort, as well as a waterway with boat service connecting all three of the new additions to Universal Studios. A Hard Rock Hotel opens this year. This new complex is called Universal Orlando, and before it is finished it will contain a total of five resorts.

One thing is for sure: Universal is no longer content to be the park you visit on the last day of your vacation, after the bulk of your time and money have gone to Disney. Universal Orlando is poised to be a destination, not an afterthought, aiming to keep guests on-site and entertained for multiday stays.

At present, Universal is offering several ticket options:

Money-Saving Tip

Tickets do not expire, so if you plan to return to Orlando in the future—and your kids won't jump from the child to adult category in the meantime—you may want to purchase the multiday pass.

- 1-day, 1-park Pass: $46 for adult, $37 for child 3 to 9— This allows you admission to either Islands of Adventure or Universal Studios.

- 2-day Escape Pass: $80 for adult, $65 for child 3 to 9— This allows you admission to both Islands of Adventure and Universal Studios.

- 3-day Escape Pass: $100 for adult, $80 for child 3 to 9— This allows you admission to both Islands of Adventure and Universal Studios.

- 5-day Escape Pass: $120 for adult, $96 for child 3 to 9— This allows you admission to both Islands of Adventure and Universal Studios.

In addition Universal offers a Flexpass, which allows you admission into other area attractions:

- 5-park Flexpass: $197 for adult, $158 for child—This allows you admission to Universal Studios, Islands of Adventure, Wet 'n Wild, and Sea World, as well as Busch Gardens Tampa Bay.

- 4-park Flexpass: $160 for adult, $128 for child—This allows you admission to Universal Studios, Islands of Adventure, Wet 'n Wild, and Sea World.

Tips for Your First Hour at Universal Studios

@ The new parking garage is in New Jersey (seems that way, anyhow), so arrive at least 30 minutes before the main gate opens. The cost is $6 a car. (Call 407-363-8000 the day before you plan to visit to confirm hours of operation.) After getting your tickets, you'll wait in a small holding area for about 10 minutes. Hanna-Barbera characters such as Woody Woodpecker and the Flint-stones often circulate among the crowd to pose for pictures and give autographs.

@ Generally guests are allowed through the main turnstiles about 20 minutes before the official opening time. If a show is filming on the day you're visiting, this will be indicated on a sign outside the Studio Audience Center, located to your far right as you enter. The attendant can tell you how to get tickets.

@ After entering the main turnstile, visitors arriving early are allowed partway down Plaza of the Stars and Rodeo Drive, the two major streets in Universal Studios. If you want to see Back to the Future, Jaws, Men in Black, or

Time-Saving Tip

Watching a taping is time-consuming. If your kids are young and will be skipping many of Universal's scary attractions anyway, you'll have the time. But if your children are older and you'll be trying to cram all the big rides into your day, it's unlikely you'll want to devote two hours to viewing a taping.

E.T. Adventure first, go down Rodeo Drive as far as you're allowed. If you'd rather see the Funtastic World of Hanna-Barbera, Kongfrontation, Twister, or Earthquake first, go down Plaza of the Stars until the ropes stop you. Families who haven't had breakfast may have time for a pastry at the Beverly Hills Boulangerie before the ropes drop.

Time-Saving Tip

Once the ropes drop, go directly to the Funtastic World of Hanna-Barbera. Because of its proximity to the main gate, this attraction draws large lines from 10 A.M. on and should be visited early. After you've saved Elroy, try to convince the kids not to linger too long in the interactive play area behind the Hanna-Barbera ride. You can always come back again in midafternoon, but now you need to move on to the other big-name attractions as quickly as possible.

◉ If your kids are old enough, ride Men in Black, Jaws, and Back to the Future in rapid succession. (At this time of day you shouldn't encounter waits longer than 15 minutes.) If your kids aren't up to the high-intensity rides, head toward E.T. Adventure, then the water ride in Fievel's Playland.

◉ If you're touring in the off-season, not all attractions will open at 9 A.M.; some open at 9, some at 10, with shows starting even later. Your touring will be pretty much dictated by which attractions are open.

Universal Studios Touring Tips

- The same basic plan you used in the Disney theme parks will also apply here. You need to visit major attractions—Men in Black, Back to the Future, Twister, E.T. Adventure, Jaws, Earthquake, and the Funtastic World of Hanna-Barbera—early in the morning or in the evening. Take in the theater-style attractions in the afternoon.

- If you miss one of the major continuously loading attractions in the morning, hold off on it until two hours before the park closes. Midday waits of up to 90 minutes are common at popular attractions such as Men in Black or Terminator 2: 3-D, but the crowds ease off a bit during the dinner hour; by the time the crowd has moved to the lake to watch the Dynamite Nights Stuntacular, the lines at major attractions have become much shorter.

- In the off-season Universal usually employs a "staggered opening" system where some attractions begin operating at 9 A.M., others at 10, and still others at 11. This will dictate your touring schedule because you can obviously see only what's open—but it's really no problem because in off-season you rarely encounter morning waits anyway.

- If you plan to see Universal in one day, it's unlikely you'll have time for a midafternoon break such as returning to your hotel or visiting a water park. But the numerous theater-style attractions at Universal offer plenty of chances to rest up and let small kids nap. A lot of shows are scheduled for around noon, and another wave begins around 2 P.M.; ride in the morning and then catch a midday show, have lunch, and see a second show.

❧ Universal clusters most of its kiddie attractions in one section: The Woody Woodpecker Kid Zone, A Day in the Park with Barney, the large play area called Curious George Goes to Town, Fievel's Playland, E.T., and the Animal Actors Stage Show are all located in the same general area of the park. This means if your children are preschoolers you can park the strollers once and then walk from attraction to attraction, letting them play as long as they want.

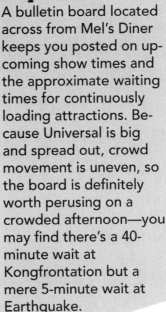

Helpful Hint
A bulletin board located across from Mel's Diner keeps you posted on upcoming show times and the approximate waiting times for continuously loading attractions. Because Universal is big and spread out, crowd movement is uneven, so the board is definitely worth perusing on a crowded afternoon—you may find there's a 40-minute wait at Kongfrontation but a mere 5-minute wait at Earthquake.

❧ The theaters that hold the Horror Makeup Show, Alfred Hitchcock, and Terminator 2: 3-D are high capacity, so even if the lines in midafternoon look discouraging, odds are you'll still be seated. Consult the entertainment schedule that you receive with your ticket or check the posterboard at the attraction entrance for show times, and then put one parent in line about 20 minutes before the show is due to start. The other can take the kids for a drink or bathroom break. If you all opt to wait in line together, be aware that Universal has placed trash cans all through the queue areas of the high-capacity attractions in acknowledgment of the fact that visitors on a tight touring schedule may well be eating or drinking in line.

Insider's Secret

If you plan to see the Dynamite Nights Stuntacular on the lake (which shows at the park closing time), be there at least 20 minutes before show time. Unlike IllumiNations or Fantasmic!, the show is a boat race and subsequent explosion that takes place at water level, so unless you're actually standing lakeside, you won't see much.

@ Headed toward Back to the Future, Men in Black, or another intense attraction? Universal employees are prepared to help families traveling with a baby or toddler do a "baby swap" so that everyone can ride.

@ Universal employs only one height restriction—40 inches on Back to the Future. But just because all kids big enough to sit up are allowed on Jaws or Kongfrontation doesn't mean it's a good idea to take them; consult the ride descriptions for information on the special effects. Other attractions such as E.T. Adventure and the Funtastic World of Hanna-Barbera provide separate sta-

Money-Saving Tip

Try not to let the kids stop to shop in the morning; not only should you keep moving between rides while the park is relatively uncrowded, but in addition the shops are located to encourage the ultimate in impulse buying. Hold off on souvenir purchases until late in the day when you've seen it all.

tionary seating for kids under 40 inches, thus allowing families to go through the attraction as a group.

❧ Almost every major attraction empties out through a shop selling merchandise related to the movie featured; you can buy Jetsons T-shirts after riding Hanna-Barbera, a stuffed shark after riding Jaws, or a Bates hotel shower curtain as you exit Alfred Hitchcock.

The Scare Factor at Universal Studios

The shows and tours are family-oriented and fine for everyone, but some of the big-name attractions are too frightening for preschoolers. The motion simulation rides, especially Back to the Future, induce queasiness in some people. And be aware that in general the rides and shows are very loud. Twister and Terminator can practically jolt the fillings from your teeth.

Universal imposes very few height restrictions and thus gives parents little guidance. Kids under 40 inches are banned

The Universal Studios Don't-Miss List

The Funtastic World of Hanna-Barbera
Kongfrontation
E. T. Adventure
Back to the Future
Jaws
The Animal Actors Stage Show
The Wild West Stunt Show
Fievel's Playland (if you have kids under 10)
Twister
Terminator 2: 3-D
Men in Black

The Universal Studios Worth-Your-While List

Earthquake

Alfred Hitchcock: The Art of Making Movies

The Horror and Makeup Show

Dynamite Nights Stuntacular

The Nickelodeon Tour (If you have kids under 10)

A Day in the Park with Barney
(If you have preschoolers with you)

Fine for Anyone

The Funtastic World of Hanna-Barbera
(if you choose the stationary seats)

E. T. Adventure

Animal Actors Stage Show

Earthquake

Lucy: A Tribute

Wild West Stunt Show

Beetlejuice's Graveyard Revue
(unless the child is afraid of loud noises)

Fievel's Playland, including the water ride

A Day in the Park with Barney

Woody Woodpecker's Kid Zone (but think about the
coaster before you board with really small kids)

from Back to the Future and required to use special seating on E.T. Adventure and the Funtastic World of Hanna-Barbera, but beyond these minimal restrictions, parents are the ones who decide who rides what.

Any child old enough to sit on his own can ride Jaws, Earthquake, and Kongfrontation. Universal seems to set the rules based on how physically wild the ride is—and none of the rides listed bounces you around too much. But they're psychologically scary, and a visit to Kongfrontation or Alfred Hitchcock may lead to more bad dreams than even the wildest of roller coasters. Although individual reactions obviously vary from child to child—my own son has adored Kongfrontation since he was 4—read the ride descriptions and consult the list that follows to help you decide.

Consider Waiting Until Your Kids Are at Least 7 to Try These

Kongfrontation

Back to the Future

Jaws

Alfred Hitchcock: The Art of Making Movies

The Horror Makeup Show

Terminator 2: 3-D

Twister

Men in Black

Favorite Preteen and Teen Attractions at Universal

Most of the visitors 11 to 17 rated Universal as "grosser and wilder" than the Disney-MGM Studios, and in this age-group, that's a compliment.

Attractions Especially Popular with Teens and Preteens

Kongfrontation

Back to the Future

Jaws

Alfred Hitchcock: The Art of Making Movies

The Horror Makeup Show

Terminator 2: 3-D

Twister

Men in Black

Dynamite Nights Stuntacular

Beetlejuice's Graveyard Revue

CityWalk, especially Hard Rock Cafe

Universal Studios Attractions

Men in Black: Alien Attack

Remember the scene in *Men in Black* where Will Smith tries out for the force? Think you could do better?

The Men in Black ride opened in April 2000. The premise is that guests are rookie agents riding through streets of New York armed with laser guns called "alienators." But unlike the tame targets in Disney's Buzz Lightyear, these aliens can strike back, sending your vehicle into an out-of-control spin.

As you shoot at the 120 Audio-Animatronic aliens, the ride keeps track of your individual score and the collective score of the six people in your vehicle. You're not only fighting off aliens, but also competing against the team of rookies in the car beside you. Here's where it gets cute. Depending on how well you and your vehicle mates do, there are alternate endings to the ride. Will you get a hero's welcome in Times Square or a loser's send-off?

Since you're actually in a video game it stands to reason that video game rules apply—that is, the more you play the better you get. Can you spell addictive? Come early if you want to ride more than once.

Scare Factor
The aliens look pretty real, but most kids take it in stride—especially if they've seen the movie and know what to expect.

Back to the Future

Flight-simulation technology makes a quantum leap forward—or is it backward?—in Back to the Future. After being briefed by Doc Brown (played by Christopher Lloyd of the movie series) in a preshow video that bad-boy Biff has sabotaged his time-travel experiments, you'll be loaded into six-passenger DeLoreans.

What follows is a high-speed chase back through the prehistoric era. The cars bounce around pretty violently, but it's the flight-simulation techniques that are the real scream-rippers, far

Quick Guide to

Attraction	Location	Height Requirement
A Day in the Park with Barney	Universal	None
Alfred Hitchcock: The Art of Making Movies	Universal	None
The Animal Actors Stage Show	Universal	None
Back to the Future	Universal	40 inches
Beetlejuice's Graveyard Revue	Universal	None
Earthquake	Universal	None
E.T. Adventure	Universal	None
Fievel's Playland	Universal	None
The Funtastic World of Hanna-Barbera	Universal	None
Men in Black	Universal	None
The Horror Makeup Show	Universal	None
Jaws	Universal	None
Kongfrontation	Universal	None
Lucy, A Tribute	Universal	None
The Nickelodeon Tour	Universal	None
Terminator 2: 3D	Universal	None
Twister	Universal	None
The Wild West Stunt Show	Universal	None
Woody Woodpecker's Kid Zone	Universal	None

Scare Factor

0 = Unlikely to scare any child of any age.
! = Has dark or loud elements; might rattle some toddlers.
!! = A couple of gotcha! moments; should be fine for school-age kids.
!!! = You need to be pretty big and pretty brave to handle this ride.

Universal Attractions

Speed of Line	Duration of Ride/Show	Scare Factor	Age Range
Fast	15 min.	0	All
Fast	40 min.	!!	7 and up
Fast	20 min.	0	All
Moderate	7 min.	!!	7 and up
Fast	20 min.	!	All
Moderate	20 min.	!	5 and up
Slow	5 min.	!	All
Moderate	n/a	0	All
Moderate	10 min.	!	5 and up
Fast	25 min.	!!	7 and up
Fast	5 min.	!!	5 and up
Moderate	7 min.	!!	7 and up
Fast	10 min.	0	All
Slow	45 min.	0	All
Moderate	30 min.	!	7 and up
Slow	15 min.	!!	7 and up
Fast	16 min.	!	All
Moderate	1 min.	0	3 and up
Moderate	6 min.	!!	7 and up

more intense than those provided by Disney's Star Tours or Body Wars. Passengers who can bear to glance away from the screen will notice that as many as 12 DeLoreans, arranged in tiers, take the trip simultaneously, making Back to the Future a sort of ultimate drive-in movie.

The Scare Factor
At one point in your trip through the prehistoric era, you're even swallowed by a dinosaur, making the ride much too much for most kids under 7, although technically anyone taller than 40 inches is allowed to board. If your child wants to try it, brief him or her that the majority of the effects can be erased simply by closing your eyes—and that's not a bad tip to keep in mind yourself if you're prone to queasiness.

Earthquake
After a preshow hosted by Charlton Heston, visitors travel through two separate theaters where they will learn how special effects and stunts were done in the *Earthquake* movie. (The special effects and intricate models of San Francisco are somewhat of a revelation to most kids because few have seen the original movie, which was made more than 20 years ago.) In the second preshow, audience volunteers are drafted to play quake victims, which is great fun for the kids who are chosen.

After the preshows, you are loaded onto your subway for the ride segment itself. Earthquake is a very short ride and less intense than you may have been led to believe from the advertisements. Most kids will hold up through the rumbles, fires, floods, and train wrecks just fine, and as one mother wrote, "It's fun to feel it really happen instead of watching it on a

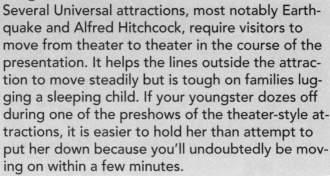

Helpful Hint

Several Universal attractions, most notably Earth-quake and Alfred Hitchcock, require visitors to move from theater to theater in the course of the presentation. It helps the lines outside the attraction to move steadily but is tough on families lugging a sleeping child. If your youngster dozes off during one of the preshows of the theater-style attractions, it is easier to hold her than attempt to put her down because you'll undoubtedly be moving on within a few minutes.

screen." And it's even more fascinating to watch the water recede, the concrete mend itself, and the broken turnstiles arise when the ride is over!

Kongfrontation

You'll go head-to-head with one of the fiercest monsters in movie history in the justifiably popular Kongfrontation. The long "underground" queue area, meant to emulate the subways of New York, sets the mood with TV cameras overhead reporting to you that the ape is loose and on a rampage. You'll eventually be loaded onto trams (which carry about 30 riders) and lifted above the fiery streets of a city under siege. Riders

The Scare Factor

This is one real-looking ape, and the ride is simply too intense for toddlers. Some parents of kids as old as 8 reported that the combination of the darkness, the bursts of flames, and of course, the mega-ape had their kids clutching their arms and ducking.

will confront Kong up close twice, coming near enough to inspect his 4-foot fangs and feel the hot blast of banana breath in their faces.

Older kids love the ride, however, and rate it extremely high—especially the finale, where Kong grabs your tram car and "drops" you back onto the street. (The actual fall is only about 6 feet; this attraction relies heavily on its atmospheric effects to scare its riders.) As your wounded tram limps to a halt, you'll learn that your close brush with disaster has made the evening news. A videocam inside your car filmed your reaction to the drop, and the tape is replayed on a TV camera above your head.

At Safari Outfitters, adjacent to Kongfrontation, you can pose clutched in the fist of King Kong himself for a family souvenir shot; the pictures are developed immediately, and at $5 per pose it's an unusual and reasonably priced memento.

The Funtastic World of Hanna-Barbera

This attraction features a high-speed cartoon flight simulation chase and is very popular with kids in every age-group.

The premise of the ride is established in the brief preshow when you learn that Dick Dastardly has kidnapped Elroy Jetson and that it is up to you, along with Yogi Bear and Boo Boo, to rescue him. You'll go on into another room to be loaded into cars that hold six to eight passengers. Because the cars lurch about a bit during the movie, children under 40 inches tall, pregnant women, anyone with back or neck problems, or those who are just plain gutless are ushered to stationary seats at the front of the theater.

The flight-simulation effects make you feel as if you're really flying, and most kids squeal with delight as they meet up with other well-known Hanna-Barbera characters such as the

Flintstones and Scooby Doo. Not surprisingly, Elroy is safely back with his family by the end of the ride. After Yogi brings you in for a rather rough landing, you go on to the interactive area, where you can make a choir of birds sing by stepping on a huge piano and color your own cartoon using computers.

Time-Saving Tip

Like other attractions along the Plaza of the Stars, lines form by 10 A.M. as late-arriving visitors walk through the front gate and simply queue up for the first attractions they see. Visit the Funtastic World of Hanna-Barbera first thing in the morning, both to avoid the crowds and to use the ride as a gauge for how well your kids will handle the more intense flight-simulation ride, Back to the Future.

Twister

After a taped intro by Bill Paxton and Helen Hunt, you're led into the main show area. There a 5-story-high tornado will be created right before your eyes. The tornado, along with accompanying fires and explosions, swirls through the building while you watch from two platforms. You'll feel the wind, the rain, and the rumbles, and yes—the flying cow from the movie comes along for the ride.

The Scare Factor

Twister is a dramatic experience—and extremely loud. The intensity is heightened by the fact you're trapped in a relatively small space for the duration of the show. The experience is too frightening for preschoolers; most kids over 7 will love it.

Terminator 2: 3-D

Universal's most high-tech action show combines 3-D effects, live actors, and movie clips. (The best special effect is the way the live actors seem to emerge from the movie screen onto the stage and then later run back "into" the movie.) The show is fast, dramatic, and loud—just like the film series it's based on—and the ending is explosive.

Terminator 2: 3-D, because of the size of the theater, is relatively easy to get into and best saved for the afternoon.

The Scare Factor

Although not as violent as the film series, the show has some startling effects that may be too much for kids under 7. Again, it is extremely loud.

E.T. Adventure

This charming ride is as technologically impressive and atmospherically seductive as anything at MGM, but, because there's nothing scary about it, the entire family can enjoy it as a group.

The attraction begins with a brief preshow featuring Steven Spielberg and E.T., after which you file through a holding area and—somewhat mysteriously at the time—are required to give your name in exchange for a small plastic "interplanetary passport." Then you move onto the queue area, which winds through the deep dark woods and is so evocative that it even smells and sounds like a forest. (Universal in general does a bang-up job of setting the moods in the queue areas; Kongfrontation has many visitors in a lather of nerves before they even board the ride, and E.T. is designed to make you feel small and childlike.)

After handing "passports" to the attendant, children under 40 inches tall or anyone elderly, heavy, pregnant, or otherwise unsteady is loaded into flying gondolas. Others get to ride bicycles, and the lead bike in each group has E.T. in the front basket. You rise up and fly over the forest in an effective simulation of the escape scene in the E.T. movie. After narrowly missing being captured by the police, you manage to return E.T. to his home planet, a magical place populated by dozens of cuddly aliens.

> ## Helpful Hint
> Unfortunately, this "personal good-bye" system is the most frequently malfunctioning part of the ride, so I wouldn't mention it to the kids at all. That way, if it works, everyone is extra-delighted, and if it doesn't, the ride is still an upbeat experience.

The ride closes on a fun note, for as you sail past E.T. for the final time, he bids you farewell by name. When you give your name to the attendant before you enter the queue area, your name is computer-coded onto the plastic passport. As you give up the passport and are loaded into your group of bicycles, the cards are fed into the computer. The ride thus "knows" who is riding in that particular batch of bicycles, which enables E.T. to say, "Good-bye Jordan, Good-bye Leigh, Good-bye Kim . . . ," and so on as your family flies past.

Alfred Hitchcock: The Art of Making Movies
You'll pick up 3-D glasses in the holding area, but only part of the film that follows requires them. This rapid-fire montage of classic scenes from Alfred Hitchcock thrillers will go right over the heads of most kids, who probably won't get much out of

this segment of the show. The brief 3-D effect, however, is a thrilling adaptation from a scene in *The Birds,* and you don't have to be a Hitchcock buff to get chills down your spine as those ravens appear to come right off the screen toward you.

After the movie, you'll be directed into a separate theater, where audience volunteers will illustrate how the infamous shower scene in *Psycho* was shot. This part may be too scary for younger children, but you can always pass through and wait for the rest of your party in the final area, which has interactive exhibits.

Jaws

As the people of Amity Beach learned, that darn shark just won't stay away.

Jaws carries you via boat through a big outdoor set. The shark rises from the water several times quite suddenly, the unseen boat before you "gets it" in a gruesome way, and there are also grenade launches, explosions, and a fuel spill. There's tremendous splashing—especially on the left side of the boat—and most of the boat captains throw themselves totally into the experience by shrieking, shouting, and firing guns on cue. It all adds up to one action-packed boat ride. Interestingly enough, Universal invested $50 million on the ride,

The Scare Factor

Kids 7 to 11 gave Jaws a strong thumbs-up, and the ride was popular with many kids under 7. The fact that you're outdoors in the daylight dilutes the intensity, meaning that some kids who freak on Kongfrontation do just fine on Jaws. The really brave should wait until evening, when the "shark in the dark" effects are much scarier.

which is more than six times what Steven Spielberg spent on the original 1975 movie.

The Horror Makeup Show

A witty pair of young actors illustrate certain makeup effects onstage, but you'll also see clips from *The Exorcist, The Fly,* and an astounding man-to-beast transformation scene from the little-known *An American Werewolf in London.*

The Scare Factor
Although the movie clips and general gore level are too intense for preschoolers, most kids over 7 can stomach the show. Better than adults, frankly.

The Animal Actors Stage Show

If your children are strung out from a combination of 90-degree heat, 3-D birds, and people-eating dinosaurs, the Animal Actors Stage Show offers a welcome change of pace. The show features apes, birds, and Benji-clone dogs and takes place in a large open-air arena. Kids in both the 4-to-7 and 7-to-11 age-groups rated the animals very highly—and adults love it too. This attraction is fun to videotape and watch again later at home.

The Wild West Stunt Show

Funny, fast-moving, and full of surprises, this show ranks at the top of the list with kids 7 to 11 and rates highly with kids under 7 as well. The shoot-'em-ups, fistfights, and explosions are played strictly for laughs, and sometimes the comedy tends to overshadow how dangerous these stunts really are. A good choice for the whole family, and as with the Animal Actors Show, it's fairly easy to get into even in the crowded parts of the afternoon.

Fievel's Playland

Fievel's Playland is a cleverly designed play area filled with western-style props, including a harmonica that plays notes as kids slide down it, a giant talking Tiger the cat, canteens to squirt, cowboy hats to bounce in, spider webs to climb, and a separate ball pit and slide area for toddlers.

The centerpiece of the playground is a 200-foot water ride in which kids and parents are loaded into two-man rafts and swept through a "sewer." The ride is zippier than it looks, will get you soaking wet, and is so addictive that most kids clamor to get back on again immediately. The water ride is very popular and loads slowly, so by afternoon the waits are prohibitive; if you come in the morning, it is possible to ride several times with minimal waits, but by afternoon one ride is all you can reasonably expect.

Time-Saving Tip

Fievel's Playland often opens an hour or two after the general park. If you ride the big-deal rides and then show up at the playground at the opening time indicated on your entertainment schedule, you'll be able to try the water ride without much of a wait.

Fievel's Playland is great fun, and most kids could happily stay for an hour or two. The only drawbacks are that, like the Honey, I Shrunk the Kids Adventure Zone at the Studios, it needs to be much, much larger and that Universal unwisely lets preteens and teens in. Their rowdy play makes the area downright unsafe for younger kids, especially in the afternoon, when the playground is crowded. How about a few reverse height restrictions, guys?

A Day in the Park with Barney

Designed to appeal to Universal's youngest guests, A Day in the Park with Barney is actually an enclosed parklike setting with pop-art-colored flowers and trees. Barney appears several times a day in a song-and-dance show, and there is also an interactive indoor play area designed for toddlers. This play area is far cooler and calmer than Fievel's next door, and the nearby shop and food stand are never crowded.

Woody Woodpecker's Kid Zone

The centerpiece of this latest addition to the kids play area is a small roller coaster. Somewhat like Goofy's Barnstormer at Disney, the ride is zippier than you'd guess. Watch it make a couple of runs before you line up with your 3-year-old.

> **Helpful Hint**
>
> Universal has located all the attractions for very young children close together; if you have preschoolers, hang an immediate right on Rodeo Drive after you enter the park and follow the signs to E.T. Adventure. The Animal Actors Stage Show, A Day In the Park with Barney, E.T. Adventure, and Fievel's Playland are all located within close proximity to one another, so a family with kids who are all under 7 can set up base here for the afternoon.

Curious George Goes To Town

Perhaps a better name would have been Curious George Goes to the Car Wash. This large interactive play area is a simulated city that includes climbing areas, ball pits, and lots of chances to get very, very wet. There are fountains in the center and water cannons up above; many parents let their kids wear bathing suits under their shorts so they can strip down and really get into the spirit of the place. A great way to cool off in the summer, but if you're going in the off-season, either save it for the warmest part of the afternoon, or keep walking.

Beetlejuice's Graveyard Revue

A rock 'n' roll dance show starring Dracula, the Wolfman, the Phantom of the Opera, and Frankenstein and his Bride, the Revue is popular with the 7-to-11 age-group and teens—although the show is so goofy and upbeat that younger kids certainly won't be frightened by the ghouls.

This is a high-tech show featuring pulsating lights, fog machines, synchronized dancing, and wry renditions of rock classics. (My personal favorite is the Bride of Frankenstein's version of "You Make Me Feel Like a Natural Woman.") Because the theater is huge and this 20-minute show plays frequently throughout the day, getting in isn't too tough—work it into your schedule whenever it happens to suit you.

Lucy, A Tribute

Fans of *I Love Lucy* should take a few minutes to walk through this exhibit, which houses memorabilia from the famous TV show, including scale models of the Tropicana and the Ricardos' apartment, clothes and jewelry worn on the show, personal pictures and letters from Lucy and Desi's home life, and the numerous Emmys that Lucille Ball won throughout the years. The "California Here We Come Game" is a treat for hard-core trivia buffs. By answering questions about episodes of *I Love Lucy*, game participants get to travel with the Mertzes and Ricardos on their first trip to California. They lost me somewhere in the desert, but perhaps you'll do better.

The Nickelodeon Tour

After reviewers and families labeled it something of a drag, this tour has been revamped and is now much more fun. Even if you opt to skip the filming of a Nick show, your kids will enjoy the 45-minute walk-through tour. You'll see the sets of shows they'll immediately recognize, perhaps get a glimpse of a show in production, and then move on to the popular Game Lab, where audience volunteers play games and one lucky kid is slopped and glopped in the best Nickelodeon tradition. Kids 7 to 11 rated the tour very highly, as did younger kids who were familiar with the Nick lineup.

If you're visiting on a day when one of the Nick shows is filming, you can also volunteer to be in the studio audience.

Helpful Hint

Even if you don't plan to take in the tour or a filming, drop by the Nick Studios entrance and check out the Green Slime Geyser, which periodically erupts and spews into the air an unearthly colored substance about the consistency of pudding.

The Best Food Bets at Universal Studios

The fastest fast food is simply a hot dog from one of the many vendors scattered throughout the park, but you'll be missing much of the fun if you eat on the run for all three meals. Universal has many appealing dining choices, and in general the food is tastier and cheaper than that found within the Disney theme parks.

In addition, because many families have a one-day ticket and are trying to cram all of Universal into to 12 straight hours of touring, few break up the day by actually leaving the park. That means you'll need to rest up in the afternoon or risk having the kids—and maybe the parents—collapse in tears of exhaustion at 6 P.M. A late lunch or early dinner is advised because it will get you off the streets during the hottest and most crowded touring times of the day and give everyone a chance to rest and regroup before heading on to the attractions you missed earlier. Some of the restaurants listed here accept reservations at the door, which is a good idea if you'll be dining at peak hours.

Finnegan's Bar and Grill ★★ $

Friendly, informal, and with the added bonus of live music during peak dining hours, Finnegan's is a great place to rest up and pig out. It's dark inside, too, even on the most blistering summer afternoons, and kids can stretch out and nap in the booths.

Hard Rock Cafe ★★ $

What's there to say? Hard Rock Cafes, found in major cities all over the world, are justifiably famous for their funky atmosphere, raucously friendly service, and tasty, unassuming food.

The problem is when to go. The Hard Rock does not take reservations, and large crowds are the norm from midafternoon on. If you have young kids along, the best bet is to eat an early lunch around 11 A.M., when the cafe isn't so crowded that you can't get up and look around. Another crowd-busting option is an early dinner around

Helpful Hint

If you only want to buy a Hard Rock T-shirt or sweatshirt, you can purchase merchandise in a separate shop without entering the restaurant.

4 P.M. Universal veterans take note: Hard Rock has moved. The new cafe is accessible either from CityWalk or from Universal Studios through an entrance located near Nickelodeon Studios.

Lombard's Landing   ★★ $$

If you crave a fancier meal, such as prime rib or fresh pompano, Lombard's Landing is a beautiful restaurant in the Fisherman's Wharf section of the San Francisco set. The service is leisurely and the atmosphere a bit more elegant than in most of the park restaurants, so opt for Lombard's only if your kids can be counted on to behave reasonably (or sleep) through a 60-minute meal. Lombard's Landing becomes quite crowded at dinner, so a late lunch or midafternoon meal is a better bet. Reservations are recommended.

Louie's   ★★ $

Louie's is a nice spot for a fast Italian dinner, especially if you're headed for the nearby Dynamite Nights Stuntacular. Louie's offers spaghetti for kids at a reasonable $3 and a choice of hearty pasta favorites for adults.

Cafe La Bamba   ★ $

This cafe is a good choice for tame Mexican food, with margaritas and live music on the patio during lunch and dinner.

Mel's Drive-In   ★ $

Unquestionably the place to go for fast food, Mel's offers home-style burgers and fries, served up with '50s music. The drive-in is based on the one in the film *American Graffiti,* and even kids far too young to remember the movie, much less the decade being spoofed, will enjoy the table-based jukeboxes and vintage cars parked outside.

Monster Cafe	★	$

Big eaters in the party? Monster Cafe runs lunch and dinner buffets, which are a good choice if you want more than a burger but still want it quick.

Helpful Hint

The opening of CityWalk in 1998 dramatically increased your dining options, with eateries such as the NASCAR Cafe and the Motown Cafe. You'll have to leave the park, but you don't have to move your car, and a visit to CityWalk can help you break up a long day of touring.

Tips for Your Last Hour at Universal Studios

- If you want to see the Dynamite Nights Stuntacular, find a spot around the lagoon at least 20 minutes before show time. After you stake out a good spot, one member of your party can go back for snacks so that you can enjoy a picnic while waiting for the show.

- If you don't care to see the lagoon show, you'll find that it draws so many people to one spot that it's now easier to get into rides like Men in Black or Jaws, which may have been swamped all day. Jaws is much more atmospheric at night, so if you're brave enough, make it your last stop.

© As you work your way toward the exit, many characters such as Ace Ventura, the Blues Brothers, and the Hanna-Barbera cartoon gang will be circulating among the crowds. If you haven't gotten pictures or auto-graphs earlier, here's your chance.

Time-Saving Tip

If you want to stop at CityWalk to eat on your way out, skip Dynamite Nights and arrive 15 minutes ahead of the crowd.

CHAPTER 15

Islands of Adventure

Islands of Adventure

Jurassic Park River Adventure

Dueling Dragons

Thunder Falls Terrace

The Enchanted Oak Tavern

Jurassic Park

Camp Jurassic

Jurassic Park Discovery Center

teranodon Flyers

Dudley Do-Right's Ripsaw Falls

Triceratops Encounter

Sindbad's Village

Mythos Restaurant

The Lost Continent

The Eighth Voyage of Sindbad

Comic Strip Cafe

Toon Lagoon

Me Ship, The Olive

Comic Strip Lane

Popeye & Bluto's Bilge-Rat Barges

Poseidon's Fury

If I Ran The Zoo

Pandemonium Theater

Green Eggs & Ham

Seuss Landing

The Amazing Adventures of Spider-Man

Island Skipper Tours

Doctor Doom's Fearfall

Marvel Super Hero Island

Cafe 4

Caro-Seuss-el

Circus McGurkus Cafe

One Fish, Two Fish, Red Fish, Blue Fish

Incredible Hulk Coaster

Port of Entry

The Cat in the Hat

Islands of Adventure

Opened next to Universal Studios in the summer of 1999, Islands of Adventure is the cornerstone of Universal's massive expansion. Now there are two theme parks as well as CityWalk, the sumptuously elegant Portofino Bay Resort, and lively Hard Rock Hotel all connected by bridges and waterways.

Parents of younger kids will appreciate the fact that at Islands of Adventure, the rides designed for younger kids are every bit as engaging and technologically complex as the fastest coasters. Many theme parks—and even Disney is somewhat guilty of this—pour their creativity and money into the teen and adult attractions, leaving the preschool set with rides where cardboard cutouts swing toward them on door hinges. But at Islands of Adventure, especially in the Seuss Landing section, Universal has created a world that is not only fun but also marvelous to look at and cleverly designed.

A one-day ticket for an adult is $46.00, $37.00 for children 3 to 9. For multiday passes, including Universal Studios, turn to page 379. Check for any changes by calling 407-363-8000 or go online at www.uescape.com.

Tips for Your First Hour at Islands of Adventure

Older kids who are up to a high-intensity experience should veer left upon leaving Port of Entry and immediately board the Amazing Adventures of Spider-Man. From there you can move on to the Incredible Hulk Coaster and Dr. Doom's Fearfall, both of which are also on Marvel Super Hero Island.

Younger kids? Turn to the right and immediately enter Seuss Landing. Let the kids build up steam on these gentle rides and then, if they've mustered up the courage for bigger thrills, scoot over to Toon Lagoon and board Popeye and Bluto's Bilge-Rat Barges.

Helpful Hint

No matter what your age or risk tolerance, ride in the morning and save the shows for the afternoon.

Islands of Adventure Touring Tips

Given its circular layout, touring Islands of Adventure is relatively easy. And the park is small enough to allow you to make several laps of the circuit without wearing yourself out too badly.

- Arrive early, especially if your focus is the coasters and the more intense rides. These can draw long crowds late in the day.

@ In your initial lap of the park, focus on the rides, especially name attractions that are likely to draw crowds by midday.

@ Stop for lunch in Port of Entry.

@ Begin your second lap of the park, this time focusing on shows and attractions like Triceratops Encounter, which can be toured in a fairly leisurely manner. If you have young kids, use this lap to also hit the interactive play areas: If I Ran the Zoo, Camp Jurassic, and the Me Ship, The Olive. Midday is also a good time to ride the water rides—getting soaked at noon is more fun than getting soaked at 9 A.M.

@ Exit the park and have dinner at CityWalk.

@ If stamina permits, reenter the park for your third and final lap. Revisit favorites, see shows, or try any attraction that had prohibitive lines earlier in the day.

Height Requirements for the
Different Attractions in Islands of Adventure

Dueling Dragons: 54 inches
Jurassic Park River Adventure: 42 inches
Dudley Do-Right's Ripsaw Falls: 44 inches
Incredible Hulk Coaster: 54 inches
The Amazing Adventures of Spider-Man: 40 inches
Popeye and Bluto's Bilge-Rat Barges: 48 inches
Dr. Doom's Fearfall: 52 inches
Pteranodon Flyers: 36 inches

Islands of Adventure Don't-Miss List

IF YOUR KIDS ARE 7 AND UNDER
One Fish, Two Fish, Red Fish, Blue Fish
Caro-Seuss-el
If I Ran the Zoo
The Cat in the Hat
Camp Jurassic
Popeye and Bluto's Bilge-Rat Barges
Me Ship, The Olive
Pandemonium Cartoon Show
Dudley Do-Right's Ripsaw Falls (for kids over 5)
The Amazing Adventures of Spider-Man
(for kids 6 or 7)

IF YOUR KIDS ARE 8 TO 11
The Amazing Adventures of Spider-Man
Dudley Do-Right's Ripsaw Falls
Popeye and Bluto's Bilge-Rat Barges
Jurassic Park River Adventure
Poseidon's Fury
Dr. Doom's FearFall
Incredible Hulk (if they're bold enough)
Dueling Dragons (ditto)

IF YOUR KIDS ARE OVER 12
Spider-Man
Dr. Doom's Fearfall
Incredible Hulk
Dudley Do-Right's Ripsaw Falls
Popeye and Bluto's Bilge-Rat Barges
Jurassic Park River Adventure
Dueling Dragons
Poseidon's Fury

Islands of Adventure Worth-Your-While List

IF YOUR KIDS ARE UNDER 7
Discovery Center
The Eighth Voyage of Sindbad (for kids over 5)
Pteranodon Fliers

IF YOUR KIDS ARE 8 TO 11
Anything in Seuss Landing that catches their fancy
Pandemonium Cartoon Show
Pteranodon Flyers
The Eighth Voyage of Sindbad

IF YOUR KIDS ARE OVER 12
Anything in Jurassic Park that catches their fancy
The Eighth Voyage of Sindbad
Anything in Seuss Landing that catches their fancy
CityWalk

The Scare Factor at Islands of Adventure

Make no mistake: The rides here are big-deal squealers, and you don't want to guess wrong about what is age-appropriate.

The Scare Factor for Kids Under 7

- @ In Seuss Landing: Everything is okay for kids.

- @ In The Lost Continent: Dueling Dragons is an extremely intense coaster, not suitable for preschoolers. The Eighth

Voyage of Sindbad is generally comic, but the final scene, in which a villainness is set on fire and dropped to her doom, may be too much for some children. Poseidon's Fury can be quite loud and intense, but should be fine for any child who doesn't have a fear of the dark.

@ In Jurassic Park: Camp Jurassic is a great play area, and unless they're afraid of heights, most kids will enjoy the Pteranodon Fliers. The Discovery Center and Triceratops Encounter are a bit educational and geared toward older kids, but they won't frighten anyone. The last drop on the River Adventure makes it too intense for your average pre-schooler. Watch a couple of boats descend and then decide.

@ In Toon Lagoon: Kids who pass the height requirement should love Popeye and Bluto's Bilge-Rat Barges, which offer plenty of action—but the fact that the whole family is aboard dilutes the scare factor. The last drop series on Dudley Do-Right's Ripsaw Falls eliminates some young riders. Watch the descent from dry land a couple of times, and then make your call.

@ In Marvel Super Hero Island: Many 6- and 7-year-olds will love Spider-Man, which bounces you around a lot, but the most dramatic effects are visual. Hulk and Dr. Doom? Just keep on walking.

The Scare Factor for Kids 8 to 11

@ In Seuss Landing: Nothing's scary here—unless they're scared of not looking cool.

@ In The Lost Continent: Older kids in this age-group may like Dueling Dragons, assuming they've been on lots of coasters and don't spook easily. The Sindbad and Poseidon shows should both be good choices for school-age kids.

Quick Guide to

Attraction	Location	Height Requirement
Amazing Adventures of Spider-Man	Super Hero Island	40 inches
Camp Jurassic	Jurassic Park	None
The Cat in the Hat	Seuss Landing	None
Caro-Seuss-el	Seuss Landing	None
Discovery Center	Jurassic Park	None
Dr. Doom's Fearfall	Super Hero Island	52 inches
Dudley Do-Right's Ripsaw Falls	Toon Lagoon	42 inches
Dueling Dragons	Lost Continent	None
The Eighth Voyage of Sindbad	Lost Continent	None
If I Ran the Zoo	Seuss Landing	None
Incredible Hulk Coaster	Super Hero Island	52 inches
Me Ship, The Olive	Toon Lagoon	None
One Fish, Two Fish Red Fish, Blue Fish	Seuss Landing	None
Popeye and Bluto's Bilge-Rat Barges	Toon Lagoon	42 inches
Poseidon's Fury	Lost Continent	None
Pteranodon Flyers	Jurassic Park	None
River Adventure	Jurassic Park	44 inches
Triceratops Encounter	Jurassic Park	None

Scare Factor

0 = Unlikely to scare any child of any age.
! = Has dark or loud elements; might rattle some toddlers.
!! = A couple of gotcha! moments; should be fine for school-age kids.
!!! = You need to be pretty big and pretty brave to handle this ride.

Islands of Adventure Attractions

Speed of Line	Duration of Ride/Show	Scare Factor	Age Range
Moderate	15 min.	!	6 and up
N/A	N/A	0	All
Moderate	6 min.	0	All
Slow	3 min.	0	All
N/A	N/A	0	All
Slow	2 min.	!!!	6 and up
Moderate	8 min.	!!	6 and up
Moderate	7 min.	!!!	6 and up
N/A	25 min.	!!	6 and up
N/A	N/A	0	All
Moderate	4 min.	!!!	10 and up
N/A	N/A	0	All
Slow	4 min.	0	All
Moderate	12 min.	!	4 and up
N/A	25 min.	!!	6 and up
Slow	6 min.	!	4 and up
Slow	N/A	!!	6 and up
Slow	20 min.	!	All

- In Jurassic Park: Kids this age will still enjoy Camp Jurassic, the Pteranodon Flyers, The Discovery Center, and Triceratops Encounter—but the River Adventure will definitely be their favorite. Unless they have a fear of heights—and dropping from heights—it's a good choice for this age group.

- In Toon Lagoon: They'll love everything here, including the numerous chances to get wet.

- In Marvel Super Hero Island: Spider-Man's a must-see, and many kids this age will like Dr. Doom's Fearfall and the Incredible Hulk Coaster as well. Both rides are fully outdoors, so watch them a while before you make your call.

The Scare Factor for Kids 12 and Older

The most intense rides are the Incredible Hulk Coaster and Dueling Dragons. On the next tier down, at least in terms of sheer scariness, are Dr. Doom's FearFall, Jurassic Park River Adventure, Spider-Man, and Dudley Do-Right's Ripsaw Falls.

Islands of Adventure Attractions

Port of Entry

As the name implies, you'll enter through this section, which resembles a wild and colorful Middle Eastern marketplace. Take a glance at the wacky bicycles and other forms of transportation lining the street as you pass. Check out Confisco's Grill, where you'll find character dining—featuring such favorites as Spider-Man, Dudley Do-Right, and The Cat in the Hat—for the same money as an ordinary lunch.

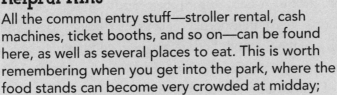

Helpful Hint

All the common entry stuff—stroller rental, cash machines, ticket booths, and so on—can be found here, as well as several places to eat. This is worth remembering when you get into the park, where the food stands can become very crowded at midday; you may want to return to Port of Entry for lunch.

Seuss Landing

You'll find nothing but pastel colors and curved lines in this world, which looks uncannily like the illustrations in the actual Dr. Seuss books.

Kids are bound to love One Fish, Two Fish, Red Fish, Blue Fish, a very innovative Dumbo-style ride where you board brightly colored fish who fly in a circle. Your fish has a joystick that controls the height of the flight, and throughout the ride you're given directions such as "Red fish, fly high." If you opt to obey the instructions—that is, go "with the book," you stay at least somewhat dry. But if you disobey and go "against the book," a bad fish will squirt water on you. The Universal people assure me this teaches kids to follow directions—I suspect it really shows them how much fun it can be to rebel—but either way, it's a terrific ride.

You'll also find the Caro-Seuss-el, composed of colorful, moveable versions of the creatures from the Seuss books. You go around and up and down

Helpful Hint

Islands of Adventure has three separate interactive play areas scattered around the park, further proof of their commitment to pleasing families with young kids.

like a classic carousel, but you can also make your beasties blink, flick their tails, or turn their heads. In The Cat and the Hat ride, you're transported on couches through scenes in the book as Things 1 and 2 create mayhem and the poor goldfish tries to keep everything orderly. Clever and colorful, the Cat puts Disney's kiddie rides to shame.

Seuss Landing is the ultimate eye candy and some of the most clever visuals—like the cars on the overhead track—aren't at eye level. The cars weave above Seuss Landing, around buildings such as the restaurant Green Eggs and Ham. (Relax; the food gets its color from parsley.) Finally, Seuss Landing has an interactive play area called If I Ran the Zoo, which offers kids plenty of chances to jump, climb, play tic-tac-toe with a Gak, and, of course, squirt and be squirted.

Helpful Hint
The lively setting of Circus McGurkus Café Stoo-pendous makes it a great stop for lunch with young kids.

The Lost Continent

Myths and legends come to life in this mysterious land, which is home to one of the Islands of Adventure headliners, the Dueling Dragons double roller coaster. Two suspension-style coasters (that is, they hang beneath the track) operate at once, coming so close in their mock battle that at three different

Insider's Secret
The red "Fire" Dragon goes a bit faster but blue "Ice" Dragon has more side to side movement. Either is enough to scare you silly, especially if you're sitting in an outside seat.

times the coasters are within 12 inches of each other, giving riders the distinct impression they're going to crash.

The Eighth Voyage of Sindbad, an outdoor stunt show with a finale that may be a bit too scary for preschoolers, is a good choice for afternoon. Another show, Poseidon's Fury, depicts sibling rivalry run amok as Zeus, using fire as his weapon, battles his brother Poseidon, armed with water, for world dominion. At one point in the show, a spiraling wall of water surrounds the audience. Mythos, the park's most elegant restaurant, is also on The Lost Continent.

Jurassic Park

The centerpiece of the Jurassic Park section is the River Adventure, a boat ride that takes you through the land of the dinosaurs—five-story-high Animatronic dinosaurs, that is. After a T-Rex decides you'd be a good snack, you escape via an 85-foot downhill plunge—the longest, fastest, and steepest water descent ever built on a theme park ride. You will get very, very, very wet.

If this sounds a bit much, consider the Pteranodon Flyers, gentle beasts that soar above the interactive play area of Camp Jurassic with riders dangling below. This attraction, because it boards slowly, draws long lines. Kids 36–56 inches are allowed to board with older kids and adults are welcome only if they're accompanying a child in that height range. Lines move incredibly slowly for this low capacity ride, so only board if the wait is 20 minutes or less.

In the Triceratops Encounter guests will come close to an animatronic dinosaur who seems to breathe, blink, sneeze, and respond to stimuli such as camera flashes. (Note: The ads imply that everyone gets to play with the dino; in reality, one or two kids are pulled from the crowd and allowed to touch and interact.) In the Discovery Center—which looks eerily like the one in the movie—kids can watch an animatronic baby raptor "hatch" from an egg, and there are some clever interactive games as well.

Camp Jurassic is a wild, wonderful play area, but because it's multi-leveled, with winding paths, it's easy to lose your kids. If they're under seven, you'll need to stay with them step by step. Watch out for the water cannons.

Toon Lagoon

Another section geared toward younger kids—although older ones will love it too—Toon Lagoon is designed to get you dripping wet.

The idea is that this is where cartoon characters live when they're not in the Sunday funnies, and the major attraction is a wild log flume ride, Dudley Do-Right's Ripsaw Falls, which culminates in a 75-foot drop that makes it look as if you're falling into a shack filled with TNT. (To give you some idea of the kind of thrill we're talking about here, Splash Mountain drops 52 feet.) Popeye and Bluto's Bilge-Rat Barges is a whitewater raft ride suitable for the whole family. Much wilder than Disney's Kali River Rapids, Popeye and Bluto's Barges will splash you silly.

Other attractions include a cartoon show, which is held in the large Pandemonium Theater and is thus another good

Helpful Hint

Younger kids will like the play area on Popeye's boat, where they can fire water guns at the passing occupants of the whitewater rafts.

choice for afternoon. The present manifestation is Cartoon Circus, starring Rocky and Bullwinkle—as well as a host of other funnies favorites.

Helpful Hint

Take your shoes and socks off while riding Popeye and stow them in the central cargo hold. A wet bottom can be annoying—but wet socks can give you blisters and ruin your whole day.

Marvel Super Hero Island

This is the land where super heroes battle super villains—and theme park riders test their mettle. The following attractions are extremely intense and certainly not for young children or anyone who's just finished a big platter of green eggs and ham.

On most coasters you slowly climb the first hill, building up speed and courage; on the Hulk Coaster you're propelled by a "cannon shot" and immediately flip over and go weightless. About two-thirds of the ride takes place over water, where you make seven different inversions at speeds of 40 miles per hour, and on two occasions you go into a subterranean trench filled with mist and fog.

Next door, Dr. Doom's Fearfall—the story is that Dr. Doom has created a machine that can suck the fear out of you, and he plans to use this accumulated fear to take over the world—shoots riders 180 feet into the air. They dangle for a minute,

Insider's Secret

Although the ride is wild, it's smooth, and some people who don't like to be jerked around swear that the Hulk is the most user-friendly coaster in the park.

Helpful Hint
Spider-Man gets my vote for the best attraction in Orlando. The special effects will convince you that you've battled super villains, rescued the Statue of Liberty, and been lifted, thrown, and caught in Spider-Man's net. But the actual movements of the ride are relatively mild, meaning kids over 5, older people, and even those with a fear of heights can ride.

sitting in chairs with nothing under their feet, and then plunge. The first 5 seconds is the scariest part of the ride; if your survive the initial ascent the remainder isn't too frightening.

But these attractions aren't even the centerpiece of Marvel Super Hero Island. That distinction goes to the Adventures of Spider-Man, the most state-of-the-art ride at Islands of Adventure. Housed in a 1.5-acre set, Spider-Man combines actual ride movement with 3-D and motion-simulation effects—ending in a simulated 400-foot drop. It's as if Universal took the most dramatic parts of Jaws, Back to the Future, and Terminator 2:3D and combined them into one powerful ride. Spider-Man is the sort of ride you can go on five times in a row (which I've done) and see something new every time.

Tips for Your Last Hour at Islands of Adventure

As of this writing, Islands of Adventure has no big closing extravaganza. That, of course, is subject to change.

On busy nights, there are sometimes a few surprises. If a fireworks display or other show is scheduled for over the water, find a good viewing spot about 20 minutes in advance.

No closing show? Evening is a good time to revisit favorites, but if you plan to eat at CityWalk on your way out, leave before closing so you won't be caught in the glut of people who hit the gates when the park shuts down.

Insider's Secret
Islands of Adventure plans to add two new kiddie attractions in 2001. Plans are incomplete as we go to press, but check the map given to you at the park for these new offerings.

CityWalk

CityWalk is the dining, shopping, and entertainment complex that links Islands of Adventure with Universal Studios. A fun destination in its own right, CityWalk also gives guests at both of the Universal Orlando theme parks many more dining options. Just have your hand stamped, exit the park, and head for lunch at CityWalk.

You can shop and dine at CityWalk for free, up until around 9 P.M., when the live music starts. Interested in club-hopping late into the night? An $8 party pass gives you unlimited access to all clubs, and a $12 pass includes admission to a movie at the giant Cineplex. Or, if your tastes are quite specific—you know you just want to hear jazz or reggae, for example—you can pay the $3–7 cover charge for admission to a single club. During the off-season, holders of a multiday Universal Orlando pass are sometimes allowed into the clubs for free.

Good choices for families include NBA City, where you can compare your palmprint to that of Patrick Ewing and other basketball stars. Inside they serve hearty chow and have shootout games and a merchandise shop. Or try the good ol' boy cuisine of NASCAR Café, where you dine in cars, the wait staff dresses like your pit crew, and the utensils look like tools. The Motown Café is another family-friendly choice, especially when the house band comes out to sing compilations of Supremes and Temptation hits. Jimmy Buffet's Marguaritaville, where taped Buffet concerts play on screens overhead between live musical acts, is my 15-year-old daughter Leigh's favorite, featuring Key West food as well as the obligatory Cheeseburgers in Paradise. Three guesses as to what the house drink here is.

More adult-oriented choices choices include Pat O'Brien's, where you'll find gumbo, jambalaya, crawfish nachos, and other Cajun appetizers to match the restaurant's New Orleans heritage. The big deal is the big drinks. Settle into the patio and order a classic Hurricane. They've been known to level people. Patio dining is also an option at Bob Marley's, where the restaurant façade is modeled on Bob's actual home in Jamaica. Down-home island food is dished up along with reggae music. The Latin Quarter is a particular favorite of mine. The shrimp appetizer wrapped in bacon is one of the best bites in all of Orlando. It's fun to watch the salsa dancers (and vacationing wanna-bes) take the stage when the music starts up. Popular with Orlando locals, the place may get a little too raucous for young kids after dark.

For a special occasion, nothing beats Emeril's, which offers the most glorious food in CityWalk. The service is friendly and the mood is casual. Not up for the full-scale full-price Emeril's experience? Sit in the large bar and order just an appetizer and dessert.

The largest Hard Rock Cafe in the world—with a correspondingly large collection of rock memorabilia and souvenirs—can be found at CityWalk. (Be sure to look up at the electronic marquee that reads things like "Green hair, tattoos, and nose rings . . . and that's just the waitress.") Next to the café is the Hard Rock Live auditorium, where both local and nationally known music acts perform. Live music is also a nightly event at City Jazz, which, since it is a performance venue and not a restaurant, opens later. To get a schedule of who is appearing at the clubs, either call 407-224-2189 or go online at www.uescape.com.

Food and music aside, there's lots in CityWalk to keep kids entertained. On weekend nights special performers like extreme sport athletes are often displaying their skills on skateboards, bikes, or jet-skis. There are fountains to play in, street music, and fun specialty shops like All Star Collectibles and Captain Crackers Toy Store, as well as a 20-screen Cineplex showing the latest movies.

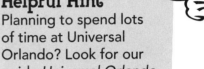

Helpful Hint
Planning to spend lots of time at Universal Orlando? Look for our guide *Universal Orlando with Kids*, published by Prima.

CHAPTER 16

Life Beyond Disney World

Sea World and Other Orlando Attractions

Sea World

Sea World is so beautifully landscaped that you often can't see one stadium from the other, and the sense of space is a welcome change after a week spent at Disney. But the openness also means that children up to age 5 will benefit from a stroller.

Sea World admission is $46.00 for adults, $37.00 for kids 3 to 9, but numerous discount coupons can be found floating around Orlando, and the park is also included in the Flexticket plan. The park opens at 9 A.M. and can be comfortably toured

Helpful Hint

Sea World is best known as the home of Shamu and the killer whales. Sea World is a low-stress experience, much less frenzied than the other Orlando parks. It can be easily seen in six or seven hours and is laid out so that the crowds pretty much flow from one scheduled show to another, working in the smaller attractions on the way.

in a single day. Call 407-351-3600 for more information. On-line information can be found at www.shamu.com.

Journey to Atlantis

On the Journey to Atlantis, guests are transported back to the lost city of Atlantis, on an attraction that combines the excitement of a high-speed water ride and a coaster. Ride designers call this hybrid a water coaster, and it is one of the most thrilling rides I've ever encountered.

Riders are boarded onto Greek fishing boats and lured by sirens into the depths of the lost city. The tiny boats twist, dodge, and dive at near-highway speeds through the water. You will see the first drop, which comes out the front of the building. But Allura pulls you back in for a second, unseen 60-foot S-shaped drop.

Coming Soon: Kraken

Sea World's first full-scale roller coaster is set to open in Summer 2000. With a speed of 65 MPH, 7 loops, and 3 underground plunges, this coaster is definitely designed for pre-teens and teens. As with all new attractions, ride early or expect long lines.

Shows

For years, Sea World's claim to fame has been its shows—especially those that feature the dolphins, the sea lions and otters, and the park icon, Shamu. Although the themes are regularly updated to keep the shows fresh, these three classics are funny, fascinating, and very worthwhile. See them if you do nothing else. All the shows take place in enormous open-air theaters, so touring Sea World is as simple as consulting your map for show times and being at the theater about 15 minutes early.

Clever preshows make the wait bearable, especially the mime at the Sea Lion and Otter Show.

Insider's Secret

Be forewarned that if you opt to sit in the "splash zone"—the first 10 rows of the stadium—Shamu's good-bye wave will leave you drenched straight through to your underwear. Kids enjoy the blast of saltwater, but if you're touring off-season or catching a nighttime show, it may be wiser to sit farther back and laugh at the unwary tourists down by the tank.

Other shows are updated on a rotating basis. There is generally a waterskiing show, an acrobatics show, films, musicals, a Polynesian revue, and a laser light show. Pets on Stage features the comic talents of a group of dogs, cats, potbelly pigs, and other animals that were rescued from animal shelters. Work these shows in as your schedule permits; they're well done but not as essential as the Sea World classics that feature dolphins, whales, and sea lions.

Standing Exhibits

Sea World is also known for its fascinating standing exhibits, such as the Penguin Encounter, where you can observe the tuxedoed charmers both above and below the ice floe—and witness their startling transformation from awkward walkers to sleek swimmers. Check your entertainment schedule for feeding time, when the trainers slip about on the iceberg with buckets of fish and the penguins waddle determinedly behind them. The birds ingest the fish in one amazing gulp, and you

can stand on the top observation level and watch for
as long as you like.

The California sea
lions are at the Pacific Point
Preserve. In Key West at
Sea World, you'll find
Florida's own endangered
species, the manatee, as

Helpful Hint
If your kids are too cool
to like cute, try the Ter-
rors of the Deep exhibit,
where you'll encounter
sharks, moray eels, and
barracudas at close
quarters.

well as sea turtles, dolphins, stingrays, and other species indige-
nous to the Florida Keys. There are also underwater viewing
tanks where you can observe many of the animals up close.
These continuous-viewing exhibits do not have special show
times and can be visited at your leisure as you circle the park.

At Wild Arctic, an exhibit dedicated to Polar Bears, you
can opt to ascend to the top of the exhibit to view the bears
either via a motion-simulation helicopter "ride" or by walking.
(Kids must be 42 inches tall to take the motion-simulation
ride.) Lines at Wild Arctic are long just after the nearby
Shamu show lets out; if you visit while one of the Shamu
shows is in progress, you'll get through much more quickly.
(Note: This attraction is a bit of a snooze in comparison to the
Disney and Universal motion-simulation rides.)

The Budweiser Clydesdales are also part of the Sea
World family, and children thrill at the chance to meet these

Helpful Hint
At certain times of the day, noted on your entertainment schedule, one of the horses is taken out into a
paddock and children are allowed to get close
enough to have a picture taken.

huge but gentle creatures. The nearby Anheuser-Busch Hospitality Center is a quiet, cool oasis from the rest of the park; beer samples are given out to adults, and the deli inside is never as crowded as other Sea World restaurants.

Preschoolers and Toddlers

Small children at Sea World welcome the numerous chances to get close to the beasties. My 4-year-old son loved feeding the harmless-looking but actually quite vicious seals and the vicious-looking but actually quite harmless stingrays. For $3 you can get three small fish and toss them to the seals, sea lions, or dolphins; the dolphins and stingrays are also in shallow tanks so that children can reach over and touch them as they glide by.

Helpful Hint

Running a hand along the flank of a dolphin or flinging a fish into the whiskered mouth of a furiously barking sea lion is a real kick for a young child, and the experience will probably stay with her long after the shows and tours have faded from memory.

Another kick for kids is Shamu's Happy Harbor, a play area that is not only happy but huge, with an elaborate web of climbing nets, a ship heavy-laden with water-firing muskets, a splashy climb-through area, a variety of ball pits to sink into, and padded pyramids to climb. After a few hours spent in shows and exhibits, stop by and just let the kids play for a while. There's a shaded area with seats below the climbing pits where parents can relax.

A separate play area for smaller kids ensures that they don't get tangled up in the webs, whacked by an older kid on a tire swing, or, worst of all, confused in the mazes and exit far from where Mom and Dad are waiting. Because several of the play areas involve water, some parents let kids wear their bathing suits under their shorts. It provides a nice in-park break on a summer day of touring. There's a midway and arcade next door, so older kids can hang out while the younger ones play.

Educational Tours

If you're feeling guilty about taking the kids out of school, Sea World offers educational tours. (Quick—can you tell the difference between a sea lion and a seal?) Tours focusing on sharks, polar bears, and Sea World's animal rescue and rehabilitation programs are available. They're reasonably priced (adults $7, children $6), and reservations are not necessary; either buy your tour ticket when you purchase your general-admission ticket or, if you get the urge to join a tour after a few hours in the park, return to Guest Relations near the main entrance.

Helpful Hint

The Dolphin Interaction Program is a special treat for kids 10 and up. Participants learn a bit about dolphins and then don wet suits and wade into the main pool at the Whale and Dolphin Stadium, where they interact with the animals under the watchful eyes of the trainers. (Kids under 10 or shorter than 52 inches are allowed to observe.) The cost is $159, and you can get more information by calling 407-370-1385.

Camp Sea World

If you think your kids would benefit from a more extensive program, call for the Camp Sea World brochure at least two months in advance of your trip (800-406-2244 or 407-363-2380). There are one-day classes geared for kids from as young as 6 up to eighth-graders ("Key West Wonders") as well as five-day classes that allow a more in-depth study of marine animals. The one-day classes for grades K–1 are $35, grades 2–5 $55. Five-day courses for grade-school kids are $140 for half days, and full days for preschoolers are $240, $100 for half days. The vast majority of the offerings take place in the summer.

Helpful Hint

Camp Sea World activities are popular, so advance reservations are a must. The wonderful brochure not only outlines the available classes for every age-group but also gets you so fired up that you want to register for everything.

Gatorland

Gatorland, surely the most Floridian of all the Florida theme parks, is best known for its Gator Jumparoo, where the beasties jump up to five feet out of the water to retrieve chickens from the hands of their trainers. The Gator Wrestlin' Show, Jungle Crocs of the World, and Snakes of Florida are also a hit with kids.

This campy little place, which you enter through a giant blue gator mouth, also has a small zoo, a kids' interactive area, a water playground, and a train ride. The park can be easily toured in three or four hours. Children might like a souvenir photo of them holding either an alligator or a boa constrictor. And although Sea World certainly doesn't serve dolphin,

Gatorland suffers no qualms about biting the hand that feeds it. You can pick up a few cans of Gator Chowder at the gift shop—surely a unique thank-you gift for the neighbors back home who are watering the plants while you're away.

Gatorland admission is $15.97 for adults, $6.94 for kids 3 to 12; one child under 3 is free with each paying adult. Call 800-393-JAWS or 407-855-5496.

Wet 'n Wild

The atmosphere doesn't stack up to the Huck Finn feel of River Country or the tropical splendor of Typhoon Lagoon, but for families staying off-site, Wet 'n Wild is a great place to cool off without getting back into the mouse race.

The Fuji Flyer toboggan ride, the twisting tubes of the Mach 5, and a spiraling descent through the Black Hole are not for the faint of heart. Wet 'n Wild's wildest attraction, the Bomb Bay, sends riders

> **Helpful Hint**
> This was the original water theme park in Orlando, and in terms of sheer thrills, the preteen crowd surveyed claim it's still the best.

on a six-second free fall down a 76-foot slide and is, like many of the other big-deal attractions, strictly off limits to children shorter than 48 inches. These rides are enough to knock the breath out of even a strong swimmer; some kids who make the height requirements still aren't up to the intensity of the attractions, so if you have doubts, steer your 8-year-old toward the smaller slides and flumes.

Small children and others who are chicken of the sea can slide along in a Bubba Tub or float down the Lazy River in a big rubber tube. Wet 'n Wild also offers a $1.5-million children's water playground, billed as a "safe, fun environment for kids 1 to 10." Preschoolers and unsteady swimmers have their own wave pool, a miniature raging rapids, and fiberglass flumes designed for riders under 48 inches tall. It's perfect for families whose children range in ages and who need a place that can be both Wet 'n Wild and Wet 'n Mild.

Admission is $28.95 for adults, $22.95 for kids 3 to 9. Discounts—which often cut admission price in half—take effect at 3 P.M. during the off-season and at 5 P.M. in summer, when the park stays open until 11 P.M. Crowds become far more manageable as the sun goes down, and summer evenings offer live entertainment, poolside karaoke, and the laid-back party atmosphere of a beach club. Or consider the Flexticket, which lets you take in Universal Orlando, Sea World, and Wet 'n Wild. Wet 'n Wild is located on International Drive, which is Exit 30A off I-4. Call 800-992-WILD or 407-351-WILD for details.

Mystery Fun House

A good place for rainy days, the Mystery Fun House is full of mazes, sloping floors, and optical illusions. It also features a Jurassic Park miniature golf course and arcade. Admission for all ages is $11. Miniature golf is $10.85.

Off-Site Dinner Shows for the Whole Family

Disney isn't the only company in Orlando that produces family dinner theater. The food is generally mediocre but plentiful, and the main attraction is the spectacle before you. Prices run about

$36 for adults and $23 for kids 3 to 11, but discount coupons (some discounting the price of an adult dinner as much as $10) can be found all around Orlando at Guest Services booths, family-style restaurants, and in those freebie magazines aimed at vacationers. There is generally one seating nightly in the off-season and two during the on-season, so you'll need to call for exact show times and to make reservations. The halls

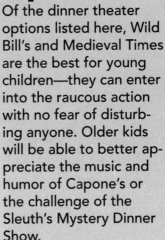

Helpful Hint
Of the dinner theater options listed here, Wild Bill's and Medieval Times are the best for young children—they can enter into the raucous action with no fear of disturbing anyone. Older kids will be able to better appreciate the music and humor of Capone's or the challenge of the Sleuth's Mystery Dinner Show.

hold between 400 and 1,000 people; come prepared to buddy up to that talkative couple from Michigan.

Arabian Nights

Arabian Nights features more than 60 horses, including white Lipizzans and a "mystical unicorn." The highlight of the evening is a high-speed chariot race re-created from the movie *Ben Hur.* The main course is prime rib. Call 800-553-6116 or 407-396-1787.

Wild Bill's Wild West Show

A favorite of younger kids, this Wild West show offers knife throwers, rain dancers, lasso twirlers, and a gaggle of comically inept soldiers. (If you remember the old *F Troop* TV show, you get the general picture.) Barbecue, fried chicken, and corn on the cob are served up chuck-wagon style. Call 800-883-8181 or 407-351-5151.

Medieval Times

Dueling swordsmen and jousting knights on horseback perform in a huge pit while guests dine on roast chicken and ribs. Medieval Times was the favorite dinner theater of kids in the 7-to-11 age range, largely because the arena is divided into competing teams bearing different colors, and the performers do a wonderful job of urging spectators to cheer for "their" knight. Call 800-229-8300 or 407-239-0214.

King Henry's Feast

The portly monarch is searching for his seventh wife—portraits of her six unlucky predecessors hang in the entry hall—as magicians, jugglers, and minstrels offer a kinder, gentler version of Medieval Times. Chicken and ribs are on hand for the revelers. Call 800-883-8181 or 407-351-5151.

Pirates Adventure

The basis of this show is interesting—it's an old B movie that suddenly comes to life on a set of an enormous pirate ship surrounded by water. The pirates engage in lots of swashbuckling stunts, and the audience is color-coded; each diner has his or her own pirate to cheer for when the competition starts. The main course is skewered meatballs and chicken—meant to simulate the losers in the sword fights? Call 407-248-0590.

Capone's

Expect Italian food and mobsters aplenty in this cheerful version of a Chicago prohibition-era speakeasy. Capone's offers musical comedy in the *Guys and Dolls* tradition and massive portions of pasta. Call 407-397-2378.

Sleuth's Mystery Dinner Show

As you munch hors d'oeuvres and mingle with suspicious characters in an English drawing room, be sure to keep your wits about you. A crime is about to unfold, and it is up to you to collect the clues, interrogate the suspects, and formulate a theory. The family who comes up with the most accurate solution wins a prize. Call 407-363-1985.

Index

Gorilla Falls Exploration Trail (Animal Kingdom), 248–249, 250, 252
Gospel Brunch (West Side), 292
Grand Cypress Resort, 82, 83
Grand Floridian, 54
  character breakfasts, 303
  character buffet, 304
  getting to Epcot, 182
  getting to Magic Kingdom, 143
  kids' club, 365–366
  quick guide, 44–45
  ratings, 60–61
  returning from Magic Kingdom, 177
  waterskiing, 307
Grand Floridian Cafe (Grand Floridian), 320–321, 333–334
Grandmother Willow's Grove (Animal Kingdom), 248–249, 255
Grandparents, tips for, 109–110
Great Ceremonial House (Polynesian Resort), 56
Great Movie Ride (MGM)
  described, 227–228
  as don't-miss attraction, 224
  quick guide, 222–223
  scare factor, 228
  touring tips, 122, 219, 220
Green Eggs and Ham (Islands of Adventure), 422
Grosvenor Hotel, 78
Guest Relations (MGM), 219, 221
Guest Services
  cash advances from, 96
  health care and, 92
  pagers from, 108–109
  park information from, 36
  priority seating through, 24
  tickets from, 21, 86

Guidebook for Disabled Visitors, 22, 110, 112
Guides, quick. *See* Quick guides
Gulliver's Grill at Garden Grove (Swan), 320–321, 334

H

Hall of Presidents (Liberty Square), 90–91, 148–149, 169–170
Hampton Inn, 83
Hand icons in this book, xx
Hard Rock Cafe (Universal Studios or CityWalk), 388, 404–405, 428–429
Hard Rock Live auditorium (CityWalk), 429
Harmony Barber Shop (Magic Kingdom), 145–146
Harry's Safari Bar and Grill (Dolphin), 320–321, 334
Haunted Mansion (Liberty Square)
  described, 170
  as don't-miss attraction, 147
  as favorite attraction, 136
  quick guide, 148–149
  scare factor, 170
  touring tips, 126
Health clubs and spas, 310–311
Hearing-impaired visitors, 113
Height requirements
  Animal Kingdom, 31, 248
  Epcot, 31, 188
  Islands of Adventure, 414, 418
  Magic Kingdom, 31, 148, 150
  MGM, 31, 222
  overview, 30–31
  Universal Studios, 385, 387, 390
Hemingway's (Grand Cypress), 82
Hertz car rental, 25–26
Heston, Charlton, 392
Hilton Disney Village, 78, 82–83, 367

M